Liquid Territories

In addition to being a fundamental concept for planning the water infrastructure which supports extensive agricultural economies across Southeast Asia, knowledge of the Mekong River's hydrological catchments has calibrated the control of land, resources and people. *Liquid Territories* shows how and why the areal dimensions of the Mekong's basin, delta and floodplain have become a critical geographic reference for human activities.

This book concentrates on the way knowledge of the river's catchments has been recorded on, and extracted from, maps. Repeatedly drawn by geographers, engineers and cartographers since before the start of European colonization, the book describes how cartographic projections of the basin, delta and floodplain have affected geopolitical strategy, the exercise of military power and anthropogenic modifications of the terrain. Drawing on the discourses of hydrology, geography and cartography, as well as military science, colonial politics and regional planning, the book explains why the spatial articulation of surface water flows is reflected in the configuration of national boundaries, soils and settlements today. Focusing on geographic concepts, the book provides insights into the process of urbanization in Southeast Asia, the region's colonial and post-colonial history, the Mekong River's political ecology, the scales of contemporary water management and the design of territory.

This book will be relevant to academics who are interested specifically in the Mekong River and Lower Mekong Basin as well as in integrated water management planning. It would be especially relevant to architects, urbanists and landscape architects.

Christoforos Romanos studied architecture in London and urban planning at the Massachusetts Institute of Technology. He completed his doctoral research at Delft University of Technology. Before returning to Europe, he directed the urban design of numerous multi-disciplinary planning projects in East Asia. He writes, draws and speaks on the intersection of geography and urbanization focusing on the way infrastructure, settlement and landscape produce and transform territory. In parallel with practice and research, he has taught urban design at MIT, the University of Hong Kong, the Berlage, the Amsterdam Academy of Architecture and Delft's School of Architecture.

Architectural Borders and Territories

Series editors: Marc Schoonderbeek, Nishat Awan and Aleksandar Staničić.

Architectural Borders and Territories offers a comprehensive series of books on architectural 'borders' and 'territories', emphasising the intrinsic critical relationship as well as the inherent complexities between these two core terms of architecture.

Topics include:

1. border and migration studies in relation to spaces of conflict;
2. the territory and architecture, infrastructure and landscape;
3. critical theories probing (the boundaries of) architecture as a discipline
4. design thinking in relation to design methodologies.

The series is theoretical and historical in its scope and presents discussions relevant to international contemporary scholarship in architecture.

Mapping in Architectural Discourse
Place-Time Discontinuities
Marc Schoonderbeek

Architectural Technicities
A Foray Into Larval Space
Stavros Kousoulas

Informal Settlements of the Global South
Edited By Gihan Karunaratne

Liquid Territories
Catchment Cartographies of the Mekong River
Christoforos Romanos

For more information about this series, please visit: Architectural Borders and Territories - Book Series - Routledge & CRC Press

Liquid Territories
Catchment Cartographies of the Mekong River

Christoforos Romanos

LONDON AND NEW YORK

Designed cover image: Christoforos Romanos

First published 2025
by Routledge
4 Park Square, Milton Park, Abingdon, Oxon OX14 4RN

and by Routledge
605 Third Avenue, New York, NY 10158

Routledge is an imprint of the Taylor & Francis Group, an informa business

© 2025 Christoforos Romanos

The right of Christoforos Romanos to be identified as author of this work has been asserted in accordance with sections 77 and 78 of the Copyright, Designs and Patents Act 1988.

All rights reserved. No part of this book may be reprinted or reproduced or utilised in any form or by any electronic, mechanical, or other means, now known or hereafter invented, including photocopying and recording, or in any information storage or retrieval system, without permission in writing from the publishers.

Trademark notice: Product or corporate names may be trademarks or registered trademarks, and are used only for identification and explanation without intent to infringe.

British Library Cataloguing-in-Publication Data
A catalogue record for this book is available from the British Library

ISBN: 978-1-032-70615-3 (hbk)
ISBN: 978-1-032-70617-7 (pbk)
ISBN: 978-1-032-70623-8 (ebk)

DOI: 10.4324/9781032706238

For Yioula, Maya and Dorella

Contents

Preface		*ix*
Introduction		1
PART A		
Basin		9
1	The Area of Water	11
2	Unifying Geographic Space	27
3	The River's Nations	45
PART B		
Delta		71
4	A Map for Water	73
5	Shaping the Delta	93
6	The Metropolis' Hinterland	114
PART C		
Floodplain		135
7	A Section in Water	139
8	Articulating Inundation	150

viii   *Contents*

9   The Region's Immergence   166

Bibliography   *179*
Cartography   *193*
Index   *196*

Preface

My earliest memory of the Mekong River is the lingering taste of coconut candy during a holiday in the wet season of 2010. As our tour group gathered enthusiastically around a boiling vat of the sweet stuff, the crowd parted and I caught a glimpse of boats floating silently along the river's flat horizon. Over the following decade I returned to the river to sketch the brick kilns of Vinh Long, to climb the karst peaks of That Son, to eat crab noodles on Can Tho floating market, to examine the disappearing waterfront in Phnom Penh and to briefly touch the parched soils of Isaan. Shared with friends, colleagues and lovers, those experiences prepared me for the moment when a planning project for the Mekong Delta was delivered to my desk at the end of 2017. Then the leader of my office's urban design team, I began a fervent search for information about those places I had visited. Maps, remote imagery and spatial data coupled with social statistics and official master plans presented this region according to the location of roads, settlement patterns, administrative units and the imaginary colours representing land uses. The Delta's particular association with the river also meant that the same region could be described with hydrological diagrams, the plans of canals and the principles of water management. Combined through the architect's eye, water, infrastructure and thousands of kilometres of canal-side settlements defined a delta of many parts that would nonetheless be collectively planned.

While our bid for the project never made it past the preliminary selection, I was left fascinated and travelled with my varied impressions of the Mekong into a PhD in the Netherlands. But less than a year after beginning the research, the start of the coronavirus lockdown cancelled all my plans. Without the possibility of conducting fieldwork, the clarity of the view constructed from the mapped information became even more urgent. Being aware that my perspective was remote (and would remain so for the duration of the lockdown) provided the incentive to reframe the initial investigation about water infrastructure through the technical tools that construct this distant view. Consequently, this book frames my attempt to understand what is made known by visualizing the flows of water but also what is made when the cartographer – like the architect – projects an image of the world onto the surface of a map.

This book is an outcome of that doctoral research project and the editorial process that followed. I consider myself very fortunate to have been guided through

x *Preface*

this entire process by Marc Schoonderbeek whose laconic demeanour, piercing intuition and warm friendship has been instrumental to this publication. In this respect, I also owe a great thanks to René van der Velde and Filip Geerts, whose insightful feedback on the content of this book allowed me to overcome my many intellectual limitations. A respectful (and cheeky) nod of thanks is also due to my friend and Rotterdam neighbour, the architect and teacher, Stefano Milani for many meaningful discussions and our various collaborations these last five years. This research would have been poorer without the generosity of the indefatigable hydrologist Thành Quốc Võ at Can Tho University, Sjoerd Swart, who introduced me to the works of Thomas Kuhn, Steffen Nijhuis of Delft's Urbanism department, who shared his time and knowledge on the practice of regional planning, and Nikos Katsikis, who inspired me to consider geography not as a mere background for design but as an active variable in the elaborate equation of planning territory. I must also mention the remarkable doctoral committee that tested the thoughts which appear in this book. Teacher, designer and invaluable source of knowledge on all things called urbanism Kelly Shannon, the great scholar of Southeast Asia's urbanization Stephen Cairns, the designer Adriaan Geuze, director of West 8, and the engineer Chris Zevenbergen, head of Delft's Delta Urbanism.

In the years of lockdown and those that followed, I was also fortunate to have the support of friends and colleagues: Salomon Frausto, director of the Berlage, François Molle for his enthusiastic dissemination of my thesis manuscript, Gianni Talamini at City University of Hong Kong for sharing his extensive knowledge and good humour, the critical wit of Alain Chiradia at the University of Hong Kong and the scholar Louie Shieh. I also want to thank Grahame Shane for his earnest attempts to read my thesis manuscript and his encouragement in my latest venture. Thanks is also due to my good friends Biao Lu and Jasper Hilkhuijsen, both veterans of our urban design team at Arup, the journalistic curiosity of The Ferg, Grazia Tona for her continued friendship and paradoxically Tram Nguyen for never reading and thus misunderstanding all of my texts.

The last to thank are always foremost in my thoughts. My singular friends, the artist and scholar Stella Bolonaki and the mystic Sebastian Heller, who kept me going in the worst of times. And my wonderful family, Andrew, Lena, Dimitris, Maya, Dorella and Yioula.

Introduction

Just as in the laboratory we create formulaic understandings of the processes of the physical world so too, in the map, nature is reduced to a graphic formula.
Deconstructing the map, John B. Harley, 1989

If maps are intended to formulate a nature visible to all, those of the Mekong River will conjure images of a mighty waterway coursing from the melting glaciers of the Tibetan Plateau to the tropical shores of the East Sea.[1] Other readers, however, will imagine the vast quantities of water flowing through a landscape of innumerable human interventions. Across parts of Thailand, Laos, Cambodia, Vietnam, Myanmar and China, the countless waterways which converge to form the Mekong's mainstream have been collected behind dams, diverted through irrigation canals, redirected by dikes and detained in endless extents of rice paddy. Supporting the livelihoods of millions of people speaking different languages, the infrastructure sustaining the region's extensive agricultural economies has been designed with the unwavering certainty granted by our accumulated knowledge of the river's surface flows. But after decades of exploitation, confidence in this knowledge is now quickly eroding. Not only has climate change severely disrupted the seasonal weather patterns which have allowed farmers to plan their harvests based on a regular supply of water. In the flatness of the deltaic lowlands, thousands of kilometres of canals have drained ancient wetlands reducing the capacity of the floodplain to detain unexpected inundations. Moreover, within the last two decades, the dams once celebrated as the most sustainable source of electrical power for rural households have been conclusively linked to unprecedented fluctuations in the quantity of water reaching downstream areas and affected the quality of sediment deposits vital for cultivation and biodiversity. As we aim to repair the catastrophic consequences of almost total water control and anticipate future conditions, *how* we know the Mekong River has become equally if not more important than *what* we know at this critical moment. The book draws a line in the present to trace the trajectory of our common knowledge about the river and explain how this knowledge has produced the vulnerable landscapes we live in today.

Organized on a regional scale, control of the Mekong's waters is underpinned by the assumption that the river occupies a very specific geographic space. Unlike the

DOI: 10.4324/9781032706238-1

2 Liquid Territories

liquid area covered by a single stream, the Mekong's hydrological *catchment areas* such as drainage basins, inundated plains and lowland delta extend far beyond the limits of the river's perennial flows. Specifying a catchment not only helps explain the way surface water behaves – from a raindrop falling on a distant mountain to the inundation experienced thousands of kilometres downstream. Conceptualized in terms of a catchment, multiple waterways of varying lengths, navigable conditions and cultural histories can be considered collectively along with the periodically wet (or dry) terrains between them. As a result a catchment area can encompass thousands of square kilometres even if the terrestrial ground permanently covered by water is only a small fraction of that extent. In a mathematical equation where the volume of water is a seasonal variable and space is a fixed constant, the catchment's geographic area quantifies how much water will be diverted, and where, within that area, canals, embankments, reservoirs and dams will be located and given corresponding dimensions. If knowledge of a catchment's hydrology is decisive for regulating the wetness of the ground in many parts of the world, knowledge of the Mekong's has served as more than a generic explanation of the way water flows. Across mainland Southeast Asia, significant sections of riparian countries' borders align with the basin's watersheds and have been historically contested as the geopolitical limits of colonial and later, national jurisdictions. Classified as geographic units, references to the Mekong's catchments have defined what constitutes the 'context' that affects planning decisions and functioned as the 'site' where those decisions are implemented. Instead of a predetermined geography, the book approaches the catchment area as one of multiple variables in a much more elaborate calculation aiming to transform social, political, environmental and technical relationships to conform with an anticipated outcome.

In hydrological relationships spanning distances beyond almost any individual's immediate first-hand experience, knowledge of what constitutes the Mekong's catchment areas is formed through the information recorded and displayed through the medium of maps.[2] Typically regarded as a scientific process that results in "a correct relational model of the terrain",[3] mapping provides valuable information describing how water flows, where people live or which infrastructure has been deployed. When the cartographic frame centres on the floodplain or on the basin, the map explains the outcome of interrelated processes that have unfolded on a geological timescale and present ground conditions that are cumulatively beyond the capacity of human technology to produce. The cartography of the catchment area, however, does not necessarily produce pictorial images of objectively perceived truths. Even though today maps are generated through remote sensing rather than the laborious topographic surveys of the past, the conditions which make a catchment 'visible' on paper or on screen are underpinned by the contingencies which distinguish wet ground from dry, a waterway from the inundated plain and one river system from all others. With each map in each era prepared for different reasons, the motives surrounding their production, as well as the agency of the cartographer to select which part and which features of the earth's surface to show, means that maps expound arguments that create connections between "conditions, states, processes, and behaviours".[4] Rather than incontrovertible representations of the terrain, references to the delta, basin or the floodplain propose different rules to edit the map's content. The region which emerges by projecting the Mekong's catchments on a map implies a context where people's activities, terrains and resources are inexorably linked to the river's surface flows. Even if these flows are too complex to depict on any one map or to include in any single hydrological model, by adopting the nomenclature of the catchment to describe where an event or ground condition is present or absent, the cartographic documentation of waterways, soil types and topographic gradients present a curated body of knowledge to assess the validity of a proposed spatial differentiation or the efficacy of a planned course of action. The question of the map's 'objectivity' is therefore less important than the set of common rules that inform the depiction of the drainage basin, coastal delta or flooded plains on maps prepared by cartographers in a different time and place. Viewed through the map-maker's eye, the reductive "graphic formula" resulting from this process does not so much simplify reality into easily digestible visual information as invoke alternative forms of spatial organization that only incidentally reflect the natural behaviour of water.

In the preparation of maps, one cartographic process stands out as most pertinent to this rarely unintentional divergence from observable experience. Indispensable to all professions that seek to explain and manipulate the condition of the ground, the act of delineation draws imaginary limits on the surface of the map. If the delineation of a catchment area may not always be presented as a boundary, the scientific allusion to a very specific, quantifiable geographic space implies the presence of an outer limit. The point where two basins meet or where land ceases to be a delta or a floodplain, the outer edges of a catchment area are brought into human consciousness "by virtue of the distribution of matter in space and time but are not themselves made of matter".[5] Thus, while soils, rivers and mountains are tangible phenomena with specific material qualities, the area described as a catchment is one of many possible conclusions drawn from observation of multiple geophysical processes. The cartographer's dependence on an epiphenomenon to specify a catchment area reverberates with a critical warning. In their voluminous study of maps, Denis Wood and John Fels have suggested that depending on the way information about the terrain is brought together within the cartographic frame maps can display different 'natures'. By claiming to explain these 'natures', the outline of embankments, the contour of slopes and the colours of the ground ascribe a cause and an expected outcome to parts of the earth's surface. In this sense, delineation is a deliberate interpretation of reality that inevitably favours the objectives of a dominant discourse. By indicating the scientific knowledge of water flows, by placing value on the entirety of the catchment area and by presenting political choices as the adherence to the qualities of a 'natural' phenomenon, the catchment's boundaries acquire authority. On a terrain that is rapidly transforming as a result of climate change and human modifications to water flows, references to the basin or delta evoke a permanent 'natural' order to adjust plans and implement a course of action. The notion that catchments signify unmediated geophysical processes is therefore tentative – merely theories that ultimately can only be falsified by recording inconsistencies in their operationalization. In times of escalating

4 *Liquid Territories*

environmental crisis such as the one we are currently experiencing, the multiple discrepancies between experience and theory are conveniently assigned to failures in implementation, and their designers – engineers, architects, planners and politicians – cast simply as blameless victims of incomplete or distorted information.

Yet even when an awareness of the possible gaps in knowledge informs design considerations, the outcomes hardly match expectations. Formulated on the map, the decision-making context given form through the catchment alone does not reflect the geography of Southeast Asia. If references to the science of geography denote knowledge of the world around us, knowledge of the Mekong's basin, delta and floodplain continues to be calibrated in relation to archetypal catchments in Europe and America. In different periods, comparisons of 'model' deltas and basins with their counterparts in Southeast Asia have glorified the benefits of the archetype's coordinated development to claim all basins and deltas are inherently designable. The technical and managerial practices compiled and commodified into "export products" for planning international basins and more recently global deltas identify the catchment with the source of 'common' problems and paradigmatic solutions. Explained with reference to the model, and despite the multiple political, economic, topographic and hydrological considerations typified by the archetypes, the Mekong's catchments are framed as the most relevant spatial extent to prescribe solutions for resource management, economic growth, climate change and urbanization. The context shaped by alignment of the Mekong's catchments with a global geography of hydrological basins, deltas and floodplains evokes a supervised geography pivoted on the expert's capacity to distinguish the spatial extents of the system being transformed.

A record and a speculation, the degree to which these maps convincingly represent reality or predict a future condition is less important than how they produce territory. On the map, the catchment area articulates what Richard Hartshorne calls the epistemic *concrete whole* or the *working object* of geography but also of geopolitics, spatial planning, infrastructure design and military control and serves to define the principles which underpin the selected area's internal coherence.[6] In this sense, the regions qualified by collecting and displaying information of catchment areas constitute hypotheses rather than unequivocal truths. Because hypotheses are created to explicate economic, social, political and environmental conditions, they can be presumably reframed – along with the region they envelop – to describe conditions which inevitably change at different rates. By intentionally maintaining the validity of the hypothesis when it is no longer descriptive, the *working object* indicates what should be rather than a current or previous condition. Once the *working object* specifies change, what may have begun as a *region* describing the context becomes a *territory* prescribing where transformation will take place. In other words, mapping designs territory by constructing the context around human activities.

The relevance of the Mekong's catchments in the production of territory does not lie solely with their power to situate transformation. Catchments are inventions of the human mind as much as outcomes of geology and hydrology. And as ideas which inform human action these too have genealogies. Arthur Lovejoy has pointed out that in the history of ideas each age appears to confront similar problems by evolving "new species of reasonings and conclusions".[7] Adherence to theories which require the map to prove however eventually mutate into dogmatic ideologies with more sinister motives. Against all proof to the contrary, the hypocritical conviction of European cartographers that the earth's natural order was maintained within *natural frontiers* (*frontières naturelles*) justified colonial powers to manufacture the limits which would contain Southeast Asia's unbounded *mandala* polities. And even as regional conflict escalated following the dissolution of French Indochina, monumental plans to drain the floodplain of 'excess' water conflated the calculable water balance with a natural equilibrium apparent only through the expert's gaze. By 'recovering' the capacity of water-logged lands to produce crops, by 'rescuing' the colonial *atopia* from the dangers posed by the action of water and by regaining control of the floodplain from the disruption caused by enemy insurgents, the delineation of the catchment differentiated the terrain to be 'reclaimed' from various threats. Articulating the response to a perceived imbalance in the natural, political and social equilibrium, cartography made the temporary accumulation of water 'visible', aligning the floodplain with the corrective operations aiming to 'redeem' the floodplain from its marginal status. Through the map, the territory produced by equating the spatial extent of these social and political concerns with the catchment did not simply anchor a course of action to a specific setting as provide the spatial parameters for their resolution. A unit of human more than geophysical activity, when the catchment becomes the plan to modify reality the possibilities inherent in mapping the flows, outflows and overflows of the river converge into the illusory certainty of a specific territory. As ideas speciate to evolve new settings, the book asks how the territories produced and maintained by the Mekong's catchments have gradually shaped the condition of the ground to resemble its mapped depiction.

The book approaches the search for answers to this question from two directions. On the one hand, the reader is invited to participate in the process of extracting knowledge through the perspective of the cartographer. Rather than photos, statistical charts or other forms of visual information, the book provides detailed descriptions of selected maps and the discourses surrounding their production bringing into simultaneous focus the minutiae which structure the depiction and the vast landscapes which they claim to explain. From the other direction, the book organizes the process of acquiring knowledge from maps by elaborating on the cartography of three types of catchment areas. Introduced to the region's geographic nomenclature as Europe's empires turned their sight eastwards, the Mekong's drainage basin, delta and floodplain are conceived on different hydrological premises and encompass more than one national jurisdiction. The repeated focus of cartographic efforts since before the violent start of colonization, maps of these catchments have also informed successive attempts at statecraft, military strategy, regional planning and water control. Graduated by their relative magnitude, the basin, delta and floodplain therefore serve as three viewpoints to examine broader questions of power, knowledge and space that will resonate with other global geographies. In this book, these are arranged in a typical sequence of spatial

6 *Liquid Territories*

analysis which proceeds from the largest to the smallest, the scale of the basin perceived as the *whole* encompassing the delta and the floodplain as the *part* from which the delta is composed. Where the sequence of chapters is intended to build a cumulative understanding of the other two catchments and the river as a whole, their capacity to act both as a scaled process and as a discrete space defies the assumption of a predetermined hierarchy describing the same single river system. Instead, the perceivable orders (of magnitude, of flows or of spatial organization) are revealed to be choices, the interdependence between upstream and downstream magnified, maintained or summarily collapsed by the deployment of a specific course of action.

What the territories of water include, if not what they signify, becomes increasingly important for the design disciplines collectively responsible for organizing society's adaptation to emerging ground conditions. Children already born will doubtless live to witness an average rise in global temperatures that will likely exceed three degrees by the end of the century and face the devastating consequences. As the urgency to confront the impacts of climate change is exponentially amplified, the ability to draw conclusions from reading maps and to formulate plans based on those conclusions is no longer a function of the map's capacity to convey accurate information or display information accurately. In the elaborate design equation which aims to transform territory, the results of mapping are merely proof of the designer's intent rather than unbiased evidence of the condition of the ground. If this sounds harsh, the book is not a condemnation of mapping or the cartographer. Just as Hannah Arendt's metaphorical *table* relates and separates at the same, the map's capacity to bring people from different disciplines and backgrounds together makes it an indispensable tool to form a shared understanding of the world and to organize collective action. As a process of acquiring knowledge, mapping can still serve to discern and assess the sometimes contradictory values which we assign to the world around us. Yet this alone is no longer enough. Dealing effectively with the territories which emerge on the map's surface requires us to look beyond the map and the divisive fixation with morphological legibility or systemic complexity. With each plot, neighbourhood, city, region or even the planet conceptualized under diverging premises, situating the individual design project – from building to landscape to infrastructure – requires us to consider which *whole* the *part* refers to. In a synthesis that eschews the distorting lens of scale, this calls us to reexamine the aspect of time, not as a managed ritual of construction phasing or material weathering but as a succession of conditions that trigger unexpected trajectories of change. If there is one thing that the liquid territories of the Mekong River can teach us, it is that this work is never done.

Notes

1 The book adopts the perspective of Southeast Asia where the South China Sea is named the East Sea.
2 Landscape architect Dilip Da Cunha has argued that the agency of cartography has been fundamental in the conceptualization of rivers. According to Da Cunha, by "separating

water from land" through the delineation of embankments mapping "invented" rivers. Dilip da Cunha (2019), *The Invention of Rivers: Alexander's Eye and Ganga's Descent*. Penn Studies in Landscape Architecture. Philadelphia, PA: University of Pennsylvania Press.

3 John B. Harley (1989), Deconstructing the Map. *Cartographica*, v. 26, n. 2, p. 3.

4 Denis Wood & John Fels (2008), The Natures of Maps: Cartographic Constructions of the Natural World. *Cartographica*, v. 43, n. 3, p. 190.

5 "In all these cases, the boundary is real but lacks physical substance; it is located in space but does not occupy space. It arises as a by-product of particular distributions of matter or energy (including human behaviour) over space and time". Antony Galton (2003), On the Ontological Status of Geographical Boundaries. In M. Duckham *et al* (eds.), *Foundations of Geographic Information Science*. London: Taylor & Francis, p. 155.

6 See Richard Hartshorne (1951), *The Nature of Geography: A Critical Survey of Current Thought in the Light of the Past*. Lancaster, PA: The Association of American Geographers, p. 39; and Lorraine Daston & Peter Galison (1992), The Image of Objectivity. *Representations*, Special Issue: Seeing Science, p. 35.

7 Arthur Lovejoy (1964), *The Great Chain of Being: A Study of the History of an Idea*. Cambridge, MA: Harvard University Press, p. 4.

Part A

Basin

Following a course that descends more than 4,000 kilometres from the Tibetan Plateau to reach the coastal lowlands of the East Sea, the mainstream of the Mekong River collects the water flowing from melting glaciers, forested mountain valleys and densely inhabited plains. The countless rivers and streams which merge to form the Mekong are the source of water for groups of people speaking multiple languages that can live thousands of kilometres away from each other. Included in the jurisdictions of separate national, social and political groups, the geographic space encompassed by these flows has been drawn on maps numerous times in different periods. The majority have focused the cartographic frame on the most densely populated sections, part of the contested historical domains of Siam, Vietnam, Cambodia and the region's multiple semi-autonomous polities. Since the violent start of European colonization, this space has been defined as the river's *basin*. Suggesting a single region unified by the flows of the river, maps of the hydrological catchment area have described a particular way of seeing the geography of Southeast Asia. If over time, the basin's limits have been refined according to improvements in cartography, the terms of this unification have also changed. But this change has not been informed solely by the evolution of scientific hydrology. The development of new techniques for regulating surface water and the conflict over the sovereignty of the terrestrial surface encompassed by the basin suggest different premises for cartographers to consider the catchment's extent. The cartography of the Mekong's basin is therefore not only a question of how best to represent the behaviour of water. Taking into account that maps of the Mekong River have also reflected the predominant technical, social and political narratives in the periods they were drawn, what land, domain or group of people is being unified or separated by delineating the catchment area is equally important.

DOI: 10.4324/9781032706238-2

10 *Liquid Territories*

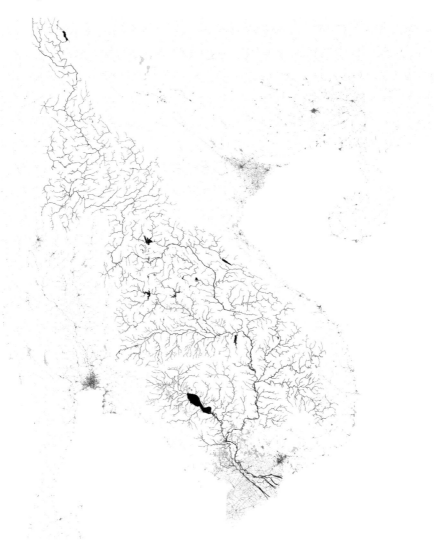

Figure A.1 **Distinguishing the Mekong River's catchments.** The map shows surface water flows (grey lines) and the footprint of urbanization (dark grey shade). According to the perspective of hydrology, the Mekong River consists of a group of waterways (black lines) that merge into a single flow carried downstream to the sea. The river courses past six countries and its drainage basin encompasses all the land between the waterways continuing northwards (beyond the edge of the map) to the Tibetan Plateau. Christoforos Romanos (2022), *The Mekong River's Flows*. [*Source:* Author]

1 The Area of Water

According to ideas purely theoretic, we should be tempted to admit, that rivers, having once issued from Alpine vallies, at the tops of which they take birth, must rapidly leave the mountains on a plane more or less inclined, the greatest declivity of which would be perpendicular to the axis of the chain, or the principal line of ridges. Such a supposition, however, would be contrary to what we observe in the most majestic rivers of India and China.

Personal narrative of travel to the equinoctial regions of the New Continent,
Alexander von Humboldt, 1822

Delimited by lines representing embankments, the way rivers are depicted on maps appears to suggest a linear body of water flowing over the terrestrial surface. Although the fixed cartographic extents of natural waterways essentially reduce their hydrological significance to the visible route of surface water, the spatial relationship between water and land is not restricted to the width and length of the river's perennial flows. Expressed as a *catchment area*, the measurable extent of geographic space contributing to the collection and drainage of a river's flows can extend far from the mainstream. Encompassing the sometimes dry terrestrial surfaces of distant mountains, inundated plains and sedimented lowlands, geographic references to a river's hydrological catchment are underpinned by specific ideas about the behaviour of surface water. Apart from describing a natural phenomenon, knowledge of the catchment's areal magnitude is necessary for the quantification of water volume in any part of a river system as well as for specifying the land affected by inundation. Articulating the catchment's boundary on maps has therefore been a preoccupation for both hydrologists and cartographers, who need to deduce the limits of these hydrological relationships from drawings of mountains, waterbodies and sediment deposits.

If this would imply that the catchment's mapped outline is simply the representative of an existing natural phenomenon, the process of translating that phenomenon into the pictorial language of cartography is not confined to the knowledge derived from scientific hydrology. Arguments equating the catchment area of rivers with the political ideology of natural frontiers or with the

DOI: 10.4324/9781032706238-3

12   *Liquid Territories*

hypothetical subdivision of the entire globe appeared almost simultaneously with the concept's theoretical inception in Enlightenment France. The basis for subsequent mappings of the Mekong River, the ability to 'see' the catchment on a map, became increasingly important for European cartographers visualizing the unexplored hinterlands of distant continents and for geographers attempting to define the epistemic *working object* of their discipline. Beginning with the emergence of the catchment area as a scientific concept, this chapter presents the hydrological, geographic and political notions which allowed sections of the terrestrial surface to be differentiated from each other in relation to a river's flows. Examining the work of European geographers prior to the colonization of Southeast Asia, the chapter asks what phenomena were being mapped with reference to the catchment: the behaviour of surface water, the apparent relationship between rivers and land or the spatial unit of political geography?

An Areal Equilibrium

Investigating the origin of rivers was a popular topic of research among scholars from the Renaissance onwards. Yet in contrast to the linear waterbody depicted on maps, to arrive at the conclusion that a river has, in some sense, an area 'belonging' to it, the river itself needs to be perceived as having areal properties. For the late 17th-century pioneers of scientific hydrology such as Edme Mariotte and Pierre Perrault, the extent where water collects as a result of rainfall or flooding, was instrumentalized in the form of a space called the *catchment* to aid in the estimation of the total volume of rainfall. Both Mariotte and Perrault structured their hydrological treatises around their response to a fundamental question: could the estimated volume of precipitation account for all the water in a river? Brother of the architect Claude Perrault who designed the Paris Observatory, made significant contribution to the study of water *On the Origin of Streams* constructed the concept of what later came to be known as the hydrological cycle. By closely studying the origins of the River Seine, he imagined the catchment area as a natural reservoir which collected all the rain that was to be distributed among the Seine's tributaries. Through observations of "the sides of its course" Perrault estimated the magnitude of an area which extended outwards from the river to nearby slopes. Refined to exclude streams and watercourses that drained in other directions, the resulting area was used to quantify the rainwater collected in the catchment. From this Perrault concluded that all the accumulated water *must serve also to supply all the losses, such as the feeding of trees, grasses, evaporation, useless flows into the River. . . .*[1] The "losses" which Perrault attributed to "useless flows", and computed to around five times the volume flowing down the Seine, served as the proof to confirm that rain could indeed supply all the water for the river.

In order to estimate this loss, however, Perrault's calculations required knowledge of an anticipated total from which to determine the deficit of water in the catchment. This total was found using a unique concept that continues to serve as a fundamental theorem of hydrology. The *principle of continuity* in the science of

The Area of Water   13

water expresses a fundamental law of mass conservation, holding that the amount of water entering a distinct system of hydraulic flows is equal to the amount of water exiting the system. This simple concept provided the study of water with a basis to consider the water volume measurable inside the catchment as an absolute total from which all other flows emerged. Enclosing a distinct hydrological continuity which included the rivers, their surrounding sides as well as precipitation and evaporation, the catchment presented a geography unified through a 'hydrocentric' lens. By imagining that the quantity of a river's flow at any one point could be approximated as the sum of the water in all upstream waterways, the catchment made distant – sometimes unnavigable – rivers immediately dependent on each other. In this sense, the principle of continuity provided the reasoning to splice together geographic spaces, thousands of kilometres apart, that were outside the immediate experience of a single average individual or beyond the control of a distinct political authority. The significance of this concept however did not anchor hydrology to an extended geographic dimension. The suggestion that a fixed total of water was distributed among river branches of varying lengths, breadths and navigable conditions presented the *part* as proportional to the *whole*. With individual waterbodies in a river system each sharing a determinable portion of the total amount, a distinct hierarchy was formed on the basis of the volume of water collected within the limits of the catchment. In this new register, rivers with larger catchments were privileged over sometimes historically significant rivers with smaller catchments, which became labelled as tributaries in relation to the main flow.

The catchment's reference to the geographic properties of a river and its conceptual dependence on an autonomous hydrological continuity suggest that the concept functioned in two ways. As a proxy for a very particular geographic space, the edge of the catchment could signify the limit of a distinct area on a map. What distinguished this area from all others that could be drawn on a map was the idea that all the water within the catchment's limit drained into one main river. The geographic space comprising the catchment was visualized according to the geometry of a bowl or basin, the sloping edges collecting and directing the water that ultimately discharged into the sea. As an area delineating the action of water, however, the catchment was also an abstraction of geographic space, a mathematical plane utilized to calculate volume, flow or evaporation. This distinction is important because while the catchment always indicated an enumerated relationship between geography and water, its delineation did not necessarily reflect the configuration of the topography. The divergence was not solely due to the dearth of reliable topographic information on 17th-century maps which could not be used for detailed calculations. Under the principle of continuity, the catchment could be conceptualized as a distinct collection of water-related phenomena without the need to acknowledge the nuances of its riverine terrain.

Yet if the principle of continuity allowed specific waterways to be thought of as a group, differentiating one particular catchment from other similar groups required a way to determine not only what was included but also what the collection of

14   *Liquid Territories*

waterways entailed when considered together. Switching his level of engagement from the river to the more general category of water, Perrault explained that:

> *the waters which remain there [in the catchment] being able to supply the continual evaporations, the sources [of rivers] which are produced from them flow in a continual and almost always equal course, because there is sufficient matter to maintain them in this state.*[2]

That the catchment delineated an area where unpredictable yet measurable atmospheric phenomena such as precipitation and evaporation would nonetheless maintain a constant flow suggests that for Perrault this grouping of rivers and slopes was something more than an assemblage of separate parts. The state of internal stability suggested by Perrault's hydrological reasoning is discussed by Christopher Duffy in relation to the broader scientific concept of the *natural balance*. Building on Joel Kaye's analysis of the notion of *balance* in Western literature, Duffy argues that early scientific hydrologists such as Perrault saw the internally self-regulating actions of water which were reflected in the principle of continuity in terms of a perceived state of equilibrium within nature.[3] This particular concept of balance becomes clearer when considering the area delineated by the catchment from the perspective of the hydrological cycle. As the plane upon which rain becomes stream, stream becomes river and river becomes sea, the topography of a river's basin encapsulated the entire range of processes related to water as a general phenomenon, as well as more particularly the journey of a single raindrop to the sea. The faith that together these processes, however turbulent, would always result in the inflow being equal to the outflow, reinforced the view of internal completeness and autonomy in relation to the catchment. Moreover, it assigned to the cumulative whole an idealized condition of balance that would have been impossible to assign to any of its individual parts.

The sense of an observable state of equilibrium in the interaction between natural phenomena developed into the laws of conservation from which the mathematical formulations for force, mass, energy and water are derived. However, as far as water is concerned, this only appears inevitable in hindsight. The historian of hydrology James Dooge has attempted to determine a genealogy for the science of water from multiple practices, treatises and computations. Comparing the critical role played by the principle of continuity in hydrology with Newton's laws of motion in astronomy, he notes how the influential Roman-era treatises by Vitruvius and the water commissioner Frontinus display no understanding of the principle.[4] The hydrological study by the architect Giovanni Fontana da Meli of the River Tiber in Rome illustrates how these ancient manuscripts still influenced hydrological practices even as late as 1598. As historian Asit Biswas explains, Fontana's study meticulously recorded the width and depth of all the streams flowing into the Tiber in an attempt to estimate their cross-sectional area.[5] According to the mathematical precedent established by Frontinus, this sectional area was considered exactly equal to the amount of water discharged through the waterway, enabling Fontana to estimate the overall water quantity affecting

The Area of Water   15

Rome during a recent flood. For Roman-era engineers, the cross section had been a critical concept to dimension infrastructure such as aqueducts that were needed to transport water across great distances. But the conceptualization of the action of water purely through the sectional area had limits that went beyond the flaws in the mathematical formulation itself. The technical focus on replicating the natural flow of rivers implied by the section limited the need for water control practices to understand phenomena that took place beyond the boundaries of the section. And even though Vitruvius was well aware of the *quadratus locus* (square area) especially with regard to agricultural fields, that particular spatial understanding remained unconnected with water. The planar conceptualization of water was therefore inaccessible to pre-17th-century architects and engineers until the introduction of the principle of continuity assigned an explicit geographic dimension to the river.

Perrault's measurements through the planar catchment did not eliminate or replace the need to consider water in terms of a cross section. But between its use as an approximation of a geographic space in perpetual equilibrium and a computable extent underpinned by the internally self-regulating action of water, the catchment could be seen to embody aspects of what Max Jammer distinguishes as the primordial values of the concept of *Area*. In an argument constructed as a precursor to the theories of space in physics, Jammer distinguishes between the *square unit* denoting an area's extent and the *areal unit* denoting an area's activity. Using metrology as his framework of comparison, Jammer notes that within the evolution of mathematics in pre-modern cultures, the units used to enumerate an extent of ground were also the units for other forms of quantification. In this sense, the same value that indicated the square area of an agricultural field could also represent the weight of the crop produced on that field or the number of seeds needed for its cultivation. By equating the value of an area's extent with the value of a specific activity enacted within the limits of that area, Jammer hypothesizes that in its conceptualization *Area* was intimately anthropocentric. Over many generations of refinement, the calibration of units of extent in relation to units of activity allowed geographic space to be approached from the perspective of the human labour involved in its domestication or cultivation.

The association between *Area* and human activity was more clearly articulated in the way hydrological theory, and the catchment in particular, could be used to cross between the confines of the experimental laboratory and the water-logged field. For engineers tasked with draining wetlands or irrigating agricultural plots, knowledge of the catchment provided a new perspective. Quantifying the impact of annual inundation in terms of a specific unit of liquid volume did not solely describe the physical condition of a landscape 'invaded' by water. The magnitude of a calculated volume of water also structured the technical requirements for the canals that needed to be excavated, or the height of the dikes that needed to be constructed. In other words, the planar catchment allowed the area of water to be imagined in terms of human activity. Traditional practices of floodplain drainage or water supply infrastructure, refined over generations, could now be adjusted according to the metric of an extended geographic relationship. As Dooge notes,

16 *Liquid Territories*

the study of water through the medium of classical mathematics was essentially deterministic. The symmetry encoded in the principle of continuity, presented hydrologists and water engineers with the opportunity to rationalize, and therefore eliminate the uncertainty posed by seemingly random natural phenomena. Control of water, and by extension control of the land affected by water, became a possibility within the boundaries of the catchment.

Nature's Frontiers

Perrault and Mariotte theorized the existence of the river's catchment in a period when cartography had only recently been elevated into a scientific pursuit. On the European continent, the centre of cartographic knowledge and where new astronomical surveying techniques were systematically adopted to prepare maps was Paris. Yet at the beginning of the Sun King's reign (1643–1715), maps of France were typically constructed at the level of provincial administrations. Prioritizing a local perspective of the terrain, these maps rarely followed any common standards in their representation of natural or man-made features. Without a consistent scale or reference system across the surface of the map, the use of cartography to communicate the measure of geographic space was limited, if not impossible. Moreover, the perspectives which informed the disposition of natural features on individual provincial maps were built on oral traditions and local histories, often presenting the location of rivers and mountains duplicating or sometimes determining the distinction between separate domains.[6] These maps were so different from each other in their representation of the terrain that they prevented the royal cartographer and first director of the Paris Observatory Jean-Dominique Cassini from combining them into a unified map of the kingdom. But these incommensurable perspectives of the same terrain were not a problem of graphical representation alone. They also involved the use of maps to convey different interpretations of the role of nature in shaping France and, more broadly, human affairs.

In the *Ancien Regime*, the discourses around France's *frontières naturelles (natural frontiers)* reflected the changing concerns of politicians, military strategists as well as scientists with regard to the manmade organization of geographic space. Politicians supporting a theory of natural frontiers such as Cardinal Richelieu considered the location of mountains and rivers as an indicator of France's innate size, placing the Pyrenees, the Rhine and the Alps at the edges of a unified terrain occupied by a distinct cultural group (the Gauls). The differentiation of France's sovereignty along these geographical features, however, defied the complexity of governing such vast natural "boundaries". This was reflected in the negotiated legal documents that resulted from conflicts between the royal courts of Europe. Signifying the end of hostilities between France and the Hapsburg dynasty, the 1648 Westphalian peace treaty legally confirmed the absolute power of sovereigns over a determined extent of land. Where it came to determining authority over the shared waterways of the Rhine, the treaty stipulated that above all "the Navigation of the Rhine be free, and none of the Parties shall be permitted to hinder Boats going up, or coming down, detain, stop, or molest them".[7] By denying the sovereign states through which the river meandered the right to block trade or impose tolls or taxes, the treatment of the Rhine in the words of the Treaty presented limits to the monarch's absolute power over his domain. The 'violation' of absolute sovereignty in the case of the Rhine was due to the importance of the river as a trade route for all riparian users along its length. Considering that barges were usually pulled by draught horses, the area addressed by the Treaty extended beyond the mapped embankments of the river. The historian Terdje Tvedt argues that where it came to the river forming a boundary, the Treaty underlined the importance of cooperation between states and the "creation of authority structures that were not coterminous with geographical borders".[8] The difference between the rhetoric of the *frontières naturelles* and the autonomous organization of the area adjacent to the Rhine illustrates the practical limitations of conceptualizing the linear boundary in terms of a natural feature. This was not because the river or mountain could not be conceptualized as an edge. Yet such a simplified separation of France from its neighbours could not account for the notional space of activity structured on the conventions of regional trade that surrounded the river. The conceptual chasm between the idea of a linear river boundary – as it continued to be portrayed on maps – and the reality of a "corridor" of riverine activity, highlights the ideological character of the discourse around *frontières naturelles*. Within this framework, the river's role in determining the boundaries of political authority was essentially passive, a rhetorical instrument to further the goal of a unified French identity and political nation-building.

Positioned on maps relative to where the boundaries "ought to be" rather than necessarily reflecting the physiognomy of the landscape, mountains and rivers continued to represent the borders of French sovereignty even as cartographic practices evolved. The founding of the French Academy of Sciences in 1666 and Observatory a few years later sought to rectify an absence of standards related to cartographic projection, surveying and representation. The new astronomical and geodetic techniques introduced to cartographic practice through the Academy rescaled the disproportionate prominence of rivers, hills and forests presented in provincial maps to fit the boundaries of a national narrative. Nonetheless, maps of France prepared by Cassini's son Jacques and based on new mathematical methods of triangulation, continued to sketch the Alps and Pyrenees as clear, linear limits, incorporating rivers and mountains into the cartographic language used to express the limits of a domain (**Figure 1.1**). The influential Genevan philosopher Jean-Jacques Rousseau, who idealized society's relationship with nature in his writing, crystallized the belief that the "political order of the Continent is in some sense the work of nature" with mountains, seas, and rivers determining forever the number and size of Europe's constituent nations.[9] Rousseau's invocation of a political order as the product of nature shifted emphasis from a question about the *frontières* to questions about the agency of nature to shape human affairs. From Rousseau's perspective the relationship between mountains and the limits of polities was observable in the mountainous configuration of the Swiss Confederacy. In the generalized condition implied by this statement, the role of Nature is not that

18 *Liquid Territories*

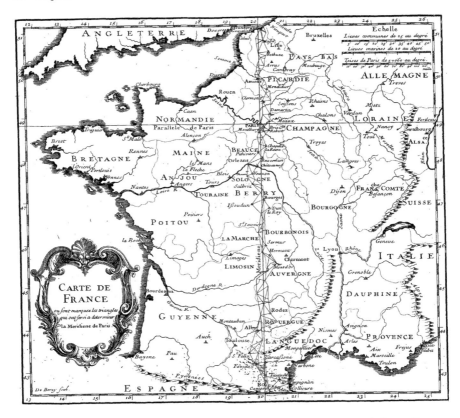

Figure 1.1 **The Cassini map of France.** Completed and published by Cassini's son Jacques, the map gives physical expression to the boundaries of France. Linear mountains (south and east) and the Rhine (north) are drawn according to the triangulated reference points of the Paris Meridien. Jacques Cassini (1723), *Carte de France ou sont marquez les triangles qui ont servi determiner la Meridiene de Paris*. [*Source:* BNF]

of a passive receptacle of human action. For Rousseau and the other *philosophes*, the environment was active in defining the character of social relationships, and stabilizing an imagined harmony with nature. In this sense, the natural boundary reflected – more than delimited – particular cultural or linguistic specificities, characteristics that for Rousseau could be further elucidated through the study of nature and its aesthetic reception by people. The conflation of natural features with sovereignty augmented the perception that the two were related. However, the implication that the product of the natural boundary was a political space rather than a geophysical area which is only subsequently given a political dimension suggests that there was limited scope to independently examine the nature to which these boundaries referred.

Theorizing the Catchment's Cartography

The nature related through maps was not always a representation of political narratives. Maps used to record the effects of recurring natural phenomena, such as floods, made cartographic practices useful for systematic observation and for the deployment of technological means to mitigate their impact. Drawings of the 1740 Paris flood, for example, showed the plan of the city along with the land inundated by the river and the cellars in which water had entered. Prepared by the architect and cartographer Philippe Buache, the drawings and the report which accompanied them gave a detailed account of his observations and recommendations based on almost ten years of mapping the Seine River. In addition to recording the location of flood waters, Buache's level surveys of the city's streets in relation to the river presented the topography beneath Paris and used it to identify the sloped ground which directed water towards the Seine. The drawing named "Second Plan" however goes some way further than simply illustrating the condition of the ground below the city's houses, streets and palaces. A distinct outline resembling a mountain ridgeline indicated the limits of the flood in relation to the slope, making apparent an areal relationship that was only possible to imagine through the medium of the map.

As the first member of the Academy to hold the title of Geographer within the newly established scientific discipline, Buache's maps resonated beyond scientific circles. Apart from publishing his research on the Parisian floods, Buache's scientific output included two maps prepared in 1744. These presented the Pacific Ocean and France subdivided according to mountain ranges and river basins, respectively. Published eight years later in the prestigious *Mémoires de l'Académie Royale des Sciences*, Buache's *Essai de Géographie Physique* appeared to synthesize the two maps into a rational geographic theory of the globe's geophysical structure. Accompanied by two new maps, his essay introduced the concept of the river basin. With almost nothing – as Buache claimed – known about geography below the 50th parallel (of latitude), his maps gave shape to distant, unknown landmasses based on the configuration of rivers and mountains. In the manner of scientific treatises dealing with a new field of knowledge, the text distinguished three categories of rivers and their respective mountains. Rather than size, the hierarchy proposed by Buache relied on the physical disposition between these three types, with the great (*grande*) rivers and mountains forming the "spines" and the lateral (*moyenne*) and coastal (*de côtes*) mountains the "branches". The structured geophysical order that emerged on the map was therefore:

> . . . according to the natural division of the Earth Globe [. . .] with the lands inclined towards each sea, and whose waters, from rivers and streams discharge therein from the chains of mountains, which are like the crest of their basin.[10]

The conception of the mountain crest as the highest part of an inclined surface that descended to the sea explained the way "rivers and streams" were part of a new geographic principle called the river basin. On the basis of the "clues provided by rivers", Buache proceeded to deduce the location of the unknown "chains

20 *Liquid Territories*

of mountains" from the location of known rivers. The dogmatic adherence to the basin as a geographic principle was reflected in the two new maps. On the global scale, mountain ribbons appeared on parts of the map where mountains would have been known not to exist, such as the range bisecting the Iberian Peninsula. These even extended into the seas to form underwater basins that subdivided the ocean according to an invisible aquatic topography. On the second map focused on the English Channel, the clearly labelled names of the river basins inside France were presented within the limits of sometimes fictional mountain ranges, such as the one dividing the Loire and Seine basins to the south of Paris (**Figure 1.2**). However, the novel planimetric projection of mountains which gave the surface of the map a sense of relational measure did not distinguish between existing and imaginary topographies. Especially in areas close to Paris where the map's information could be easily verified, the misrepresentation of the terrain's configuration would have been difficult to reconcile with Buache's position as the head of a scientific discipline devoted to improve the accuracy of cartographic depiction.

What prompted Buache to distort geography in such a way? His *Essai de Géographie* clarified that his intention was to contribute to the field of *physical*

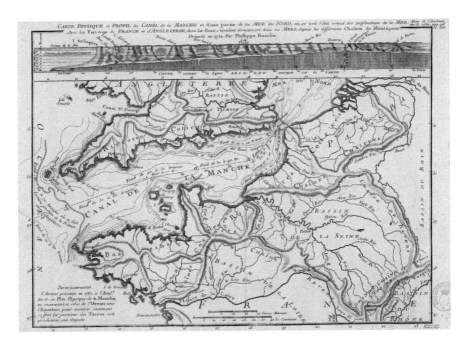

Figure 1.2 **The imaginary topography of catchments.** Using mountains to signify the hypothetical limits of river basins in France, Buache's map presents a topography that does not distinguish between existing and imaginary elevations such as the fictional range dividing the catchments of the Seine and Loire rivers. Philippe Buache (1752), *Carte Physique et Profil de la Manche*. [*Source*: BNF]

geography, which he distinguished from the political and cultural references of *historical* geography and the technical, theory-laden methods of *mathematical* geography. In his role as Academician, the disciplinary specificity is important. It served to ground his work in the practical knowledge that "can be known simply and as all men use it more or less", and to distinguish it from the Academy's related fields of knowledge such as astronomy.[11] The allusion to a collective sphere of geographic knowledge presented these maps as the visualization of a common reality that could be objectively understood. Objectivity in the mid- to late 18th century, however, was not the same epistemic value as it is today. Lorraine Daston and Peter Galison, who examined the historical evolution of objectivity, point out the difference between a later idea of a "morality of self-restraint" and an earlier notion of "truth to nature".[12] This 'nature' however is not a reference to the non-human world. Ernst Cassirer, in his study of Enlightenment thinking, suggests that *natural* refers to all knowledge "as long as it springs from human reason and does not rely on other foundations for certainty".[13] This suggests a truth bounded by the scientist's comprehension of reality rather than a specific group of objects. Thus, while in the second half of the 19th century, the creation and collection of scientific images went through a process of expunging the curatorial eye of the expert, in Buache's time the role of the scientist was to interpret natural phenomena and explain them through new cognitive types and categories. Evaluating the maps in terms of their objectivity is therefore different from understanding the information they depict as an accurate representation of nature. Faithfulness or truth to nature functioned *through* the interpretative action of the expert and not as a value-free "view from nowhere". As Daston and Galison argue, this did not mean that early scientific work was abandoned to the subjective caprices of the scientist. Rather the standard ensuring the objectivity of the depiction was the consistency of the scientist's approach towards the primary source of investigation, namely the non-human world. From this perspective, the fictional representation of mountains, which resulted from the rigorous application of the theory of basins, was evidence of the author's objectivity and in that sense, a necessary deceit for the maps to maintain their scientific value.

However theoretically credible, the drawings of mountains which acted as much to separate river basins from each other as to provide each river with its own catchment area posited a possible geophysical configuration that contradicted experience. In the hypothetical world presented on the surface of the map, mountains were not only depictions of natural barriers but also the structural elements for rational geographic conjecture. Buache's use of cartographic methods for speculative purposes was not unique. Cartographers focusing on physical geography would invariably speculate on the geography of parts of the globe even where their knowledge was non-existent, or as in the case of adherents to the ideology of the *frontières naturelles*, use maps to underpin abstract political arguments. Where Buache's maps differ, however, are in their uncompromising deployment of a specific, scientific theory even where this appeared to contradict common knowledge. The devotion to the theory of the basin is not limited to how the maps themselves demonstrate a scientific concept related to water. Referring to his proposed

22 *Liquid Territories*

framework of mountains in terms of a *système* indicates that for Buache at least, the interrelationships reflected on the maps were as important as the results they produced. Moreover, his evocation of a *natural* geophysical order encompassing the entire globe suggests that the value of the conceptual basin included its ability to provide the reference for a scientifically determinable subdivision of the world. By using the basin as the model to configure this subdivision, authorship of the monumental ribbons of elevated ground crossing the map is shared between the perceived agency of nature and the agency of the cartographer to predict nature's underlying patterns.

Perhaps the most famous student of Buache's work on river basins was Alexander von Humboldt. Highly influential to the subsequent study of geography and mountains in particular, Humboldt considered the French cartographer a man of science referencing his maps in his travels through South America. His survey of the Orinoco River however challenged the fundamental assumptions in Buache's theory. In Humboldt's personal narratives, he noted that in the low-lying landscape of the New World "small risings of counter-slopes" occurred more frequently than monumental chains of mountains. His criticism, aimed towards the inaccuracy of Buache's deductions, was particularly directed at the foundational principle of 'containing' the basin between two ridge lines. This idea clashed with the experience of the Orinoco delta where the confluences of rivers and streams, flowing from multiple directions, intertwined to make the distinction between basins impossible and perhaps meaningless.[14] Reflecting on these differences, he remarked that

> . . . *it is a false application of the principles of hydrography, when geographers attempt to determine the chains of mountains in countries of which they suppose they know the course of the rivers.*[15]

This would appear to lay the responsibility for the mistaken location of mountains on the limited knowledge of distant rivers from which the catchment area was deduced. But following his own surveys, Humboldt observed that the use of theoretical ideas to construct physical maps was problematic in general. The most interesting part of this critique was the identification of where the problem had originated. Looking closely at the assumptions governing the delineation of the basin, Humboldt clarified that these were based on the 'enclosed' valley, a model inspired by the European Alpine landscape that had little resemblance with the environments he was examining. In contrast to the theories of European 'arm-chair' geographers, Humboldt's own cartographic work aspired towards a "truth to nature" based on close personal observation and direct experience. Mountains, which for Buache formed a geophysical division of global dimensions, were for Humboldt a specific type of landscape to be studied and not a substitute for an edge or the limit of a natural phenomenon. Buache's theory was therefore useful only in so far as it indicated where mountains were located and less so with regard to describing a universal principle of hydrology. But where the theory of the basin failed to resonate with the actual experience of nature, its suggestion of a primordial subdivision of the Earth was met with far greater interest, especially among the growing community of scientists calling themselves geographers.

Even before the establishment of the Academy, geographic knowledge corresponded with the information displayed on maps. The way cartographers organized the world into political divisions was also the way to study and teach geography in the universities and royal courts of 18th-century Europe. The elevation of geography in 1730 into a new branch of science within the Academy's carefully defined categories of knowledge created the need for an epistemically structured approach to the subject. Yet unlike anatomy or astronomy that could assuredly affirm the human body or the star as the unit of research, geographers had yet to establish what Daston and Galison call their *working object*. In its role as an epistemic unit, the *working object* of geography would need to distinguish the object of study from all other possible natural objects and phenomena and to function as the area from which theories are formed and to which they are applied. As the representative of the science of geography within the Academy, Buache's public role made him at least partially responsible for the formulation of the epistemic unit. Invariably, however, this required consensus on which phenomena, out of all other perceivable transformations in the physical and social environment, were considered important enough to inform the constitution of the *working object*'s area. One of the few subjects of agreement was the doubt surrounding the use of political boundaries to constitute the unit of study. The speed by which jurisdictions changed as a result of wars or alliances, and the indefinite relationship of borders with other historical, cultural or even geophysical relationships, motivated geographers to look elsewhere for their scientific frame. The limits of basins that appeared on Buache's maps were therefore more than a theory of geophysical relationships. For geographers and quite possibly Buache himself, they reflected the potential for a naturally delineated unit on which to base geographic study that would replace the ephemerality of political borders.

But although rivers themselves were intimately connected with the human settlements in their proximity, the space encompassed by the basin often extended to include distant inaccessible terrains, linked to each other only by the notional flows of water depicted on maps. As such, although the basin provided a scientific theory for geospatial subdivision, it had limited resonance as an areal unit for the study of human relationships. For the eminent geographer Carl Ritter, the technical basis for the delineation of the basin was considered too simplistic to be acceptable as the common unit for the study of geography.[16] His alternative to the basin, the *region*, was expressly based on the belief that the areal dimension of natural *and* social phenomena coalesced into distinguishable 'organic' unities.[17] His inclusion of rivers – as well as basins – among the instruments which delineated regions confirmed the importance he assigned to the relationship between the social and natural environment. Nonetheless, the idea that the region's outline would form a permanent areal standard had less to do with how cultural ideas or historical facts appeared to transform in relation to a fixed geographic space, as it did with where some part of these social qualities was perceived to be spatially concentrated. If the articulation of the region specified the domain of phenomena worthy of study on the one hand,

24   *Liquid Territories*

on the other, it also functioned as the reference from which to analyse those same phenomena. In this sense, the epistemic act of formulating the boundaries of the region was also a hypothesis *about* the region, an argument validated through the consistency of the narratives that structured its internal coherence. Since objectivity was relative to the persuasive arguments and credentials of the geographer, this conundrum revealed the subjective hand of geographers in shaping how the scientific *working object* was conceived.

The determination of the region had one further intellectual consequence. In separating one part of the surface of the earth from all others, it raised, once more, the question of how that part was related to the whole. Was it an autonomous fragment as Buache's deterministic logic had implied or an interdependent component? For Ritter the earth as a whole was an "organism", with the continents and smaller regions related as organs would be to a body.[18] This organic analogy however does not help, since a common understanding of what "organism" implied for different geographers was as elusive as determining a commonly acceptable *working object*. Yet, the difference between a part deduced from an idea of the whole and a whole inferred from an analysis of the part is important. According to Cassirer, the "truth of nature" was not demonstrable through the deterministic processes of deductive reasoning which follow almost as proofs of a preconceived structure of relationships but could only be surmised from systematic analysis of the part.[19] Seen from the perspective that an ultimate, objective "truth" was at stake in the scientific examinations of the Enlightenment, Buache's work was compromised by his belief in an existing global structure from which the part is derived. But while his maps' focus is on the location of mountains what is presented is nonetheless a *système* that relies on basins – the existence of mountains being so inexorably linked to the existence of rivers that one cannot make sense on the map without the other.

Conclusion

Buache's theory of the basin had a basis in the hydrological ideas developed by Perrault and Mariotte. But where the two hydrologists deduced the quantity of water from the hypothetical catchment, Buache deduced the shape of the basin from the course of the river. Geography, responsible for the study of the earth and distinguishable from 'mere' cartography, was the science best equipped to speculate on these issues. Employing cartographic methods to communicate the geographic theory of global subdivision suggests that the maps accompanying Buache's thesis were themselves tools or instruments of the argument, pictorial evidence of the theory's reflection of the 'truth'. For those inspired by this vision of reality, the accuracy of the maps' depiction of mountains was less important than the greater 'truth' of a world neatly subdivided by natural forces. The epistemic arguments around partitioning the earth's surface reinforced the idea that what accounted for the integrity of the part was its place within a greater whole.

Ultimately, however, the configuration of any regional 'object' distinguished in this way would always be contingent on the geographer's ability to convincingly construct a narrative of internal coherence. Peter Galison has pointed out that the

The Area of Water 25

way *working objects* were depicted tells us much about the scientific world, but what constitutes the standards of "right" depiction tells us more about the scientists involved.[20] Thus, if the map of the basin mirrored any 'truth', it was not the agency of mountains and rivers to divide the globe into discernible units. Rather, it reflected the human need to perceive the distant, unknown and uncharted parts of the world according to what was already known. From this angle, the geography of other continents became categorized according to the classificatory registers first observed and confirmed within the European scientific tradition. With very limited first-hand experience of these places, Africa, the Americas and Asia became knowable through the subdivision of a regional *working object* conceived in Europe. The rational scientific presentation of history, society and nature became entwined with what the region included and excluded, making little-known areas such as the Mekong River present within a global geographic discourse. Yet between the comfort of writing about places on the other side of the world and how that written knowledge was instrumentalized on the ground, the distance was surprisingly short. As European geographers explicated their understanding of Southeast Asia's rarely visited hinterlands through maps and texts, the impression they created was of a place familiar and simultaneously unknown.

Notes

1 *"Toute cètte eau ainsi ramassée en la quantité· que nous venons de dire, est ce qui doit servir à faire couler cette Rivière pendant une année, depuis la source jusques au lieu que nous avons designé, & qui doit servir aussi à suppléer à tout ce qu'il peut y avoir de dechets, comme aliments d'arbres, plantes, herbes, évaporations, écoulemens inutiles dans la Rivière qui ne sont que la grossir pour un temps & pendant qu'il pleut . . .".* Pierre Perrault (1674), *De l'origine des fontaines.* Paris: Impri. Pierre le Petit, p. 258.

2 Perrault writes: *"les eaux qui y demeurent pouvant fournir aux évaporations continuelles, les sources qui en sont produites coulent d'un cours continuel & presque toûjours égal, à cause qu'il y à de la matiere suffisante pour les entretenir en cet estat . . .".* ibid., pp. 251–252.

3 Christopher Duffy (2017), The Terrestrial Hydrologic Cycle: An Historical Sense of Balance. *WIREs Water*, v. 4, e1216, pp. 14–17.

4 James Dooge (1988), Hydrology in Perspective. *Hydrological Sciences Journal*, v. 33, n. 1, p. 64.

5 Asit Biswas (1970), *History of Hydrology.* Amsterdam & London: North-Holland Publishing Company, p. 202.

6 Peter Sahlins (1990), Natural Frontiers Revisited: France's Boundaries Since the Seventeenth Century. *The American Historical Review*, v. 95, n. 5, p. 1428.

7 T. Tvedt, O. McIntyre & T.K. Woldestsadik (2011), Sovereignty, the Web of Water and the Myth of Westphalia. In T. Tvedt, O. McIntyre & T.K. Woldestsadik (eds.), *A History of Water, Series 3, v. 2, Sovereignty and International Water Law.* London & New York: IB Tauris, p. 7.

8 *ibid.*

9 Quoted from Sahlins, *op. cit.*, p. 1436.

10 *"Une connoissance plus détaillée pourroit être donnée en trois cartes, qui, selon la division naturelle, du Globe terrestre représenteroient à part, chacune des trois grands mers, avec les terrains inclines vers chaque mer, et dont les eaux des fleuves et rivieres s'y dechargent depuis les chaines de montagnes, qui sont comme la crete de leurs bassins".*

26   *Liquid Territories*

Philippe Buache (1752), Essai de géographie physique. *Mémoires de l'Académie royale des sciences*, pp. 407–408.

11 *"La Géographie physique ou naturelle peut etre considérée simplement et telle que tous les hommes en font plus ou moins d'usage: C'est alors la connoissance de Ia situation et du sol extérieur des lieux qu'ils habitent, et de ceux qui les environnent". Ibid.*, p. 400.

12 Lorraine Daston & Peter Galison (1992), The Image of Objectivity. *Representations*, n. 40, Special Issue: Seeing Science, p. 84.

13 Ernst Cassirer (1951), *The Philosophy of the Enlightenment*. Princeton, NJ: Princeton University Press, p. 39.

14 *"Accustomed to consider the rivers of Europe only in that part of their course where they are contained between two lines of ridges [lignes de faites], consequently enclosed in valleys; and forgetting, that the obstacles which inflect both the tributary streams and principal recipients are less frequently chains of mountains, than small risings of counter-slopes; we find a difficulty in conceiving the simultaneous existence of these windings, these bifurcations, these communications of rivers in the New World".* Alexander von Humboldt 1814–1829 (1827), *Personal Narratives of Travel to the Equinoctial Regions of the New Continent During the Years 1799–1804 by A. de Humboldt and Aimé Bonpland with Maps and Plans*. London, Longman, translated by H.M. Williams, 2nd edition, 7 vols, v. 5. London: Longman, Hurst, Rees, Orme and Brown, p. 450.

15 Alexander von Humboldt (1811), *Essai politique sur le royaume de la nouvelle Espagne*. Paris: F. Schoell. Quoted from Bernard Debarbieux, The Various Figures of Mountains in Humboldt's Science and Rhetoric. *Cybergeo: European Journal of Geography, Epistemology, History, Teaching*, doc 618 (Online since 21 August 2012).

16 Richard Hartshorne (1951), *The Nature of Geography: A Critical Survey of Current Thought in the Light of the Past*. Lancaster, PA: The Association of American Geographers, p. 39. Hartshorne devotes a considerable portion of his book on natural boundaries and the conception of the 'concrete whole' in the evolution of scientific geography, approaching the subject mainly from the works of German geographers.

17 *Ibid.*, p. 67.

18 *Ibid.*, p. 256.

19 Cassirer's study of Enlightenment nature and natural science draws out the contrasts between the Cartesian deductive thinking derived from 'first principles' and Newtonian inductive reasoning that accounted for phenomena on "the sole basis of the observable facts and general principles of natural science". Cassirer, *op. cit.*, p. 49.

20 Peter Galison (2010), *The Objective Image*. Inaugural Address for Treaty of Utrecht Chair at Utrecht University, Universiteit Utrecht, Faculteit Geesteswetenschappen, Utrecht, p. 30.

2 Unifying Geographic Space

People mingle with people like streams with streams, rivers with rivers; sooner or later they will form a single nation, just as all the waters of the same basin end up merging into a single river.

Histoire d'un ruisseau,
Élisée Reclus, 1869

If the area enclosed between two mountains and bisected by a river appeared as a catchment to an engineer or a hydrologist, then for many geographers the same area was more commonly identified as a *valley*. Although Humboldt had noticed the Eurocentric bias of relying on the geomorphology of the valley to delineate river catchments, he did not hesitate to characterize a wider area related to rivers as valleys, reserving the term *basin* for more technical relationships between slope and water flow. The geophysical basis for considering valleys, featured prominently in Carl Ritter's influential textbook *Comparative Geography* where along with fissures, chasms and abysses, the valley described a broader category of geological phenomena known as mountains or used as an alternative term for river basins. Prominent in the toponymy of numerous places within continental Europe, valleys featured in the European names for geographic areas in Africa and Asia. From narrow Alpine openings to the vast riparian lands included within historical landscapes such as the Nile Valley, the types of geography denominated by the term varied widely. The ideas articulating the valley's extent on the map however did not necessarily equate with the hydrological principles underpinning the outline of the basin. Maps of the Mekong Valley prepared using the late 19th century's latest surveying techniques claimed to also reflect a particular relationship between topography and power. Drawn to suggest the geography of Southeast Asia's hinterlands was a function of sovereignty, cartographers working on behalf of the French, Siamese and Vietnamese operationalized the idea of the river's catchment to respond to the questions of power ignited by European colonization. Denoted by cartographic boundaries, the European conceptualization of authority over geographic space contrasted with Southeast Asia's boundaryless *mandala* polities and the overlapping dominions of the region's kings. If not descriptive of an existing geophysical condition, the chapter asks what else was being outlined within the

DOI: 10.4324/9781032706238-4

28 *Liquid Territories*

shape of the Mekong's basin. The context of geopolitical strategies and the setting for cartographic expeditions? Or the spatial extent of particular courses of action that endeavoured to extricate and organize a single territory from a vast and diverse terrain inhabited by millions of people speaking multiple languages?

The Geography of Authority

European colonization of peninsular Southeast Asia began with the British invasion of Burma in 1824. Situated along the trade route between British-ruled India and the Qing dynasty of China, British embassies to the Burmese royal court had been regular since the late 18th century. With a long tradition in producing maps, the Burmese were interested in the new ways of cartographic representation on European maps. Conversely, in the journals of Ambassador Francis Hamilton, Burmese maps were viewed as fascinating cultural artefacts but inaccurate portrayals of the peninsula's geography. This was especially the case for maps showing Burma in relation to neighbouring kingdoms. Of the Burmese maps reproduced and published by Hamilton, those depicting the geography eastwards of the Salween River showed the Mekong disproportionately shorter than waterways within Burma and far closer to Rangoon than British cartographers estimated. Yet first-hand knowledge of these distant places would have been extraordinary for any single Burmese cartographer. The inclusion of the Mekong or the even more distant Country of the Kiokachin Shan (Cochin China) within the map indicate that geographic knowledge in pre-colonial Burma was collected and compiled from multiple sources. Despite the divergence of local maps from the coastal observations made by sailors, rival European merchants competed for information about hinterland polities and terrains to assemble the most accurate maps of Southeast Asia and reveal new trade routes to the lands ruled from Beijing.

The result of one of these syntheses was the map of Siam prepared by the cartographic office of John Walker. Drawn on behalf of the British Ambassador John Crawfurd, the map was considered the most accurate representation of the peninsula during that period. Relying on sources collected by Crawfurd during his ambassadorship to the kingdom, the Walkers' depiction of Southeast Asia's hinterlands also drew on Hamilton's reproductions of Burmese maps as well as a much older map from 1691 prepared on behalf of the French Ambassador to Siam, Simon de La Loubère, by the royal cartographer Jean-Dominique Cassini. Published in a celebrated account of his three-month stay in the country, La Loubère's map drew from limited first-hand observations sailing along the Menam (Chao Phraya) River and the anecdotal impression that "The Country of Siam is only a Valley".[1] Compiled according to the cartographic conventions Cassini had helped establish through the Academy, La Loubère's map presented peninsular Southeast Asia structured by linear mountain ranges that aligned perfectly with the dotted line denoting the limits of the kingdom. Siam itself was depicted almost like Buache would later design his maps of river basins, with the Chao Phraya as a central spine and the river's branches extending to touch an enclosing wall of mountains to the east and west. Using mountains to indicate the limits of countries where the

Unifying Geographic Space 29

geography was unknown, the cartographic tropes of the *frontières naturelles* gave Siam an illusory physical presence on the map that resembled the civilized, 'naturally' delimited kingdoms of Europe.

With source maps already distorted by either the French or the Burmese perspective, it was left up to the cartographer to determine how these materials could construct the visual representation of inland areas that could not be visually verified by sailing along the coast. In its final iteration, the Walkers' map included the north-south linear mountains from La Loubère's publication, repositioned according to a new cartographic system of global coordinates and the carefully delineated coastal edge (**Figure 2.1**). Main rivers and their branches – the Chao Phraya, Mekong and Irrawaddy – appeared to be framed by mountain ranges all the way from their estuaries to their sources in the distant north. To this depiction the Walkers added information of neighbouring kingdoms and, like Siam, these kingdoms also appeared to be confined within areas separated from each other by the planimetric projections of mountain ranges centred around rivers. First translated into English six years earlier, Humboldt's warnings regarding the Eurocentric biases of the theory of the basin were either unknown to the cartographer or, convinced by the reality of Cassini's mountainous frontier, simply ignored. However inadvertently, the reproduction of the conventions of *frontières naturelles* reintroduced the politics of geography into a new generation of mapping practices that had promised increased accuracy.

For the French, the map's presentation of the Mekong as a navigable corridor supported a long-theorized link between the river's estuary and China. The lands through which the river meandered however remained beyond the first-hand experience of European cartographers. Confined to the mountainous 'bowl' bisected by the Chao Phraya, the European image of Siam did not reflect the different types of authority exercised by the Siamese crown beyond this imaginary delineation.[2] Unlike the absolute sovereignty of European states over a delineated national space, the Siamese overlordship over multiple smaller kingdoms was often shared with other powerful kingdoms such as Burma or Vietnam.[3] The condition of multiple sovereignty, through which local chiefs paid tribute to two or three overlords, meant that the authority of the region's powerful kingdoms often overlapped. Mapped boundaries indicating the absolute limits of sovereignty were therefore incompatible with the actual political situation along the Mekong's riparian areas. Without reliable first-hand information or other reference maps, the courses of the region's major rivers like the Mekong were all depicted lying almost equidistant between the mountainous boundaries. And while the mapped location of rivers could have been a result of the cartographer's aesthetic decisions when confronted with a blank canvas which had to be filled, the delineation of rivers in relation to mountains also suggests that the cartographer was attempting to depict a very specific geographic relationship.

In the European context, this relationship was evolving in two distinct trajectories: one based on engineering water flows and one which appreciated the basin as an opportunity for decentralizing political power. The engineering trajectory was underpinned by continuous improvements in the computation of the river's hydrology and a new-found faith in the power of industrialists to improve social conditions

30 *Liquid Territories*

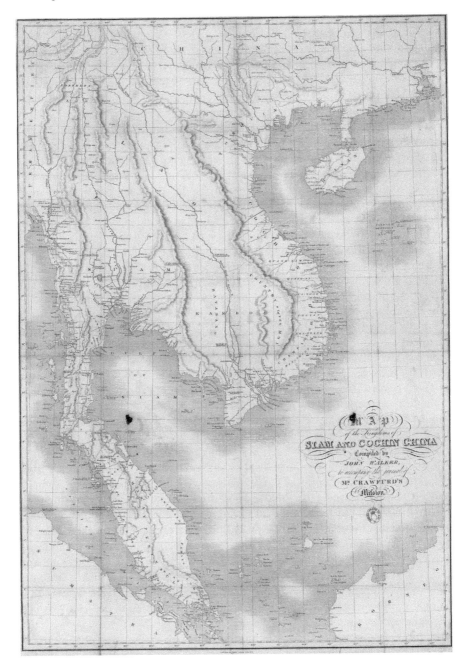

Figure 2.1 **John Walker's map of Siam and Cochin China.** Extolled for its accurate portrayal of the coastline, especially the Gulf of Siam, this was considered the most authoritative map of the Southeast Asia peninsula for decades. John Walker (1830), *Map of the Kingdoms of Siam and Cochin China.* [*Source:* BNF]

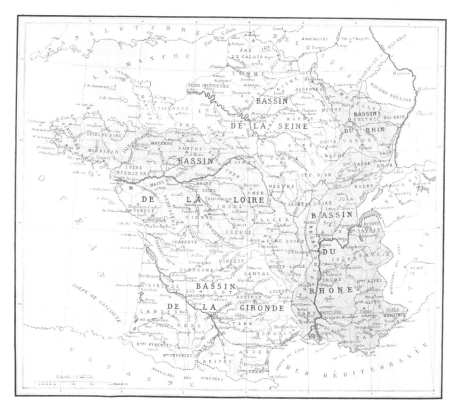

Figure 2.2 **Engineered basins.** Imagining France subdivided according to the logic of catchment areas, Gamond emphasized the economic potential of harnessing the flows of the country's rivers. Later considered visionary for his proposal to tunnel under the English Channel, Gamond's plan prefigured not only the multi-purpose water infrastructure of the Tennessee Valley but also the corporate model for financing and managing the project. Thomé de Gamond (1871), *Carte de France indiquant la division des principaux bassins hydrographiques pour la transformation et l'exploitation du Regime des Eaux courantes.* [*Source:* T. de Gamond]

through technical means.[4] In France, a plan to organize the relationship between waterways and human activity was compiled by Thomé de Gamond (**Figure 2.2**). Trained in engineering in the Netherlands, Gamond's plan was presented in 1832 and sought to capitalize on France's natural topography to restructure the country's waterways for multiple purposes including household use, irrigation, navigation and the generation of motor force.[5] To achieve this restructuring, France's waterways would be modified into *hydraulic staircases (escalier hydraulique)* according to the inclined slope followed by surface water on its journey to the sea.[6] Although, as acknowledged by Gamond, France possessed nine hydrographic catchments, to enable their exploitation his plan readily reduced them into five "basins", each

32 Liquid Territories

administered separately by private or public companies.[7] Where the plan for controlling water became a map for the region was in how settlement and industrial production were reorganized as a consequence of the proposed hydraulic 'cascade'. Dams, interspersed throughout the new system and equipped with mills and turbines, would form the centres of new industrial facilities where up to 15 million people would be relocated. Transforming industrial production in France according to the outline of his basins, Gamond's vision bestowed onto hydrological catchments the significance of an administrative region.

In France, the idea that the state's administrative units could equate to the shape of river basins came partially as a reaction to the centralization of power in Paris during the Napoleonic era. Historian Ozouf-Marignier has pointed out that for local elites, the geographic space encompassed by catchments sometimes contradicted with the notion of rivers acting as boundaries between two regions.[8] As she goes on to explain, focus on the watershed as the dividing line between administrative compartments was supported by the widespread perception that small towns commanded geographic spaces that, if not coterminous with the basin, were in line with the principles that saw mountains as the edge of a distinct domain. The perception of "commanding" such a space was exemplified by the spatial distribution of social practices which, measured in relation to rivers, gave weight to the circulation of products and people via waterways.[9] The subtle change in focus from the basin's outline to the internal structure of the basin's geography, presented the waterbodies included within the outline as distinct collections of infrastructure enabling economic and social activities. Considering that social and economic activities were not uniformly dependent on activities confined within two ridgelines, the relationship between France's network of waterways, groups of people and the theory of the basin was not structured purely on the logic of a river's flows but also on the assumption that these flows unified distinct sections of the country.

The vague relationship between the river basin and human activity was given a new political clarity by one of Carl Ritter's students. A noted geographer and political activist Élisée Reclus's 1868 book *Histoire d'un Ruisseau* presented a geographic narrative of people and places centred around the journey of water from its mountain sources to the sea. Recalling the poetic language of Humboldt, Reclus' detailed gaze described the multiple manifestations of flowing water and the cultural, social and technical adaptations made in response. Focused on social interactions with the environment, the geography practised by Reclus was significantly different from that practised by Humboldt, and to describe the outer limit of his narrative, Reclus did not rely on maps. Instead, he expressed the relationship between people, land and water through a human perspective. In an early chapter, he described where mountain streams were born:

> . . . *if we were swinging in the basket of a balloon, we would see that the limits of the basin are rounded off around all the sources of the stream like an amphitheatre and that all the valleys open in the vast roundness bow down, converging towards each other and meet in a common valley.*[10]

Unifying Geographic Space   33

Reclus' aerial angle brought the vast terrain referenced by the river basin into a new realm of human experience made popular by Jules Verne's *Five Weeks in a Balloon*. The characterization of the basin as a "common valley" (*vallée commune*) comprised of individual valleys circumscribing their own spatial domain elevated the basin into a constituent part of a larger geography shaped by nature to funnel water downstream. The limits of that even larger geography were expressed in the final chapter of the book. Taking the ocean as the starting point where "thousands and millions of streams" ended up, the movement of water through evaporation, rain, surface and underground flows was framed on an abstract planetary scale. Projected through a global lens, Reclus imagined the basin as the place where the world's people merged into one nation just as all the waters merged into one river.[11] Linking the emergence of the nation with the notional area of the river basin rather than the boundaries of the state, the metaphor of the valley as an inclusive communal space framed Reclus' anarchist politics and "non-statist" approach to geographic analysis. This perspective was especially directed at the examination of societies in East Asia where global imperial rivalries were reshaping the extents of state authority far beyond their national borders. Understood through European eyes, the political geography of Southeast Asia was dominated by the fall and rise of great empires and prehistoric kingdoms which shared some of the same qualities as European kingdoms with fixed boundaries, non-overlapping sovereignty and state bureaucracies. The criteria set by the imagination of European geographers however were arguably the opposite of Southeast Asia's reality. Most contemporary scholars of the region agree that what was perceived as an Asian "state" in the 19th century shared few characteristics with European or even Chinese kingdoms, lacking political centralization, defined borders, dynastic succession or an organized bureaucracy.[12] Especially after World War II, western historians examining Southeast Asia developed an alternative model for Southeast Asian polities based on the Indian concept of the circle or *mandala*.

What has come to be known as a *mandala* or *galactic polity* describes the overlapping political relationship between individual leaders, a "circle of power" without predetermined geographical limits on authority.[13] Each *mandala* polity was centred on an individual hegemon, with the polities of lesser kings forming the constituent parts while remaining nominally autonomous to switch allegiances or challenge the dominant leader. This politically unstable relationship however was perceived quite differently by foreign emissaries. Oliver Wolters hypothesized that Chinese ambassadors reporting on southern Cambodia in the 3rd century, ascribed the features of the Chinese dynastic kingdom to the region's loose *mandala*. The "kingdom of Funan" which was reported by the Chinese – and still persists in the region's historiography – attributed to the "kingdom" features the Chinese assumed it should possess in order to conform with their view of the world. With the region's political history reflecting the observer's viewpoint rather than facts, Reclus' intuitive rejection of colonial boundaries to describe geographic relationships can be seen as an early attempt to approach the subject matter on its own terms. Understood from this perspective, the river basin to which Reclus ascribed inclusive political ideals was less a geographic area and more a spatial container within

34   *Liquid Territories*

which social relationship could be structured without reference to the prejudices of European nation-states. The allusion to a natural commons shared by the peoples of different nations was not unique. From a different direction the same views were echoed in the French Empire's colonization of the Mekong's cartographic valley that appeared, on maps at least, to enclose a distinct domain of its own.

Mapping the Mekong's Valley

In the three decades leading up to the invasion of Vietnam, the British trading outposts in Hong Kong, Singapore and Malaya increasingly dominated European maritime trade with the Qing dynasty of China. Hoping to replicate their success, a concerted effort to establish a permanent French presence in Southeast Asia began in 1858. Meeting fierce resistance in the north, the French and Spanish navies eventually defeated the Vietnamese garrison at the trading port of Gia Dinh, renaming the town Saigon. For French diplomats, the Mekong River was increasingly seen as a strategic inland route to China that bypassed their geopolitical rivals in British Burma.[14] Maps that (erroneously) located Saigon at the Mekong's navigable estuary also showed that further upstream the river traversed through the lands of the former Khmer Empire and the power base of Cambodia's king close to Phnom Penh.[15] However, European knowledge of the river upstream from Phnom Penh was extremely limited making the organized exploration of the lucrative route to China a risky and therefore unattractive prospect.

The attitude towards exploration changed as the expenses of the military campaign increasingly began to make the colonial enterprise a financial liability for the French state. Lured by the potential upstream commerce, the *Commission d'exploration du Mékong* set off in 1866 to explore the trade route to China. The person responsible for the preparation of the mission's maps was the young lieutenant Francis Garnier. Trained in hydrography at one of France's naval academies, Garnier had been one of those urging for the exploration of the rivers flowing from Tibet, imagining an "unknown wealth" in the "valleys and the mountains that enclose them".[16] Colonial hopes for a commercial gateway to Chinese markets however were soon quashed when further upstream the mission encountered new obstacles to riverine navigation. Confronted with the Mekong's extensive cataracts, attention was redirected to the mission's scientific scope, and over the next two years, Garnier and his colleagues produced hundreds of charts of the Mekong's course. Published after his death, Garnier's widely read account of the journey, structured the spatial sequence of his narrative on the expedition's movement through smaller valleys included within the greater geographic space of the *vallée du Cambodge* or *Mékong*. For Garnier *valleys* were not simply subdivisions of an unknown terrain. In the first footnote to an account of the Siamese court's claims over north Cambodia, he explained:

> *We perhaps too forget today, by theoretically dividing Indo-China between France and England, that the kingdom of Siam is, at least in part, a natural annex of the valley of the Mekong.*[17]

Unifying Geographic Space 35

The conceptualization of the valley as a determinant of sovereign authority is surprising, especially since in their journey outside the theoretical limits of Siam, the expedition's movements were controlled by passports issued by the Siamese. Based simply on Garnier's first-hand experience, the opposite relationship should have been true: that is, at least part of the Mekong's valley was an annex – natural or not – of the kingdom of Siam. The footnote however reveals that the value given to the river valley (*vallée du fleuve*) exceeded the term's geophysical definition. Calibrated in relation to the state's 'natural' limits, the valley referenced by Garnier echoed the imagined reality of an 'enclosed' Siam that had appeared on Walker's earlier map. The idea of the valley also informed the construction of the maps charting the course of the Mekong as the team journeyed further upstream. Especially in the more mountainous areas of Laos, the topographic delineation of the river valley appeared equally as important as the hydrographic survey of the river itself. Of the seven maps published in the folio of 1873, the drawing showing the mountainous kingdom of Luang Prabang – a Siamese vassal state claimed also by Vietnam – was framed to suggest that the focus of attention should be shared between the river's meander and the mountains (**Figure 2.3**).[18] The exaggerated linear representation of the mountain chain indicated the hypothetical separation between the waters flowing towards the Mekong and those flowing to the Chao Phraya.[19] Following closely along both embankments of the Mekong, the map depicted the depth of the gorge in which the river was situated. The sides of the gorge obstructed the view to the distant mountain peaks across almost the entire length of the river shown on the map, making them an unusual feature to include since they had limited value as navigational references.[20] Considering the fact that the expedition did not survey the mountains, the delineation of the valley's limit was most likely conjecture on the part of the Garnier.

From this perspective, Garnier's cartographic representation of the distant mountains which for him – and perhaps for other military men – also symbolized the limits of Siam's authority, may not have been a strictly scientific depiction of the area's geography. Rather, it could be concluded that the purpose of including those mountain "lines" in the cartographic frame was strategic. With the watershed acting as a proxy for jurisdiction, the map displayed a topographic 'reality' in which Siam's political authority was 'contained' by the location of mountains. While the decision of what was included in the maps may not have been Garnier's alone given his military commission, arguably these were the first surveyed drawings of inland Southeast Asia and the most accurate depictions of the region since Walker's map. The subsequent recognition by the prestigious *Société de géographie* of Garnier's contributions to the science of geography confirmed the value of his mapping efforts as objective scientific portrayals according to the methodical standards of the Academy. In this sense, any information displayed on the map's surface would have been perceived as equally 'real' irrespective of how the individual parts were surveyed. As the most updated reference for the Mekong's geography, anyone seriously interested in the region would eventually have had to turn to these maps. And there, the viewer would have been confronted with the mountainous limits which, despite being labelled *supposée* (hypothetical), appeared to

36   *Liquid Territories*

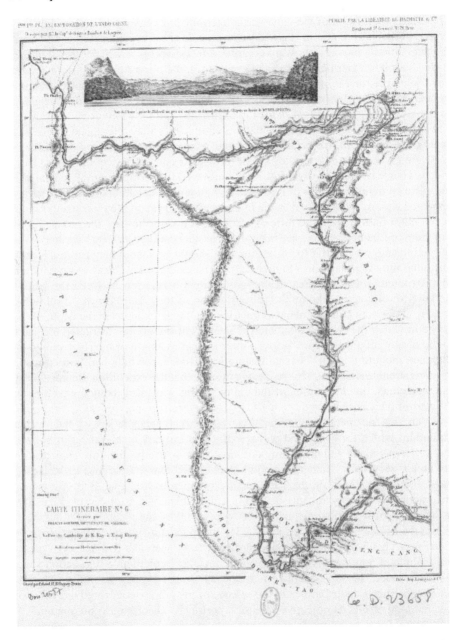

Figure 2.3 **The upper reaches of the Mekong's valley.** The map's framing centres the eye's focus on the space between the river (right) and mountain range (left). It is the first map to note the curve of the Mekong at Luang Prabang. Note the steep slopes of the canyon surrounding the Mekong which blocked the view of the distant mountain range. Francis Garnier (1873), *Carte itinéraire No. 6. Vallée de K. Kay á Xieng Khong.* [*Source:* BNF]

Unifying Geographic Space 37

refine rather than dismiss the information presented in the previous map by Walker. Even if the limits of the valley had yet to be surveyed, the map presented a reality in which a wall of mountains was somewhere present. In a multi-ethnic region where the relationship between kingdoms and vassal polities was not based on fixed political boundaries, the edge of the Mekong's imagined valley indicated a possible frontier for French influence in the region.

The most immediate consequence of Garnier's journey was that attention towards finding a river route to China switched from the Mekong to North Vietnam. Under French rule, the Empire of Vietnam was split into three *pays* (regions): Cochinchine to the south, Tonkin in the north and Annam in the centre.[21] With Cambodia's inclusion in colonial maps, boundaries confirming the limits of Siamese authority became necessary. But what exactly constituted the Siam that would be depicted was not a certainty. Advised by the British that were keeping a concerned eye on French expansion in the region, expert foreign surveyors were hired by the Siamese to train teams of cartographers in western mapping techniques. However, as the pressure increased to delimit Siam's boundaries with the British colonies in Burma and Malaya as well as the newly established French colony, attention became focused on surveying the mountains which could mark the outer extents of the kingdom's sovereignty. Working from the framework of the British geodetic triangulation, the cartographer James McCarthy undertook surveys of the distant mountainous regions claimed by Siam. Claims to these areas however were not prescribed by existing maps. As the *mandala* polity theory reflects, relationships between kingdoms of any size were underpinned by individual leaders identifying an area as belonging to their authority rather than an existing fixed boundary. Moreover, given that the allegiances of smaller kingdoms could change, areas of individual authority could extend to places that were not spatially contiguous with the kingdom's centre. With no commonly agreed location for a boundary line, McCarthy's surveys would need to provide cartographic clarity to a political question that had multiple 'right' answers.[22]

McCarthy understood that the semi-autonomous Laotian polities or *muangs* which formed Siam's eastern frontiers provided tribute to multiple overlords, but also that in turn, these polities dominated even smaller kingdoms. Relying on local information to ascertain the boundary's position, he described being guided to the geographic feature which functioned as the border for a particular tribe or village.[23] Arriving at Luang Prabang, for example, he noted:

> *[The boundary] then recrossed the Nam Ta [river], and followed a line which had always been disputed between Nan and Luang Prabang. Nan asserted its claim to the Nam Ta, while Luang Prabang, on the other hand, affirmed that the presence of Nan in the valley of the Nam Ta was an encroachment.*[24]

But while locals defined their claims based on the area encompassed by an entire valley, McCarthy could conceive of boundaries as imaginary lines that followed or crossed rivers. As such, there were diverging conceptions of how to constitute the domain of the kingdom's sovereignty – the areal unit or the line – which did not

38   *Liquid Territories*

always correspond with each other. There were however places on the surface of maps where the space assigned to the valley and the linear boundary converged. McCarthy recognized mountain ridges as *watersheds*, identifying this imaginary hydrological line with the frontiers of smaller kingdoms. The value of the watershed as a means of marking a frontier varied considerably and for local people was often incompatible with boundaries.[25] For the surveyor however the frequent ascent to the crests of mountains was a fundamental part of the mapping process where he could see the distant balloon signals that marked known points within the British geodetic triangulation. With few indisputable claims on which to base his work, McCarthy's delineation would essentially require him to speculate on where Siam's frontier could be.

What Thongchai Winichakul calls "interpretations of the ambiguous territorial margins by the new code of space" is displayed on the first Siamese map to show the limits of the country (**Figure 2.4**).[26] Published by McCarthy in 1888 primarily for a European audience, the map showed Siam straddling both the Chao Phraya and Mekong river valleys. But while the western frontier followed the ridgelines that had been part of Walker's older map, the eastern frontier aligned with the ridges of the Annamite Mountains which had not yet been surveyed.[27] Significantly,

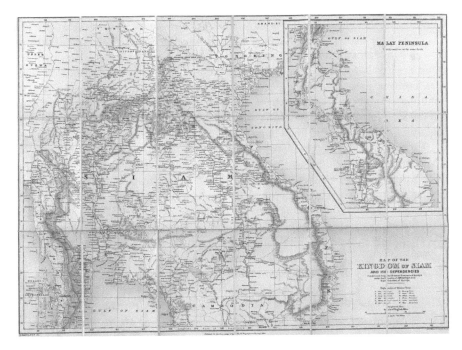

Figure 2.4 **McCarthy's Siamese Siam.** The first modern map of the kingdom speculates on the frontiers of Siam. These are shown to extend across both the Mekong and Menam river valleys. James McCarthy (1888), *Map of the Kingdom of Siam and Its Dependencies*. [*Source:* National Library of Australia]

the new map appeared to dissolve the linear mountainous boundary dividing the Chao Phraya and Mekong which had restricted Siam's extent in European eyes. In the context presented by the drawing, rather than two separate valleys the eastern limits of Siam were implicitly located on the edge of a greater *vallée du Mékong* which extended across Southeast Asia. Delineated according to the same geophysical principle as Garnier, McCarthy's interpretation of what constituted the unit of the valley was equally as imaginary as the French explorer's.[28] From this perspective, the focus on the eastern frontier could be described as just another speculation by McCarthy. But was the correlation of the Annamite Mountains with the extent of Siam simply McCarthy's technically driven imagination regarding watersheds, the expectation by the kingdom's elites that Siam encompass the entire river "valley" or a cartographic technique to counter French claims?

Winichakul reports that shortly prior to the commencement of McCarthy's surveys, members of the Siamese elite advocated specifically for the mapping of the Mekong's basin. Around the same time, the creation of Siam's Royal Survey Department integrated the European cartographic 'language' into the state's institutions. This indicates that, to some extent at least, the river valley was an important reference for what constituted the terrain claimed by the country even though that space was never wholly secured militarily. Furthermore, the Mekong's eastern watershed was not just the limit of the 'valley' but also of the French colonies of Tonkin and Annam situated on the other side of the Annamite Mountains. Placing the hypothetical frontier along this line therefore presented the Siamese claim from two sides. On the one hand, it anchored Siam to the notion of the valley, whose natural boundaries were recognized by Europeans as the legitimate extent of the country. On the other hand, it reflected the principle of political boundaries which – abhorring the vacuum of 'unclaimed' terrain – required placement coterminous to existing borders. The first glimpse of a Siamese Siam arguably used the period's predominant geographic discourses to present the country as a 'natural' part of the region's political geography. The internal division of Siam enabled by cartography began a fundamental transformation in the relationship between the central authority and peripheral 'lesser' kingdoms. It allowed for the whole country to begin the "shift from the traditional hierarchical relationships of rulers to the new administration on a territorial basis".[29]

Mountains and Water

The shift towards a territorial administrative structure was not unique to Siam. After 1822, the Vietnamese began to publish detailed geographic accounts of their consolidated empire from the new Historical Archive (*Quốc sử quán*) located in the imperial capital at Huế.[30] During this period, contact with Europeans, and in particular French missionaries, had allowed Vietnam's imperial cartographers to present their claims over the Laotian *muangs* on the surface of the map. Among the names used to reference the land under their exclusive cultural influence was *non nước*, literally *mountain and water.* The origin of this cosmographic idea is perhaps obvious if considered in relation to the two defining characteristics of the

40   *Liquid Territories*

empire's topography: the Annamite Mountain range stretching along the length of their entire domain and the numerous rivers and streams descending from the mountains to the East Sea. Vietnamese representation of these topographic features developed within the broader regional influence of China's Ming dynasty which included adoption of Confucian bureaucratic administration and the conventions of Chinese cartography. The tasks of state cartographers included the preparation of geographic atlases that combined maps and written descriptions of settlements, mountains and rivers.

As Vietnam's administration became increasingly integrated, maps portraying the entire extent of the emperor's sovereignty began to appear.[31] Among these, the 1838 map attributed to the Vietnamese mandarin Phan Huy Chú combined the European projection of the coastline with landscape features in the traditional Chinese style. Showing the empire's 32 provinces and the names of main river estuaries along the entire coastline, the map's ridge-style elevations denoting mountains were depicted lying both vertically and horizontally, portraying the 'direction' of mountain ranges which appeared to enclose the terrain into vaguely delineated rectilinear compartments. The implication of an empire perceived to extend beyond the mountainous confines of the Annamites is evident in the map's inclusion of these distant areas. The depiction of the same subject in a distinctly European style was published in Calcutta the same year by the French missionary Jean-Louis Taberd. Presenting the Vietnamese claims to the Mekong through the cartographic medium of boundaries, the *muangs* paying tribute to the emperor were included within a vast area labelled *Annam Quốc* (Country of Annam). Recognizing perhaps that either the mountain boundary demarcating Siam was fictional or Siam's jurisdiction extended beyond that limit, Taberd's visual description of Vietnam was not drawn as a valley. Distinct from the delineation of the provinces contained along the coast, these hinterlands were displayed as if part of a different level of authority, yet firmly within a perceived sphere of influence centred on the Emperor's seat in Hué. Considering that the *muangs'* allegiances could switch between rival kingdoms, Taberd's map was essentially a snapshot of the political condition at that specific time, as seen from the Vietnamese perspective.

The political narrative underpinning these depictions of the entire country was readily adopted by a colonial administration seeking to extend French control beyond coastal areas. However, growing anti-colonial sentiment and widespread condemnation of the *politique d'aventures* by the French public halted any immediate action towards expansionism.[32] Following the annexation of North Vietnam, arguments for a calculated campaign to integrate the *muangs* into colonial holdings revolved around the strategic importance of the hinterland to the coastal colonies and the wishful desire to 'steal' Siam from under British influence. Well aware of the contested suzerainty over vassal states, the tendency to see the *muangs* that appeared on Taberd's map as part of the former empire allowed the French to imagine the extent of their own influence in the region. Having seized Vietnam through force and coercion, the French now adopted the role of a 'protector' against Siamese aggression upholding Vietnamese claims over the different *muangs* in the Mekong's upstream. A persuasive case supporting France's inheritance of

Unifying Geographic Space 41

Vietnam's rights over this region was compiled into a report for the colonial governor, which resonated with the altruistic notion that the French were duty-bound to protect the Vietnamese people's right to settle unconstrained throughout the region. By appearing to act on behalf of Vietnam, France reinforced the dubious claims of exclusive control over the *muangs* which had been presented on Taberd's and Phan Huy Chú's maps.

As the growing geopolitical rivalry with the British revived public support in France for strategic counteraction, the remote Laotian *muangs* became the subject of colonial interests and the objective of the Siamese military action during which McCarthy's surveys were prepared. Arbitrated by a panel of experts, the negotiated boundary treaty of 1893 between Siam and France, located the disputed frontier along the Mekong, inevitably partitioning the smaller kingdoms for whose people the river was the centre of their domain. The sparsely populated new colonial state of Laos encompassed the areas east of the Mekong until the ridges of the Annamite Range and northwards to include the kingdom of Luang Prabang until the border with China. In the French geopolitical equation of Southeast Asia, Laos appeared as a tactical buffer between Vietnam and Siam but also between the productive colonial holdings along the coast of the East Sea and their rivals in British Burma. The location of the boundary between Laos and Vietnam, replicated McCarthy's watershed but this time – rather than an outer frontier – as the internal boundary between three of the five *pays* of French Indochina. Despite their pretentions towards scientific integrity, when it came to the transition between a topographic and a boundary map, cartographers did not hesitate to deploy the qualities of visual representation to reinforce their conclusions. As such, the subtle shading of the landscape immediately adjacent to either side of the imaginary frontier appeared to claim that a single distinct ridgeline joined multiple mountains, highlighting the value of the natural boundary to offer a solution to disputed areas of authority. In a similar manner, authoritative depictions of French Indochina in 1916 exaggerated the topographic reality of the altered boundary with colour, giving the manmade limit the same geographic gravity as the watershed dividing Laos from Vietnam. Furthermore, even when the clearly identified 'walls' of the valley separating the Mekong and Chao Phraya were surveyed out of existence, new mountain ranges were born or old ones redrawn on other maps to perpetuate the idea of a contiguous space unified by natural forces. The 'natural' background against which all claims were calibrated changed accordingly to incorporate the desired political narrative.

Conclusion

The partially fictional cartographic depictions which accompanied concepts such as the valley and catchment were not solely a result of insufficient information about the configuration of the terrain. If for Buache, placing mountains where none existed upheld a theory of the basin, in Southeast Asia the river valley, basin or watershed became convenient tools for dividing the terrain into separate domains. Imposed through sometimes subtle and sometimes blatant manipulations of the map's surface, identifying the limits of authority through the disposition of natural

42　*Liquid Territories*

features was a European fantasy promoted by the dogma of the *frontieres naturelles*. The conviction that a valley – the terrestrial interpretation of the river basin – was already there to be discovered and mapped, gave the Mekong's European surveyors a specific frame with which to rationalize what – for them – was a perplexing condition of multiple and overlapping sovereignties.

Considering how late 19th-century scientific standards of objectivity embraced the mechanical metaphors of the industrial revolution, it is unlikely that any of the authors would recognize their own, sometimes extravagant manipulation of topographic facts as anything except an earnest attempt to show what was there. For them, the mere presence of a river implied that somewhere a mountain would need to exist to form the edge of the inclined plane driving water towards its ultimate oceanic destination. Rather than inducing the limits of the river basin from knowledge of how water flowed, the valley was deduced from the simple geographic fact that if there was a river there had to be an enclosing valley. And if guaranteeing the spatial integrity of the valley required ridgelines to be imagined in the flat coastal lowlands where the river met the sea, the warnings of a Eurocentric bias identified by Humboldt could be easily dismissed since the rational theorization of the catchment made it imperative that a watershed surrounded the entirety of the river system. It is therefore doubtful that between Siam's identification with McCarthy's mega-valley and the French claims to the *Vallée du Mékong* someone could perceive the hydrological concepts that informed the action of water. Yet by aligning the shaded, pictorial gravity of the watershed with the separation of authority, the areal unit derived from observing the behaviour of water became embedded in the spatial units of political control.

Notes

1　Simon de La Loubère (1693), *A New Historical Relation of the Kingdom of Siam*. London: Printed by F.L. for Tho. Horne, Francis Saunders, and Tho. Bennet, p. 3.

2　Nor did it reflect the possibility that, since La Loubère's time, the borders of Siam may have changed. It's as if the permanence of mountains made the kingdom itself unchangeable in the European imagination.

3　Thongchai Winichakul (1994), *Siam Mapped: A History of the Geo-Body of a Nation*. Honolulu: University of Hawaii Press, pp. 30–31.

4　At the end of the 18th century, the English polymath John Dalton confirmed the calculability of the "water balance" within distinct river basins. Relying on maps to distinguish between the catchments of different hydrological systems, Dalton classified the qualities of the terrain into "three principal varieties of surface" to which he assigned general properties related to precipitation, dew and the rate of evaporation. His geographic subdivision of England and Wales into seven spatially distinct hydrological areas allowed him to estimate surface run-off in each catchment as a proportion of the Thames' better known catchment. According to the historian James Dooge, Dalton based his calculation on Halley's century-old estimations of the Thames River's runoff but was careful in specifying the extent of geographic space that runoff was derived from. James Dooge (1974), The Development of Hydrological Concepts in Britain and Ireland Between 1674 and 1874. *Hydrological Sciences Journal*, v. 19, n. 3, pp. 287–292.

5　Thomé de Gamond (1871), *Mémoire sur le régime général des eaux courantes: Plan d'ensemble pour la transformation de l'appareil hydraulique de la France*. Paris: Dunod, p. 2.

Unifying Geographic Space   43

6   *"Ce serail, en d'autres termes, la transformation du plan incliné de nos rivières en un escalier hydraulique". ibid.*, p. 12.

7   *". . . notre territoire comprend neuf bassins hydrographiques naturels et distincts: Ceux de la Seine, de la Loire, de la Gironde, du Rhône, du Rhin, de l'Escaut, de la Manche, de l'Océan et de la Mediterranée. Mais nous avons pensé qu'il serait grandement préférable, en vue d'une meilleure exploitation, de réduire à cinq et peutêtre même à quatre le nombre de ces bassins". ibid.*, p. 75.

8   Marie-Vic Ozouf-Marignier (2002), "Bassins hydrographiques et divisions administratives en France (XIXe–XXe siècle)". *Trames*, n. 10, p. 64.

9   *Ibid.*, p. 71.

10 Élisée Reclus (1868), *Histoire d'un Ruisseau. Impri.* Paris: Générale de Ch. Lahure, pp. 49–50.

11 *"Les peuples se melent aux peuples comme les ruisseaux aux ruiseaux, les rivieres aux rivieres; tôt ou tard, ils ne formeront plus qu'une seule nation, de même que toutes les eaux d'un même bassin finissent par se confondre en un seul fleuve". ibid.*, pp. 316–317.

12 Oliver Wolters (1999), *History, Culture and Religion in Southeast Asian Perspectives*, Revised edition. Ithaca, NY: Southeast Asia Program Publications (SEAP), p. 27.

13 Wolters, who coined the term "mandala" in the late 1960s, related early Sanskrit inscriptions mentioning "a pure circle of kings and brahmans" with the historical formation of the Khmer Empire based in Angkor. *ibid.*

14 From their missionaries established in Vietnam, the French received regular information on the region's politics and people, who on maps appeared concentrated in a narrow strip of land between the Annamite mountains and the coast of the East Sea (South China Sea). Ostensibly for the execution of these missionaries, the French had mounted three consecutive naval expeditions during the 1840s against the Empire of Vietnam. See Milton Osborne (1999), *River Road to China: The Search for the Source of the Mekong, 1866–73*. New York: Atlantic Monthly Press.

15 The riverine links to inland kingdoms had made the Mekong's delta a crossroads for Chinese, Khmer, Vietnamese and Malay merchants for centuries. For an understanding of the ethnic diversity of riverine commerce in the pre-colonial lower delta of the Mekong, see Nola Cooke & Tana Li (eds.) (2004), *Water Frontier: Commerce and the Chinese in the Lower Mekong Region, 1750–1880*. Singapore: Singapore University Press.

16 G. Francis (1864), *La Cochinchine française en 1864*. Paris: E. Dentu, p. 32.

17 *"On oublie peut-être trop aujourd'hui, en partageant théoriquement l'Indo-Chine entre la France et l'Angleterre, que le royaume de Siam est, au moins en partie, une anuexe naturelle de la vallée du Mékong". ibid.*, p. 14.

18 Francis Garnier, Ernest Doudart de Lagrée & Erhard Schieble (1873), *Exploration de l'Indochine. Dirigée par Mr. le Cape. de frégate Doudart de Lagrée*. Paris: Hachette.

19 On the map, mountains are annotated as *"Ligne supposee de partage des eaux de la vallée du cambodge et de la vallée du menam"*.

20 Related to, but ultimately different from the discipline of cartography, hydrographic surveys were intended to provide sailors with the information necessary for riverine navigation. These maps rarely depicted mountains or topographic information situated beyond the river unless these were vital navigation reference points or potential hazards. With the maps published in 1844's *Le Pilote Français*, the academician Charles-François Beautemps-Beaupré set a new standard for the depiction of marine coastal surveys. Garnier's survey of the Khong waterfalls a few days upstream from Phnom Penh was in many ways typical of this approach, focusing on the delineation of embankments and recording bottom measures to gauge depth.

21 In addition to Cochinchine, the French hold over the Mekong valley included the protectorate of the kingdom of Cambodia which had been under the overlordship of both Vietnam and Siam prior to colonization.

22 McCarthy's surveys were carried out simultaneously with a protracted military campaign against semi-autonomous Laotian polities or *muangs*. Nonetheless, even when

44 *Liquid Territories*

the decision was made to include a conquered kingdom into Siam's sovereignty, the question of where that kingdom's boundaries should be drawn remained unresolved.

23 James McCarthy (1900), *Surveying and Exploring in Siam*. London: William Clowes & Sons, p. 191.

24 *Ibid.*, p. 163.

25 In one incident, the surveyor reported that stone pillars marking a boundary "had been removed by the Lu that they might with greater boldness cross the watershed" while in another that the "boundary of Sibsawng Pana [*Sipsòng Panna*] crossed the watershed". *ibid.*, pp. 161, 166.

26 Winichakul, *op. cit.*, pp. 124–125.

27 The determination of these boundaries did not reflect any survey or the Siamese military campaign, since the escalating political conflict with France prevented McCarthy from travelling through these areas. Besides, the map's blank spaces adjacent to the Annamites clearly indicated that the consideration of where to locate this notional frontier was not based on any local information or the topography of individual valleys.

28 In contrast to the speculative determination of the eastern frontier, the survey results from the north were not visible on the map. Instead, the frontier extended indistinctly northwards to eventually disappear into the mountain areas under Chinese authority. It is not clear from McCarthy's narrative if this was a deliberate omission or the inability to mark a definitive boundary on the map that reflected political reality. Most probably it suggests a lack of urgency to determine Siamese sovereignty in relation to China, an erstwhile ally in the resistance to French colonization as well as the king's explicit desire to map the frontier as a measure to counter the French.

29 Winichakul, *op. cit.*, p. 120.

30 In Vietnam, the control of official publications including maps was centred in the imperial capital at *Huê*. There in 1822, the emperor Minh Mang created a new Historical Archive (*Quôc su quán*) which over the course of the next six decades published detailed geographic accounts of the newly consolidated empire. Although mostly textual, geographic knowledge in Vietnam was associated with cartography since at least the 15th century. This followed the gradual consolidation of *mandala* polities into a new imperial organization with a clear perception of its own area of authority and a sense of the cultures that lay beyond.

31 John Whitmore (1994), Cartography in Vietnam. In J.B. Harley & David Woodward (eds.), *The History of Cartography, v. 2, b. 2: Cartography in the Traditional East and Southeast Asian Societies*. Chicago, IL: University of Chicago Press, p. 502.

32 A final attempt in 1880 to revive the importance of the Mekong's riparian hinterlands had failed to gather enough votes to fund a proposed railway from Cochinchina to south China through the Mekong's valley. See C.M. Andrew & A.S. Kanya-Forstner (1971), The French 'Colonial Party': Its Composition, Aims and Influence, 1885–1914. *The Historical Journal*, v. 14, n. 1, p. 99.

3 The River's Nations

In the elaboration of this concept, as in most creations of the human mind, one can discover an element which escapes both logic and technique and which to a degree transcends both. The part played by this element, which might almost be termed mystical, has not been negligible.

Integrated river basin development,
UN Panel of Experts, 1958

The assumption that the organized exploitation of the catchment area was possessed with an undefinable, otherworldly value reflected much more than a momentary deviation from the UN's technocratic ideals. In the closest thing to an intellectual history of the river basin, François Molle argues that the manifestation of the concept after World War II pivoted on the application of the planning principles set by the Tennessee Valley Authority (TVA).[1] Described by historians as a "new export commodity" showcasing American technical knowledge of water control, today the TVA is widely acknowledged as the paradigm on which plans to exploit the Mekong River were conceived and executed during the Cold War.[2] Commenced in the United States during the Great Depression that detrimentally affected the rice-growing economy of colonial Indochina, the distinct infrastructure projects implemented by the TVA were presented on maps that highlighted the Tennessee River's eponymous valley. Equating the valley's cartographic outline with the extent of the hydrological catchment however would overlook that the mapped representation of river basins in the American context was not solely intended to show an existing natural condition. If 19th-century French geographers, engineers and cartographers referencing the basin's outline on a map could perceive a natural commons, a self-regulating equilibrium or a political boundary, the systematic cartography of basins in America's *arid region* had recognized the importance of mapping catchment areas for regional resource planning, for establishing irrigated farming units and for public participation in water management. Reflecting the period's technical knowledge of water control, the TVA's mandate to generate hydropower, stop flooding and improve navigation within the extent of the Tennessee Valley made the basin symbolic of the 'unity' between nature and mankind and influenced the way planners and engineers envisioned 'harnessing' the Mekong's flows.

DOI: 10.4324/9781032706238-5

46 *Liquid Territories*

Yet without any evident and immediate need to produce electricity, mitigate inundation or improve water-borne transport, the incentive to study the Mekong's basin as the site for regional planning arose under different premises. Within a period of escalating Cold War antagonism, the unity suggested by the basin's outline resonated with the mission to arrest Soviet influence on the independent countries which emerged from the dissolution of Indochina. Under the auspices of the United Nations, the determination of what constituted the 'entirety' of the river's drainage area was elaborated in response to political conditions and the expert opinions framing the basin as the spatial unit for international development and collaboration. Based on maps and plans prepared by American geographers and international teams of engineers, this chapter examines the ideas which allowed the Mekong basin to be considered the most suitable scale for the collective planning of water infrastructure. The chapter asks how the imagined geographic unity implied by adherence to the theory of the basin was expressed in the projects for dams and irrigation that have come to characterize the post-war exploitation of the Mekong's water.

Planning *Unity*

Located on the opposite side of the planet from the Mekong River, the waterways flowing through America's western 'arid region' became increasingly important after the end of the Civil War (1861–1865). These rivers were fed almost exclusively from the melting snows of the Rocky mountains rather than the precipitation which made knowledge of the catchment's square area valuable for enumerating water volume. But as multitudes of new settlers headed west to appropriate Native American lands and establish new homesteads, the equitable distribution of water from existing rivers was recognized as critical for economic activity and the establishment of viable settlements. Arguing that the basins of these rivers formed autonomous "natural districts" where residents faced discrete resource management problems, influential government bureaucrats such as John Powell advocated for the organization of settlers within each river's catchment area into a self-regulating "body politic" with the right to collectively decide on land.[3] Envisioning the formation of *pasturage districts* for grazing and *irrigation districts* for agriculture, Powell's proposal aimed to address the interrelated concerns of people dependent on the same source of water but living across state or county boundaries. Convinced that the hydrographic basin was the geographic setting where these issues converged, Powell directed the cartographers of the US Geological Survey (USGS) to prepare detailed maps of catchment areas. With water necessary for farming, industrial production and social well-being, the federal government's engineers would ensure fair allocation by constructing the "common use" infrastructure for every basin. The extent to which such districts could also function as units of governance was therefore confined to the technical autonomy granted by the government infrastructure. The same type of areal, bounded and internally contiguous delineation utilized for administrative subdivision would differentiate irrigation constituencies and governmental responsibilities.

Rather than the arbitrary delineation of America's administrative boundaries, for Powell the geographic unit encompassed by the basin better reflected the needs of settlements in a region of sparse rainfall. With all things (the action of water, the planning for water and the social group controlling water) measured and regulated with respect to that one type of hydrological subdivision, the probability of all interests – both natural and manmade – converging was far higher than that if each had a different spatial reference. For government scientists in positions to influence policy like Powell, the geological subdivision of the territory appeared to be most efficient (or least wasteful) not only because referencing watersheds – rather than administrative boundaries – avoided the distorting politics of land. But equally, because synchronizing human actions with the agency of water guaranteed these same actions would be coordinated with reference to the motions of nature. Nonetheless, the concept of the basin was far from being acclaimed as universally valuable for agriculture. Basins were almost imperceivable as unified geographic entities from first-hand experience and maps displaying them too rare for the concept to become popularly accepted. Even within government, only the technical and legal implications were essential for county engineers or state technicians to plan and operate the infrastructure. Apportioning water, forests and even land with reference to the basin however was not just a different way for government bureaucrats to subdivide a vast and largely unknown territory. If in Europe the basin was – at least temporarily – the *working object* of a new geographic science, in the United States it became the reference for the *working object* of scientific governance which espoused control of the physical environment through the lens of nature's laws.

With the establishment of the TVA in 1933, the imagined geographic convergence between nature and human actions was operationalized for regional planning. In the 40 years since Powell had expounded his ideas to Congress, public and political awareness of the significance of basins was increasingly framed through a waterway's potential to generate electricity. By the launch of Roosevelt's New Deal, the scope of federal intervention in the economically depressed Tennessee Valley aimed to improve riverine navigation, control floods and produce hydropower.[4] Drawn on maps, the infrastructure projects the TVA was tasked to construct and operate were presented within the context of the Tennessee River's basin (**Figure 3.1**). Symbolic of hydrological knowledge of the entire river system's flows, cartographic references to the basin's extent appeared to frame the TVA's mandate in terms of an area of water. However, the geographic correlation of the basin with the full range of social, technical and environmental problems the TVA was assigned to resolve was more complicated. Exacerbated by the impacts of the Great Depression, perennial issues of poverty, crop failure and soil erosion were not exclusive to the Tennessee Valley nor were the extents of these problems concentrated within the valley's boundaries. Even problems associated with the Tennessee River itself – such as flooding or navigating shallows – were not system-wide phenomena but concentrated along particular stretches of the mainstream and the river's tributaries. Thus, while the basin's outline delineated a region of interrelated problems, these were not uniformly distributed within the catchment nor a common concern for all the Valley's residents.

48 *Liquid Territories*

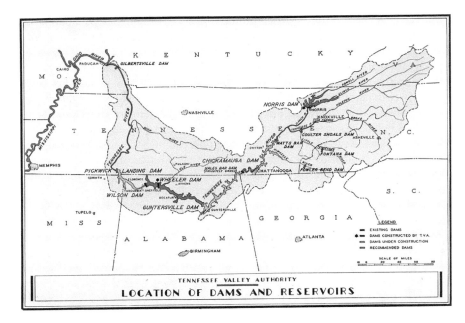

Figure 3.1 **Dams and rivers of the Tennessee Valley.** Accompanying the TVA's infrastructure masterplan, the map depicts the location of planned dams. The presence of the watershed conceptually redefines the content it frames, making the collection of hydraulic infrastructure and the river appear as a single system that is neither wholly natural nor wholly manmade. Tennessee Valley Authority (1936), *Location of Dams and Reservoirs*. [*Source:* TVA]

Despite the uneven spatial distribution of identified problems, the approach to dealing with these diverse social and environmental conditions involved fundamental changes to the entirety of the river system. To control inundation, the designed volumetric capacity of new dams and reservoirs included provisions for retaining floodwater during the wet season. Albert Fry, the TVA's expert in flood engineering described a landscape where dams had transformed the river into a series of lakes with the surface run-off continuously flowing.[5] To engineer the new flood-proof 'equilibrium' of constantly flowing water, the river's existing waterways and new infrastructure were considered collectively as part of the same hydraulic system. With each reservoir temporarily detaining and redirecting a calculated portion of the overall run-off, water control operations were distributed across the entire river catchment. Yet having made flood control dependent on manmade changes to water flows, maintaining the new equilibrium required detailed knowledge of all the streams flowing through the basin. In distant locations where first-hand observations were unavailable for forecasting stream flows, a new mapping tool became particularly useful. Developed before 1932, Leroy Sherman's *unit hydrograph* allowed the river's overflow to be quantified assuming uniform rainfall across the entire basin. Using measures from stream gauges, the mean daily discharges of individual streams could be plotted and then extrapolated to compute the river's runoff history for rainfall of any duration or degree of intensity.[6] While the scientific image of the basin captured by the axes of the hydrograph did not directly incorporate any parameters relating to topography, it allowed a glimpse into the invisible world of subterranean water flows which were critical for detailed flood forecasts (**Figure 3.2**).[7] The idea that the hydrological catchment could be known through the representation of information on a graph allowed technical decisions to be made on the basis of the graphical configuration of data. Mapping, which would once have recorded the visible extents of pondage and overflow for individual streams, would now be accompanied – and in one sense substituted – by the geometric properties of the hydrograph's lines. By envisioning the path to attain complete knowledge of the basin, engineers were brought one step closer to accomplishing total control over the river's resources.

Paradoxically for a planning project, the determination of the extent and location of land uses by the TVA clashed with the ideological leanings of the organization's director. As a lawyer and advocate for voluntary, bottom-up participation in planning, David Lilienthal believed the TVA had acted to geographically distribute the powers held in Washington and to repair what he saw as a deficit in local democracy. What had enabled the successful leap to a decentralized mode of administrative control was the way the focus of these efforts had been constructed. Claiming that geographic and economic relationships were perhaps more indicative of conditions on the ground than state boundaries, in Lilienthal's opinion, the magnitude of the TVA's area of operations was calibrated to be of "workable" size and allow close contact with people and their problems.[8] Not only to necessitate, but also to justify the application of a new system of regional administrative control, these separate issues would need to be considered and resolved collectively. Consciously dealing with diverse problems however does not immediately translate into seeing them as 'integrated', except perhaps in the philosophical sense of a broader national interest. Except for seasonal flooding, few of the social or economic problems faced by the residents of Tennessee could be attributed directly to the river's flows. Moreover, even if each of the many "parts" could be grouped, they would still have been understood to have their own unique causes.[9] A synthesis of factors was therefore required to define the area in which federal control was exercised, if this area was to reflect the problems collectively experienced by the region's residents. Yet unlike Powell, who defined participation as the people exercising a measure of direct control over local resources, Lilienthal was less concerned with the civic responsibilities of the region's residents. Rather, his argument to regionalize federal administrative powers was framed as a pragmatic way to coordinate the resolution of composite problems. Calling on the *concept of integration*, Lilienthal explained that the multiple and geographically dispersed problems of the Tennessee Valley should be "viewed as a single problem of many integrated parts".[10] A single agency such as the TVA would therefore be better suited to manage and resolve these problems rather than existing governmental instrumentalities. Acknowledging that in some respects the Tennessee River system was not a self-contained unit, the Directors' 1936 report to Congress stressed that the problems the TVA was

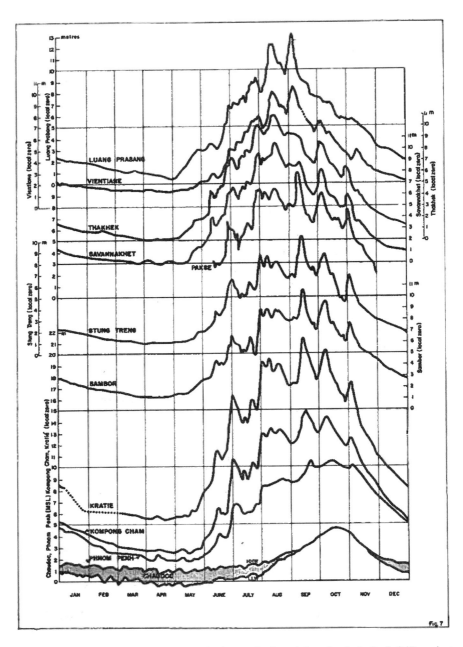

Figure 3.2 **Classifying flows.** The unit-hydrograph plotted time (period of rainfall) against the volume of water per second of rainfall allowing hydrologists to forecast the anticipated impact of a weather event of any duration or intensity. This chart of the Lower Mekong's stage hydrographs shows peak water flows at measuring points along the river. The variability in the maximum water volume at each location displayed the uneven severity of flood levels within the river's basin. UN Economic Commission for Asia and the Far East (1957), *Stage Hydrographs of the Lower Mekong 1950*. [*Source:* United Nations]

tasked to resolve were not only inter-related but also extended across individual states.[11] What made the many parts into a single problem that could be conceptualized as a whole was therefore a matter of perspective.[12] This perspective had been established by the conservation movement's concern over the private ownership of natural resources and the realization that dams, when also used for hydropower generation, were infrastructural investments that performed well against multiple social and economic goals. Yet does this mean that the specific extent of the basin presented on maps was only incidental to the establishment of regional control?

Where administration was concerned, the TVA Act had vested federal control over resource management directly to the organization, giving legal power to the TVA to mediate between those levels and departments of government whose jurisdictions intersected in the Tennessee Valley. From Lilienthal's point of view, the Tennessee Valley marked an area where for the specific functions it was mandated to perform, the TVA had exclusive, non-overlapping control. What perhaps had changed in the intervening years was a shift in focus from the length of the river's waterways to the extent of the Valley. Hydrologists and military engineers claimed that the basin was an environment with specific rules, that those rules could be known and that once known, the basin, or rather the flows of water within the basin, could be controlled. The administrative focus on an engineerable terrain suggests that it was regionalized control that initially found a home in the shape of the basin rather than the other way around. The alignment between control and the river basin was vividly expressed by Lilienthal:

> *For the first time in the history of the nation, the resources of a river were not only to be "envisioned in their entirety"; they were to be developed in* that unity with which nature herself regards her resources – *the waters, the land, and the forests together.*[13]

Yet the *unity* to which the development aspired was not the creation of the nature that Lilienthal described. From the perspective of engineers such as Albert Fry, the terrain no longer resembled the hydrological operations of the basin's primordial geography but rather the plans on which those operations had been transformed. With the assurance that increasing scientific knowledge of the basin's hydrology could explicate the interrelationship between the Tennessee's thousands of streams and waterways, the TVA engineered the flows of water in multiple locations to behave as a single unit. If water, land and forests were to be considered collectively as nature, then this nature would thereafter be dependent on technicians closing floodgates or on maintenance crews removing storm debris to maintain the equilibrium which unity implied.

From Drainage Area to Development Unit

The reputation of the TVA as a model of global development began as the Second World War ended. Lilienthal's widely distributed book *TVA – Democracy on the March* expanded on the benefits of ground-roots participation, highlighting the

52 *Liquid Territories*

project's paradigmatic purpose to unite "Nature and Mankind" within the "oneness" of the river's valley.[14] Stressing that implementation required the formation of an international agency structured on the TVA's "public-private prototype", Lilienthal's rhetoric of democracy and self-sufficiency found appeal among the leaders of newly independent nations seeking to legitimize their post-colonial authority with infrastructure investment. Thus, while the TVA experience was never repeated within the United States, the 1940s already saw the concept of unified river basin development applied in India and Mexico.[15] The elevation of the TVA into a template for world-wide water infrastructure development was not solely the result of Lilienthal's book. Exemplifying an approach rooted in technical and scientific expertise, the idea that river basins could situate modernization efforts in the world's least-developed countries within a specific geographic space was promoted in various programmes and by the Agency for International Development (USAID).[16] As research by the historian Vincent Lagendijk has shown, "TVA-like" solutions to the problems of socioeconomic distress became the cornerstone of American foreign policy, especially as Cold War tension with the Soviet bloc escalated into a battle for influence. Even as the TVA's technical concepts were adopted into the planning of the Damodar Valley in northeast India, the idea that the engineering of water infrastructure within the cartographic outline of a river basin could also help engineer peace resonated with new global organizations such as the United Nations and the World Bank.

The conceptualization of the basin as the setting for collaboration between opposing parties emerged where post-colonial national boundaries apportioned control of rivers according to sovereignty over the land through which the river flowed. On this principle, the division of the Kashmir Valley into Indian and Pakistani jurisdictions had left India in control over the highland sources of the Indus River that were critical to Pakistan's downstream agricultural economy. Faced with an unresolvable political and military situation, Lilienthal proposed to use the Indus River's basin as the basis for a common project. In an article published in 1951, Lilienthal asserted that the joint technical venture – similar to the "seven-state TVA" – would aim to develop the whole Indus system as a single unit for the benefit of both countries.[17] Even though work on planning the Indus Valley commenced under the auspices of the UN, the optimism that engineering could in some way mitigate the political deadlock over Kashmir was premature. Seen from the UN's perspective, international cooperation was a prerequisite for economic growth and social stability. The continental scope of organizations such as the UN Economic Commission for Asia and the Far East (ECAFE) sought to generate a "common interest" between Asian countries contending with significant food shortages inherited from vastly different experiences of Western colonization and Japanese wartime occupation. The post-war multiplication of internationally recognized sovereign jurisdictions and the fragmentation of internally interdependent colonial economies meant that the UN's post-war *reconstruction* of Asia would necessarily involve more than supporting a single state. But with international support usually delivered through central governments, the geographic extent of multilateral assistance more often aligned with the limits of national sovereignty. With the river's catchment framing the possibility of collaboration across multiple national jurisdictions, the concept of the basin acquired a diplomatic aura.

Perhaps not surprisingly, the political dimension of basin-scale development remained secondary to the social benefits that the technical control of water could produce. Writing in 1957, the geographer Gilbert White attempted to define the global principles that multi-purpose river development had adopted over the past 25 years. Already a consultant with the United Nations, White defined the ideally regulated stream as one that would fluctuate only to supply water for societal needs and productive uses with all "the natural variations having been evened out".[18] Acknowledging that this perspective effectively idealized the power of engineering, White argued that planning according to the extent of the entire catchment was not simply a technical concern. Influenced by his appreciation of the TVA's social programmes, he presented the engineered control of rivers as one of several possible instruments including land use regulations that would serve the greater purpose of development.[19] Accordingly, the goals of basin planning such as accelerating food production or distributing electricity took precedence over the total physical control of the river. Thus, rather than the river's volume or seasonal flow, a new set of calculable indicators were adopted to estimate the power generated by a stream, to define the land area irrigated by a waterway and to quantify consumptive uses.[20] With each waterway classifiable by its definitive maximum power output and its potential maximum consumption, the role of planning would be to efficiently organize the achievement of these measurable objectives. Determined with reference to the entire hydrological catchment, the enumerated aims of production and consumption were not simply the goals of a specific planning exercise undertaken at particular historical moment by particular people. Given that once a waterway was regulated it would underpin subsequent economic or social changes, the impact of regulating the entire collection of waterways within the basin would be permanent.

Appreciated on a map, the areal outline of the mapped basin suggested the model of a spatial unit in which the river's flows were organized to serve societal needs. Concentrated within that unit's area, diverse phenomena such as settlement or infrastructure could be assessed according to their relationship with water. Because rivers could be regulated, it was entirely possible to imagine that by controlling water changes in those other phenomena could also be determined. Acting as both the reference from which objectives were derived and results evaluated, as well as the unit of planning through which those measures were operationalized in various distinct projects, ensured that – in theory at least – the outcomes of planning aligned with the objectives. The analytical distinction which identified river basin development as the collection of projects designed with reference to the same hydrological catchment revealed the challenge of applying the concept across multiple jurisdictions. Based on the planetary background of maps accompanying the discussion of basin development, White depicted the world's international drainage basins covering a significant proportion of the continents' surface. Yet among these, only nine of the world's great rivers were "free from the complication of crossing. man-made borders", while none were considered effectively planned

54 *Liquid Territories*

across frontiers.[21] White's argument highlighted that the complexities of jurisdiction were augmented by the idea of multiple-use regulation in which an individual project addressed different functions. With each function potentially referencing economic, social or political relationships that could extend beyond the basin's limits, the idea of a unified – that is international – administration controlling a river's waters inspired controversy rather than imitation.

Even so, White's maps illustrated more than the underexploited potential of international rivers. Although his drawings referenced the extents of hydrological catchments, these catchments were presented as "drainage areas" on one map and as "basins" on the other. Despite these terms being synonymous in the text, in their cartographic articulation "drainage areas" were depicted as vast surfaces of continental extent whose scale dwarfed the individual countries they encompassed. "Basins", hosting integrated development on the other hand, were displayed compartmentalized into technically manageable subdivisions that reflected the scale, if not the shape, of national or regional administrative units. Inasmuch as these maps were primarily pictorial clarifications of the text, they also suggested that basins and the world's vast, unharnessed drainage areas were registered in different spatial categories. Taken as a sequence of two maps, the delineation of *basins* appeared to represent the spatial extent of an amorphous *drainage area's* domesticated portion. The cartographic representation expounded a pictorial argument in which global geography and technical knowledge together produced a particular unit of the earth's surface.

A similar cartographic argument accompanied the UN's recommendations on integrated river basin development published one year later (**Figure 3.3**). In the report co-authored by White, two separate maps outline the global extents of river basins with one entitled "Major Drainage Areas of the World" and the other "International River Basins". Without the overlap in the displayed information making one of the two maps redundant, each drawing expands on different aspects of the argument. Drainage areas displayed in relation to arid or permafrost regions in one map evoked habitability, the propensity for a specific type of geographic space to host human activities enabled by a regular supply of water. The depiction of only international river basins on the other map appeared to highlight their geostrategic location. Especially over Asia, the focus on catchments of a specific magnitude defined regions whose extents crossed between the geological spaces of otherwise Cold War adversaries.[22] Acknowledging that such regions and even individual projects were impossible to develop simultaneously to their full capacity, the report recommended phasing, or alternatively concentration on the largest basins that were "so large that for certain planning purposes their sub-basins can be developed with a large degree of independence".[23] By focus on a local project within the plan for the larger basin, the report's authors anticipated a chain of development that would eventually accelerate implementation of the main project. An entire basin could therefore have an integrated plan, but one designed to be executed within separate geopolitical domains.

As the most influential global organization leading the multinational agenda, the UN's recommendations served to inform governments and initiate discussions

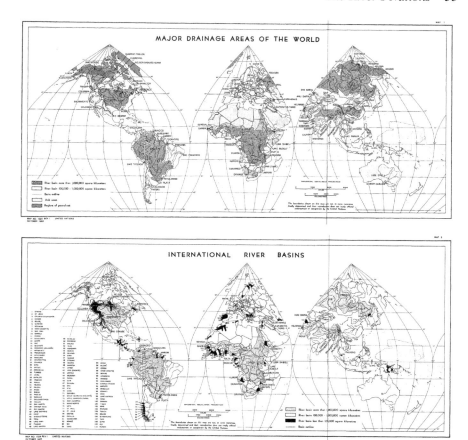

Figure 3.3 **Global distribution of drainage basins.** The maps show the world's drainage areas (above) and international river basins (below). Considered together, the two maps visualize the spatial transition from naturally occurring catchments to the more specific technical units of river basin development. United Nations (1970), *Drainage Areas of the World & International River Basins*. [*Source:* United Nations]

on potential new projects. Translated versions of these reports were disseminated globally, the maps serving as valuable pictorial tools to transmit information.[24] Following publication, the report was adopted by the UN Council with particular attention given to the formulation of legal principles for the use and joint development of international rivers.[25] During the 1958 conference of the International Law Association in New York, interest in basins crossing legal jurisdictions prompted a new definition of this term to emerge. From the UN's perspective, the "global concept of 'river basin' includes not only surface water, whether running or stagnant (lakes), but also the contiguous ground water, and even the meteoric waters (clouds, etc.) which may influence the physical and economic characteristics of the

56 *Liquid Territories*

river basin".[26] With this definition in mind, the UN's global maps of basins not only represented a 'horizontal' areal extent but also indicated the epicentre of discrete vertical relationships that bound together subterranean and atmospheric space with the earth's surface. With neither the extent of aquifers nor the position of clouds 'contained' within the basin's mapped outline, what the concept referred to was also a process bound to the terrestrial theory of the hydrological cycle. Notwithstanding the multiple legal regimes such an expansive definition of the term would have needed to comply with, the basic suggestion was simple: a specific basin was one possible delineated relationship emerging from the juxtaposition of continental surface flows, groundwater reserves and meteorological patterns. With the scale of developmental considerations no longer centred within an individual state's boundaries, rather than an aggregation of regional units from different countries the river basin equally appeared to be a single region partitioned into geopolitical units. The dialectic between basin development and state organization went even further with the UN urging the adjustment of administrative but also social and economic structures to the "system of integrated basin development".[27] The idea that a manmade development "system" rather than the existing natural basin itself could initiate structural changes in a state's internal organization arguably shifted attention to the one who was responsible for the system's design in the first place.

Formulating the *'Lower'* Mekong's Basin

Multi-purpose river development was introduced to Southeast Asia during the upheaval of the First Indochina War. The increased international recognition of the river basin's value however, did not immediately translate to the concept's application in France's Asian colonies. Although the *Compagnie Nationale du Rhône* was already developing hydropower, navigation and irrigation along one of France's longest rivers, by the end of World War II there were only two hydropower generators in French Indochina located in relatively distant mountain regions. Electricity, mainly produced with diesel engines, was distributed within proximity of the source although much more extended networks were deployed in the flat, low-lying terrain around Hanoi and Saigon.[28] With demand concentrated within the colony's dispersed urban centres, exploitation of the Mekong for power generation was not deemed a priority. As far as navigation or floods were concerned, among Southeast Asia's governments these were not universally considered problems requiring resolution through the TVA model.

Having envisioned the flood control of the Yangtze River, Chinese scientists P.T. Tan and Dr Shen-Yi founded the ECAFE's Flood Control Bureau, shifting their attention to the Mekong after Mao's communist army consolidated power in China. Mirroring the objectives of the TVA, engineering flood control in Asia was presented as an opportunity to unlock the economic and social benefits of 'harnessing' the river. For at least some of the ECAFE's members, floods were not typically considered threatening and, where exceptional inundations were periodically recorded, they were more often reported when they had catastrophic impacts on settlements and crops. As far as floods were concerned, the common "problem" shared by East Asia's nations was not the relatively remote risk of damage from inundations. Calibrated according to the period's technical knowledge, the infrastructure proposed to control wet season floods across the Mekong's vast geographic extents could also produce electricity, improve navigation and irrigate fields. To realize a river's full value however would require post-colonial states to invest their limited resources in new dams, reservoirs and canals. Although often motivated by Cold War imperatives, finance through the World Bank and engineering expertise from international scientists became increasingly available. With flood protection institutionalized, the control of rivers was presented as an internationally acceptable trajectory for economic development and famine alleviation.

The dearth of detailed hydrological information of both the mainstream and the Mekong's longest tributaries however limited what could immediately begin to be designed. Led by Tan, concerted attempts to survey the river and its surrounding geology began with a reconnaissance mission in 1951. Nonetheless, the spatial configuration of regional political interests born during the conflict on the Korean Peninsula meant that the basin could not be known as a single space. International recognition of the nationalist Chinese government based in Taiwan excluded Mainland China from participation in the UN and ECAFE.[29] Thus, neither hydraulic data nor updated maps could be obtained for the entire stretch from the Mekong's sources in the Tibetan glaciers to the tropical rainforests marking the border between China and Laos. As a result, the Lancang – the Mekong's Chinese section – along with its corresponding catchment area was omitted from international surveys. Partitioned according to the realities of politics rather than the inclined plane directing the flows of water, the exclusion of almost a quarter of the entire basin's square area was inconsistent with the calculability promised by the theory of the hydrological catchment. As only one part of the basin's entirety, a new conceptual basis became necessary that would allow not only engineers and planners but also politicians to operationalize the river's southern portion as an internally coherent – if not totally autonomous – geographic whole.

On maps, this geopolitical condition was reflected most vividly in the cartographic construction of the *Lower Mekong Basin*. A relatively typical geographic notation for rivers in Western cartography, the conceptualization of the Mekong as having an upper section and a lower section was not simply the result of excluding the Lancang. The 'lower' part of the Mekong had been highlighted on maps since colonial days, initially to describe the French section of the Mekong. As France expanded its influence into Southeast Asia, 'lower' came to distinguish the fertile agricultural region where the river emerged from the highlands of Laos to drain through Siam. What was considered the lower portion of the river was essentially determined by the mountainous land borders established decades earlier between colonial France and China's Qing dynasty rulers. Shifting cartographic focus southwards, maps presented the Lower Mekong Basin within a new cartographic frame deliberately cropped to exclude communist China to the north. As a consequence of this abrupt 'cut', maps of the river failed to show portions of the catchment included within the discursive notion of the Lower Mekong Basin.

58 *Liquid Territories*

The argument that the north-south division of the river was not ideal but an acceptable compromise for geographic and cartographic reasons was supported by Gilbert White. Examining the Lancang's steep mountainous terrain from the distance of military maps, White argued that the upper basin offered few opportunities for dense settlement leaving the mainstream flows reaching Laos from China relatively unaffected, even if, as he conjectured, dams were to be constructed there in the future.[30] Unable to formulate a convincing hydrological distinction between the upper and lower basins, White presented the geopolitical partition as a reflection of social and economic issues linked to land availability, development potential and population density. Although these relationships did not terminate at the land border, establishing the primary beneficiaries of the river's flows as those people living within the basin's defined outline conferred onto the construct of the 'lower basin' a concrete statistical reality (**Figure 3.4**). With the difference between those using the river's water visually confirmed through the reality presented by maps, the two quantifiable groups of flows could be considered separately, each in reference to the beneficiaries within its own domain. More a cartographic frame than an outlined extent, references to the Lower Mekong Basin suggested a distinct if not internally coherent geographic area, an assumption nonetheless contingent on the flows of the Mekong north of Laos remaining forever unchanged.

Producing Geography

Confirmed as the extent of international involvement in the development of the region's water resources, the Lower Mekong Basin created a common political interest between the four countries whose mapped sovereignty overlapped with its geographic area. With the majority of Laos and Cambodia as well as a significant portion of post-colonial South Vietnam encompassed within the Lower Mekong Basin, development of those countries and the river became almost synonymous. Following the formal independence of Indochina's constituent regions with the Geneva Convention, the pace of investigation into the basin's topography accelerated. The first comprehensive survey launched with a reconnaissance visit in 1956. Led by General Wheeler of the American Corps of Engineers, the survey team travelled to the few identified locations where the volume of flowing water and the slope of the ground offered a low-risk opportunity to construct dams. On the way the international team had the opportunity to glimpse how people interacted with the wet monsoon terrain reporting that protective measures against flooding were rare in the places they visited. In fact, the authors claimed that local people had "adapted" to wet season inundations, relying on them for fishing, replenishing soil nutrients and transport.[31] Appearing to contradict the urgency with which the Flood Control Bureau framed the need to control the river, the report concluded that flood control was not a subject of interest in the Mekong basin. This was,

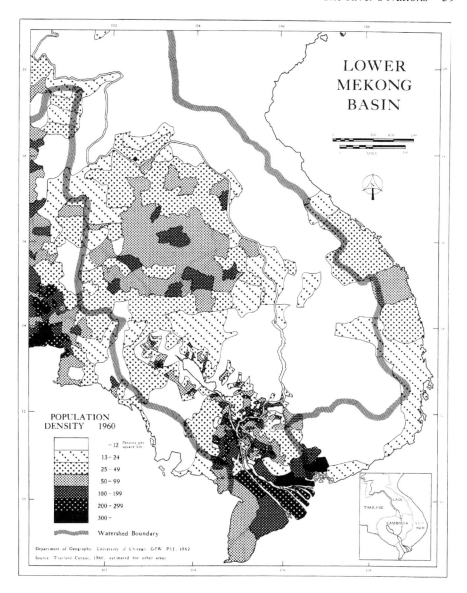

Figure 3.4 **Knowledge of the Lower Mekong Basin.** The outline of the Mekong's basin is presented in relation to population density. The absence of a statistically detectable population in the Northern Mountains allows the viewer to perceive the displayed population clusters as distinct areal continuities with no relationship to what is happening further north. White *et al* (1962), *Population Density 1960.* [*Source:* United Nations]

60 *Liquid Territories*

however, neither due to people's indifference for technical solutions nor because of an absence of catastrophic inundations. Major floods, while not uncommon, were always due to both regional meteorological phenomena such as typhoons and the particularities of the topography.[32] With some governments' officials even asking for more flooding rather than containment or diversion, a basin-wide approach to dealing with the river was not apparent to the reconnaissance team. Moreover, with inadequate topographic surveys and only sparse records of actual discharge levels, the enormous task of mapping the river at a consistent level of detail would need to precede the commencement of any planning.

Through multilateral contributions towards their expense, the ECAFE's *Committee for Coordination of Investigations of the Lower Mekong Basin* (Mekong Committee) was able to finance an international collection of experts to map the region. The task of capturing images of the terrain from the air, interpreting and then converting the aerial photographs into topographic maps was taken up by a Canadian team with Filipino cartographers. Primarily responsible for surveying the Mekong's tributaries, the team needed to establish the reference system of controls almost from scratch from which to map over 46,000 km^2, about one-twelfth of the 'lower basin'. The majority of these were photographed at a scale of $1:40,000$, and focus areas surrounding three potential dam sites covering about 160 km^2 were mapped at a scale of $1:2000$.[33] The baseline information compiled through these surveys of Pa Mong, the Khone rapids and Sambor underpinned thematic maps for hydrology or geology that would accompany preliminary technical studies of the water infrastructure itself. Unlike the cartographic focus of Powell's USGS 70 years earlier, none of the new collections of topographic data covered the extent of an entire catchment area.

Mapping the topography solved only part of the problem. Producing quality information regarding water volumes, sediment loads, precipitation and evaporation was equally as important as knowing the contours of submerged river sections. Ideally, data collection required uniform geographic distribution of measuring instruments to achieve an isotropic understanding of the entire basin's seasonal wetness. Intended to record measures in relation to both the *length* of the river (flow and sediment) and the *area* of the basin (precipitation), the redistribution of existing gauges and the creation of new measuring points became necessary to guarantee that the collected data could support assessments and planning.[34] Following the turmoil of the world war and anti-colonial struggle, however, only 135 gauges were still in operation throughout the 'lower basin' with no more than 50 years of continuous streamflow data recorded by 1956. More than half of these were located in Thailand and around Tonle Sap, or concentrated along the major rivers flowing into the Mekong. Conversely, information about rivers in the highland areas of Laos where precipitation was highest was sparse. Thus, while existing data were considered of good quality, the limited coverage meant that vast regions within the basin were poorly known or effectively not known at all. Moreover, even if data collection would begin immediately, it would take years of repeated measurements for the information produced to reliably model a mountain stream's hydraulic behaviour.

The long-term commitment to any basin scale planning was recognized by the four countries sharing the Mekong's catchment, and in 1958, they officially agreed to cooperate on the investigation and development of the river's resources. Drawing international attention to the Lower Mekong Basin's "development", the Mekong Committee prepared an initial plan for the region focused on the river's mainstream (**Figure 3.5**). Intended to guide further investigations and feasibility studies rather than to act as a definitive technical document, the plan depicted the river organized into regulated compartments. With each manmade section controlled by a dam, electricity would be generated from the flows, while reservoirs enabled navigation and stored water to irrigate adjacent command areas. Situated in relatively remote stretches of the Mekong, proposed hydropower facilities were sometimes paired with new industrial centres, to function as nodes within a network providing electricity to major cities within and beyond the basin's limits. Considering the intentional exclusion of potential projects along tributaries from the plan pending further surveys, the mainstream's visual prominence in the drawing is not surprising. But as incomplete as the plan may be, the relationship it framed between the basin, the river and the region is consequential. With the value of the Mekong's linear continuity depicted as superseding the separation of national boundaries, the mainstream's flows were shown subsumed within the engineered subdivisions created by water infrastructure. Rather than merely reflecting geopolitical reality, the plan appeared to create the conditions for the spatial integration of the larger geographic space impacted by development of the river, extending from the mainstream to the existing industrial centres beyond the limit of the basin.[35] If the concept of integration was intended to underpin planning on the scale of the catchment, then the proposal drew attention to the river's significance for development in the broader Southeast Asia region. Collectively considered as the Mekong Scheme, as the components from which an integrated plan was composed, individual projects symbolized the international collaboration promoted by the UN.[36] The idea that projects planned, built and operated in distant locations and over a period of decades could nonetheless be coordinated to optimize output, underpinned the notion of a common endeavour.[37]

Throughout the 1960s, as new topographic maps and hydraulic data were compiled, more detailed proposals for controlling the flows of both the mainstream and tributary rivers emerged. Early implementation of dams on the three sites surveyed first was intended to catalyse industrialization and stimulate modern irrigation development.[38] Proposed by the Mekong Committee, the Pa Mong project was conceived to be – by far – the largest of all the proposed projects and its significance was appreciated from a basin-wide perspective. Discussing the Pa Mong reservoir's potential to store and then discharge enormous volumes of water during the dry season, the Committee highlighted the benefits to downstream multi-purpose projects for power production, flood protection and reduction of salt water intrusion.[39] Even if only conceptual, in addressing issues such as salinization in the distant delta or inundation in the floodplain, the project's impact appeared to extend thousands of kilometres away, revealing at the same time the strategic value of a dam that could be used to exercise control across the entire downstream. Composed

62 *Liquid Territories*

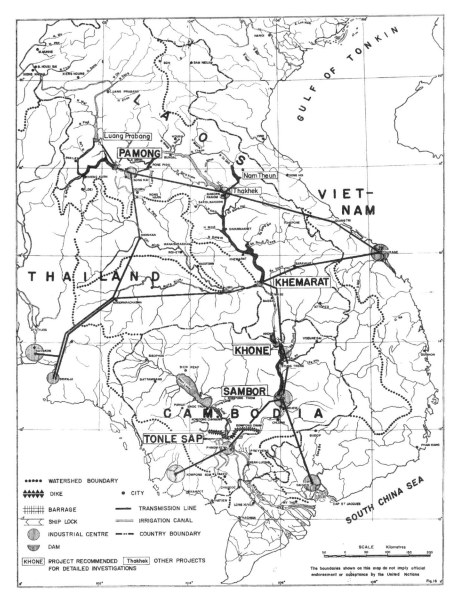

Figure 3.5 **Planning the Lower Mekong Basin.** The map displays the Mekong's mainstream compartmentalized into discrete, navigable sections by the six proposed dams. Transmission lines extend to existing regional centres (Saigon, Bangkok, Sihanoukville and Da Nang) beyond the Mekong's catchment. In the hierarchy of lines, the "watershed boundary" is highly visible and differentiated from national borders. Note the similarity of the depicted river segments, including the alternating colours/shades of the mainstream, with the Tennessee Valley shown in Figure 3.1. UN Economic Commission for Asia and the Far East (1957), *Map Showing Development Projects in the Lower Mekong Basin Recommended for Detailed Investigation*. [*Source:* United Nations]

The River's Nations 63

of dams on the mainstream and along two tributaries, the Pa Mong reservoir would detain more water than Tonle Sap, storing enough to irrigate 1,000,000 ha and to produce more electricity than the region demanded.[40] Promoted by the US State Department to influence regional Cold War ideologies, the project's planning was undertaken by the engineers of America's Bureau of Reclamation with the support of Thai and Laotian technicians.[41]

The first stage of the Bureau's Pa Mong study confirmed earlier estimations and even surpassed them. The keystone in a "cascade" of downstream projects, Pa Mong certainly epitomized the aspirations of planning a unified system of water flows. The idea that individual projects could, because of their location within the same basin, ultimately operate in relation to each other was critical to the thesis of an imagined geography synonymous with the coordinated control of water and the distribution of power. While the Bureau's reports often cited coordination or integration with downstream facilities, Pa Mong's specific role in any overall system was not determined when the project was designed leaving the relationship between individual projects and the cumulative objective of developing the basin for later studies.[42] Published in 1970, the Committee's Indicative Basin Plan compiled the new hydrological, meteorological and social investigations from the preceding ten years to propose more than 100 separate projects, aimed at collectively satisfying the anticipated regional demand for power over a period of 30 years. Divided into short-term and long-term strategies, the implementation sequence of the Basin Plan was organized around three core projects: Pa Mong, Sambor and the development of irrigation in the delta. Upstream from Pa Mong and downstream to Sambor, combinations of hydropower dams were selected for implementation based on their cumulative capacity to generate power. Between projects, what the plan termed "hydraulic integration" would relate upstream water releases to downstream power generation or irrigation requirements.[43] The operation of projects along the same watercourse or located within the same catchment area was therefore contingent on when – and if – a different project would be implemented elsewhere.[44] This suggests that deciding where and how the reservoir's water would be distributed was not the only issue. Based on their location, each installation would need to consider a different catchment area.[45] Thus, to calculate the annual anticipated volume of water detained by the reservoir, engineers would base their estimations on the entirety of upstream flows from where the dam intersected the river. Those working on projects located downstream along the same waterway would undertake reciprocal alterations, reconfiguring the extent of the catchment area they needed to consider in relation to the upstream diversion. The connection between upstream and downstream established by a single project would therefore affect – to different degrees – all subsequent proposals that relied on the same, fixed total volume of water to operate.[46] In the context of the project's planning, *integration* therefore referred to the projects' cumulative capacity to produce power, as well as the adaptation of a single project to the conditions engendered by its location within a definable collection of water flows.

The plan's spatial interpretation of integration can be discerned in the configuration of the map accompanying the planning report (**Figure 3.6**). Presenting the location of all the proposed infrastructure projects – including those that a specific

64 *Liquid Territories*

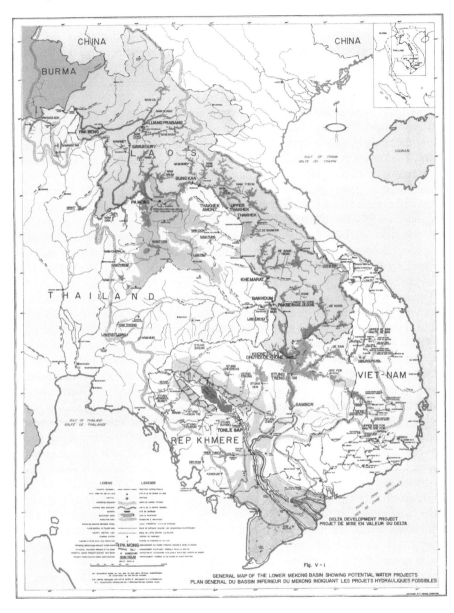

Figure 3.6 **Indicative basin plan.** With an unusual degree of geographic specificity for a cartographic projection of this scale, the map vividly represents water surfaces and irrigation areas if all projects were to be constructed and simultaneously operated. Phased according to the proposed scenarios, only those projects required to meet the cumulative goals of power generation would have been constructed. Mekong Committee (1970), *General Map of the Lower Mekong Basin Showing Potential Water Projects.* [*Source:* United Nations]

implementation sequence would exclude – the drawing depicts with a significant degree of specificity the new water bodies that would be formed from the simultaneous operation of all the dams. These are especially prominent in the mountains of Laos as well as the enormous surface of the Stung Treng reservoir in Cambodia which appears to dwarf Tonle Sap.[47] Clearly defined, extensive irrigated areas are shown surrounding the Pa Mong dam, the delta and Tonle Sap which, apart from countries, are individually the largest continuous coloured surfaces denoting a particular geographic space. Central to the hypothesis of coordinated control, on the map, the delimitation of the watershed boundary is almost imperceptible. When considered as collections of projects, however, a different pattern emerges. Unlike the groups of hydropower dams in Laos whose product would be distributed far from the project itself, irrigation implied intensified agricultural production. Consequently the concentration of settlement and the economy of these specific areas would also be affected. As such, due in no small part to their magnitude, irrigation areas along with their accompanying reservoirs appear to denote specific subregions within the basin. Shown crossing national boundaries these subregions assert a degree of geographic autonomy. Along with the reservoir formed by dams at Stung Treng, Sambor and Khone, the implication is of a different order of relationships that does not adhere to national subdivisions. From this perspective, the indicative plan presents a new scale of geographic space articulated by the impact of individual projects operating collectively.

Two different areas of water can therefore be identified. On the one hand, the extent of the river basin, dictating the total volume of water in the catchment and thus a project's relative value in the system, but which also allowed maximum power production to be estimated and demographic impacts to be measured. On the other hand, the geographic aggregate of catchment areas – modified by infrastructure – dependent on each other for their operation rather than the entire river's flows. On the surface of the map, the area occupied by these interrelated notions overlapped. Tonle Sap's extensive irrigation area was considered from the perspective of the discrete group of canals, dikes and reservoirs designed to contain floods and distribute water from surrounding rivers, but also in relation to upstream storage at Stung Treng and flood control at Sambor. Thus, if an imagined geography had emerged from the cartographic construction of the Lower Mekong Basin, it reflected a spatial subdivision produced by the deployment of infrastructure rather than the compartmentalization of national boundaries or the configuration of the topography. The aspirational unity Lilienthal imagined seeing in the Tennessee Valley was a better description of the result of concerted technical manipulation by the TVA than a general condition inherent to basins. And unlike the technocratic classification of basins as geographic units, what constituted 'nature' much less 'society' across the entire extent of the Mekong's catchment was arguably non-uniform and highly differentiated.[48] Maps portraying the Lower Mekong Basin therefore presented a potentially new, albeit discursive geographic cohesion. The cartographic framing of Southeast Asia through the lens of the 'lower' basin allowed the territory encompassed by the watershed to be visualized as the domesticated portion of the entire drainage area.

66 *Liquid Territories*

Conclusion

Writing about the utilitarian state in the context of Europe, James Scott has argued that "the vocabulary used to organize nature typically betrays the overriding interests of its human users".[49] From this perspective, the repeated use of two maps to expand the UN's global thesis of integrated basin development was not merely illustrative of a change in the natural condition of a river's flows. The transition between a 'drainage area' stretching across national boundaries and an 'international basin' entailed a political and physical transformation. The cartographic construction of the Lower Mekong Basin repositioned the regional centre of focus according to the demands of Cold War geopolitics, shaping the hydrological catchment to engineer a promised prosperity. An extent made known through the compilation of surveys conducted along the length of the mainstream and its most important tributaries rather than the area of the basin, this hydrological reference was equivalent to the cumulative total of all catchment areas encompassed by the Mekong's flows.

Yet, while the total of the units into which the basin could be subdivided was numerically equal to the combined total of all hydrological catchments, the components from which the total was computed did not remain the same. Modified according to the locations of upstream dams and the volumetric capacity of reservoirs, the catchment areas referred to by individual projects encompassed a different geographic extent from what maps of the terrain's inclined slopes depicted. And, where groups of infrastructure installations were coordinated to irrigate land or to contain floods, the cumulative impact of these alterations arguably manifested around new regional entities, distinct from adjacent geographic spaces insofar as infrastructure was needed to maintain the appropriate level of wetness on the ground in perpetuity. The Swiss geographer Claude Raffestin has defined the condition of ecosystems that would otherwise disappear without humans to maintain them as *domestication*. Since their adaptation to both the preferences and rhythms of human utility has privileged certain characteristics and eliminated others, Raffestin argues that domesticated ecosystems could be considered as new objects that "reflect the mark of the system of intentions framed by the culture of the group".[50] A geographic unit denoting the interaction between human users and water resources, the cartographic basin of the Mekong River projected the manmade order which would emerge once the river was controlled.

Notes

1 François Molle (2009), River-Basin Planning and Management: The Social Life of a Concept. *Geoforum*, v. 40, pp. 488–489.
2 David Ekbladh (2002), "Mr. TVA". Grass-Root Development, David Lilienthal, and the Rise and Fall of the Tennessee Valley Authority as a Symbol for U.S. Overseas Development, 1933–1973. *Diplomatic History*, v. 26, n. 3, p. 346.
3 J.W. Powell (1891), *Eleventh Annual Report of the Director of the United States Geological Survey. Part II – Irrigation: 1889–1890*. Washington: Government Printing Office, p. 215.

The River's Nations 67

4 The 1933 Act provided primarily for the river to be brought under control and to be made navigable. According to the law scholar Martin, "only after the requirements of flood control and navigation should have been met, it named as a purpose the production and sale of electric power". Moreover, the only provision made in the Act concerning agriculture was the production of fertilizer at Muscle Shoals. See Roscoe C. Martin (1957), The Tennessee Valley Authority: A Study of Federal Control. *Law and Contemporary Problems*, v. 22, Summer, p. 361; Norman Wengert (1952), Antecedents of TVA: The Legislative History of Muscle Shoals. *Agricultural History*, v. 26, n. 4, p. 141.

5 "Through this system of reservoirs and the interconnecting natural channels, the run-off from the 41.000 square miles of drainage area within the Tennessee Basin is continuously flowing". Albert Fry (1948), *Recent Developments in Hydrology with Respect to Stream Flow Forecasting*. IAHS Congress, Oslo, p. 143.

6 LeRoy Sherman (1932), Streamflow from Rainfall by Unit-Graph Method. *Engineering News Record*, v. 108, April 11, p. 501.

7 Fry, *op. cit.*, p. 148. The development of a theory of infiltration by Robert Horton divided the study of rainfall into two distinct phenomena: surface runoff and groundwater. Having determined the volume of total rainfall not contributing to surface runoff through stream flow observations, the anticipated groundwater volumes could also be plotted across the duration of a storm.

8 David Lilienthal (1944), *TVA Democracy on the March*. New York & London: Harper Brothers, p. 154.

9 The serious erosion threatening farmers, for example, was the result of cultivating the forested slopes of the narrow valleys with rain-fed row crops such as corn and tobacco and was not limited to the region encompassed by the Tennessee Valley. Similarly, the absence of an electricity network to serve remote settlements was a result of the state-regulated power supply market dominated by private, profit-seeking corporations.

10 David Lilienthal (1940), The TVA and Decentralization. *Survey Graphic*, v. 24, n. 6, p. 337.

11 Tennessee Valley Authority (1936), *Report to the Congress on the Unified Development of the Tennessee River System*. Knoxville, TN: Tennessee Valley Authority, p. 41.

12 "I have no confidence in the elaborate rituals by which some technicians think they can determine what constitutes a region. No one can work out a formula for what is in reality a judgment that does not lend itself to such precise measurement". Lilienthal (1944), *op. cit.*, p. 153.

13 Emphasis in original. *Ibid.*, p. 48.

14 "In the unified development of resources there is such a Great Plan: the Unity of Nature and Mankind. Under such a Plan in our valley we move forward". *ibid.*, p. 197.

15 In Europe, resolving problems related to drainage, sewerage and power generation from rivers was accompanied by institutional changes. Between the world wars, water management, either by cooperatives or by government authorities, became aligned with the geographic extent of the hydrological catchment in Germany and Spain. See Molle, *op. cit.*, p. 488.

16 Vincent Lagendijk (2019), Streams of Knowledge: River Development Knowledge and the TVA on the River Mekong. *History and Technology*, v. 35, n. 3, p. 321.

17 David Lilienthal (1951), Another Korea in the Making? *Collier's Weekly*, August 4, p. 58.

18 Gilbert White (1957), A Perspective of River Basin Development. *Law and Contemporary Problems*, v. 22, n. 2, River Basin Development, p. 158.

19 *Ibid.*, p. 174.

20 "the total amount of electric power which a stream is capable of generating may be calculated: The amount of power is a function of volume of natural flow, fall, and regulation. It is possible, as well, to calculate the total acreage of land which may be irrigated from a stream, if fully regulated, taking into account the consumptive use made by different assumed crops and cropping practices". *ibid.*, p. 158.

68   Liquid Territories

21 *Ibid.*, p. 180.
22 Within the category of mid-sized basins emphasized by the map, 880,000 km² separated the smallest (Maroni river) from the largest basin (Tocantins), U.N. Department of Economic and Social Affairs (1958), *Integrated River Basin Development: Report by a Panel of Experts*. New York: United Nations, p. 7.
23 *Ibid.*, p. 6.
24 Cartographers at the United Nations had been producing maps since 1946, and a Cartographic Unit was established in 1951 with a limited team of three. According to the cartographic department's logbook, the UN's first map was a world map of *Drainage Basins, Aridity and Irrigation* produced in July 1946. See Ayako Kagawa & Guillaume Le Sourd (2017), Mapping the World: Cartographic and Geographic Visualization by the United Nations Geospatial Information Section (Formerly Cartographic Section). *Proceedings of the International Cartographic Association*, n. 1, p. 3.
25 United Nations Office of Public Information (1959), *Yearbook of the United Nations 1958*. New York: United Nations, p. 155.
26 U.N. Economic Commission for Latin America (1959), *Preliminary Review of Questions Relating to the Development of International River Basins in Latin America (E/CN.12/511)*. Panama City: United Nations, p. 2.
27 "More vital even is the need to adjust existing social, economic and administrative structures to any system of integrated river basin development". U.N. Department of Economic and Social Affairs, *op. cit.*, p. vi (Foreword).
28 See Hugues Tertrais (2002), L'électrification de l'Indochine, *Outre-mers*, v. 89, n. 334–335, L'électrification Outremer de la fin du XIXe siècle aux premières décolonisations. pp. 591–592.
29 "The term ECAFE region . . . excludes mainland China, Mongolia, North Korea and North Viet-Nam, all centrally planned economies for which adequate information or comparable statistics are not available". Even not including the people of those excluded countries, the estimated population encompassed by the ECAFE was about half the world's total living on about a fifth of the total land. United Nations (1968), *Economic Survey of Asia and the Far East 1967: Economic Bulletin for Asia and the Far East (E/CN.11/825)*. Bangkok: United Nations, p. iv (explanatory note).
30 Gilbert White (1963), The Mekong River Plan. *Ekistics*, v. 16, n. 96, p. 310.
31 US Bureau of Reclamation (1956), *Reconnaissance Report: Lower Mekong River Basin*. Denver, CO: United States Department of the Interior, Bureau of Reclamation, p. 27.
32 From 1924 to 2008, the MRC lists ten "extreme" floods at two measuring locations along the river's mainstream. These are flood events in which the annual maximum discharge of the river (water volume) exceeds 120% of the average annualized discharge. MRC (2015), *Annual Mekong Flood Report 2013*. Vientiane: Mekong River Commission, p. 26.
33 R.A. Brocklebank (1961), The Mekong Survey. *The Canadian Surveyor*, March issue, p. 404.
34 US Bureau of Reclamation, *op. cit.*, p. 50 & Appendix A (4–21).
35 The report from which the plan is drawn interprets integration as almost a voluntary act of technical coordination between different projects: "It is desirable that plans for the development of the tributaries . . . should be properly co-ordinated and integrated with those for the main river, thus forming a comprehensive plan for the entire lower basin". U.N. Department of Economic and Social Affairs, *op. cit.*, p. 42.
36 W.R. Derrick Sewell (1968), The Mekong Scheme: Guideline for a Solution to Strife in Southeast Asia. *Asian Survey*, v. 8, n. 6, p. 452.
37 For example, in a 1968 review of the Scheme for the periodical Asian Survey, the author notes that while in different countries, basins and hundreds of kilometres apart "Co-ordination between the Pa Mong and Sambor operations, for example, will permit much greater power production at the latter project than would otherwise be possible".

ibid., p. 453. Similarly a different article reporting on the Scheme stated that the "Sambor and Pa Mong dams will function together, and during the dry season the water released upstream will maintain the level in the Sambor reservoir, preventing a reduction in its power output". David Jenkins (1968), The Lower Mekong Scheme. *Asian Survey*, v. 8, n. 6, p. 457.

38 Chris Sneddon (2012), The 'Sinew of Development': Cold War Geopolitics Technical Expertise, and Water Resource Development in Southeast Asia, 1954–1975. *Social Studies of Science*, v. 42, n. 4, Water Worlds, p. 577.

39 Mekong Committee (1961), *Brief Description of the Pa Mong Project*. Bangkok: UN, p. 2. Quoted from Sneddon, *op. cit.*, p. 577.

40 Originally estimated at 1,800 MW, the production capacity of Pa Mong's hydroelectric facilities was subsequently revised after more detailed planning to 5,400 MW. *ibid.*

41 Famous for the construction of the Hoover Dam, the Bureau's global reputation for hydraulic engineering had been built on the control of the arid region's Columbia River. In comparison to the US Corps of Engineers, the Bureau of Reclamation had not been directly involved in the planning of the TVA.

42 As the Bureau itself admitted: "In the future, assuming that the Pa Mong Project becomes the first of several such developments in the Lower Mekong Basin, it will be necessary to fit the operation of Pa Mong into a basin system, which will mean that optimum future operation could be greatly different than that envisioned for a single unit". US Bureau of Reclamation, *op. cit.*, pp. VIII–1.

43 Committee for Coordination of Investigations of the Lower Mekong Basin (1970), *Report on Indicative Basin Plan: A Proposed Framework for the Development of Water and Related Resources of the Lower Mekong Basin (E/CN.ll/WRD/MKG/L.340)*. Bangkok: United Nations, pp. V–146.

44 For example, in relation to downstream development the plan considered that "full development of the floodplain may proceed by two phases successively if Pa Mong comes into the system before Stung Treng; and the two phases concurrently if Stung Treng comes before Pa Mong". *Ibid.*, pp. V–85.

45 "Streamflow at project sites on tributaries has been determined by proportioning the catchment area and rainfall with respect to tributary area, using an appropriate runoff co-efficient". *Ibid.*, pp. V–15.

46 Preserving the water balance within a tributary's basin was considered vital to limit consequences on the overall basin from withdrawals. *Ibid.*, pp. V–50.

47 The Committee's Japanese Chief Planning Engineer Hiroshi Hori explained that many of the dams, especially those planned in the Laotian highlands, were mostly theoretical "paper plans" that would require further technical substantiation before moving ahead with their design. In this sense, they were conceived to fulfil part of a cumulative purpose. Hiroshi Hori (2000), *The Mekong: Environment and Development*. Hong Kong: United Nations University Press, p. 151.

48 With regard to the regional differentiation of society in the Mekong's basin see G. White, E. de Vries, H. Dunkerley & J. Krutilla (1962), *Economic and Social Aspects of Lower Mekong Development (Report for the Committee for Co-Ordination of Investigations of the Lower Mekong Basin)*. Bangkok: United Nations.

49 James C. Scott (1998), *Seeing Like a State: How Certain Schemes to Improve the Human Condition Have Failed*. New Haven, CT: Yale University Press, p. 13.

50 Claude Raffestin (2012), Space, Territory and Territoriality. *Environment and Planning D: Society and Space*, v. 30, p. 137.

Part B

Delta

Along with the water added to the flows of the river, a single stream also contributes land. Washed across the inclined terrain by seasonal rains, particles of soil eventually join the Mekong's mainstream. As these particles travel downstream, they are gradually deposited, accumulating into sand banks or islands that eventually displace water as the dominant condition describing the ground. Yet this incremental and sometimes imperceptible configuration of wet and dry is only transitional. As soil displaces water, the river's course shifts and as a result, the location of sediment accumulation changes. If such numerous accretions of land describe a ceaseless geological process, the sedimented lowlands of the Mekong only incidentally resemble the archetypal landform signified by the Greek letter Δ. A delta's association with the mathematical geometry of a triangle however has notional implications. The imaginary aerial viewpoint denoted by the triangle alludes to a geographic space that is differentiated from its immediate surroundings, encompassing a distinct, internally coherent entirety. The planimetric conception of the delta on the other hand suggests the importance of cartography and the eye of the map-maker to make such distinctions visible. Yet unlike valleys demarcated by the visible crests of mountains, in the flat lowlands formed by the river's sediment, the identification of a delta's extent is not just a matter of identifying where the river's sediments are deposited. Historically related with the inhabitation of the most agriculturally fertile extent of riparian land accessible from the sea, the geographic delta determined by hydrology and topography and the inhabited geography *of* the delta prescribed by boundaries and infrastructure appear to describe two different notions. Either as the stable conceptual frame within which particular human activities unfold or as the surface area shaped by the unceasing action of water, the intersection of these ideas within the outline of the delta suggests an interpretation of the phenomena presented on maps. Which part of the Mekong's lowlands became labelled or identified *as a delta* is therefore equally as important as the reasons why the cartographic depiction of sediment deposits, waterway networks and settlement patterns could differentiate the extent of a delta on the Mekong River from all other geographic spaces.

DOI: 10.4324/9781032706238-6

72 *Liquid Territories*

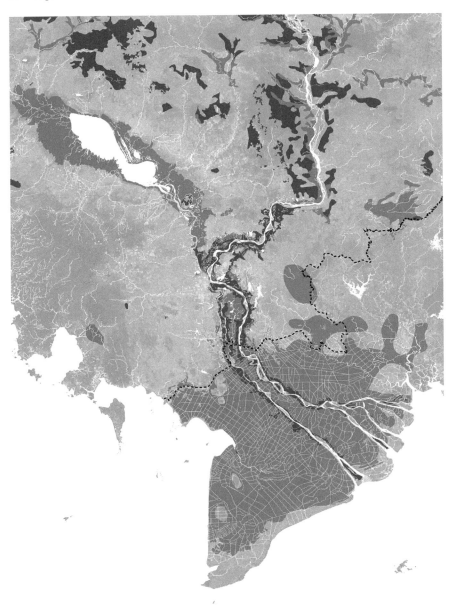

Figure B.1 **A delta on the Mekong's outflows.** The map shows the areas where two soil types are predominant, projected on an aerial image of the terrain. Fertile *cambisols* are shown in the darker grey and *gleysols*, which require drainage to be productive and deteriorate in quality if constantly submerged, in the lighter shade. *Cambisols* are found along the Mekong River or spread on Cambodia's mountains. Gleysols define the surroundings of Tonle Sap and the Mekong's outflows into the East Sea, appearing to be concentrated within the national boundaries (black line) of Vietnam. [*Source:* Author]

4   A Map for Water

The third branch or Anterior River . . . forms four arms at Vinh-long and flows into the China Sea through six mouths forming a delta.

Petit cours de géographie de la Basse-Cochinchine,
Trương Vĩnh (Petrus) Ky, 1875

If today numerous maps, hydrological studies, doctoral theses and environmental assessments are focused on the people, the water and ground conditions of the Mekong River's delta, the area these refer to was perceived differently on the eve of French colonization. This is not only due to the ceaseless accretions of sediment that gradually or suddenly transform the topography depicted on maps. Presenting rivers as wet and land as dry provides only one perspective of the way references to water construct territory. For the Khmer villagers living along the Mekong's tidal waterways, streams are conceived as salt water conduits extending from the ocean.[1] For Vietnamese settlers on the other hand, the 'garden lands' (*miệt vườn*) between the river's main flows have long been considered the most fertile regions for cultivation and the preferred location for settlement. The diverging significance of waterways and the sedimented land they create suggests that in order to hypothesize that a particular extent of the Mekong's lowlands could be differentiated from its surrounding terrain and identified as a delta, the interconnected water flows displayed on maps would need to be thought of as collectively forming a discrete part of a river system.

Yet in order to deduce that multiple waterways, in different locations and coursing through varied terrains, could constitute a distinct territory would not be possible without a prior assumption of how water connects (or divides) the areas through which it flows. Such knowledge is derived equally by direct observation of the area in question and by comparison with a paradigmatic condition which displays all the common properties considered necessary for such distinctions to be made.[2] Before the Mekong's outflows were collectively perceived as a delta, the archetypes used as the basis for comparison by the Khmer, Vietnamese and French were based on different principles. Thus, while in European atlases the Mekong's outflows were considered in relation to the inhabited extents of the Nile's cultivated sediments, the Khmer kingdom that nominally exercised authority over the same area ascribed

DOI: 10.4324/9781032706238-7

74 *Liquid Territories*

value to the cosmographic cartography of water embedded in the architecture of Angkor. For the Vietnamese on the other hand, maps presented the Mekong as the southernmost part of a strategic domain centred on the network of military infrastructure stretching southwards from the outflows of the Red and Perfume rivers. Considering that these viewpoints effectively differentiated the same geographic space, the value assigned to waterways either as limits or as conduits has arguably played a role in the way the delta's extent is imagined today. Divided into three parts that correspond to geographic, cosmographic and strategic perspectives, the chapter asks what territory was being mapped or imagined in the cartographic depictions of the Mekong's lowlands that later would appear on maps as the river's delta.

Curating Cartographic Knowledge

The use of the term *delta* to describe a particular ground condition was derived from the place-name denoted by the Nile River's triangular Delta.[3] Associated with pharaonic Egypt's most fertile agricultural region, the Nile Delta referenced an inhabited domain encompassing extents of desert and the ground watered by the annual flood. Located between the dynastic kingdom's upstream centres of power and the outside world of merchants and invaders, the vast breadth of cultivated land would have appeared in sharp contrast to the upstream settlements clustered between the mainstream and the desert. As Francis Celoria's analysis of ancient Greek literature suggests, the need to describe the distant lands conquered by Alexander the Great's army possibly led contemporary writers to compare the outflows of rivers such as the Indus with the geometric form of the Nile. The comparison between a glorious Egyptian civilization situated along the banks of the Nile and the polities located along the Indus framed the notion of the delta from the perspective of a broader inhabited region that extended far upstream.

Despite accounts of *deltas* within the classical literature that underpinned European scientific knowledge, the term only became part of geographic nomenclature in the 18th century.[4] As cartographers increasingly attempted to visually record information about distant locations on the earth's surface, deltas replaced or appeared alongside the idea of a river's 'mouth' (*embouchure*). Famous for compiling maps based only on information that could be verified from multiple sources, Jean-Baptiste Bourguignon d'Anville structured his geographic descriptions of India's deltas on the dimensions of the Nile's.[5] The late 18th century's most prominent French cartographer d'Anville's comparison of deltas brought locales on different continents into simultaneous focus. This allowed readers to develop an understanding of geographic conditions by considering specific features (such as the bifurcation of the river) that geographers considered important. As recent studies have explained, the objectives of the comparative method in geography are both *nomothetic* and *idiographic*.[6] Comparing and contrasting places provides universal explanations and establishes ideal-types, while at the same time attempting to demonstrate the uniqueness of particular regions by framing observable phenomena as variations of a basic paradigm. In a period when the proliferation of printing allowed an increasingly larger audience to access scientific knowledge, a geographer's written description of distant places was usually accompanied by newly prepared maps compiled within a single volume. Known as an *atlas*, a book of maps generated meaning for the reader on two levels. On the one hand, within the cartographic frame of a single map, depictions of coastlines, towns, rivers and the limits of sovereignty presented information regarding physical and political conditions. On the other hand, the selection, framing and sequential arrangement of maps within the pages of the atlas, as well as the textual, encyclopaedic descriptions which referenced collections of maps, structured knowledge according to the cumulative experience of reading a book. Within what Ackerman calls the *metaspace* of an atlas, maps and the places they represented became comparable to each other, allowing different conclusions to be reached than what was possible through the appreciation of a single map.[7]

For those regions known solely through the information compiled within such volumes, the value of a collection of maps or textual descriptions was potentially greater than the sum of its parts. Daston and Galison have observed that the mission of 19th-century scientific atlases was not only to inventory but also to characterize phenomena, replacing raw observation with the "digested" knowledge provided by the expert's eye.[8] The association between the cartographic depiction of a geographic space and the facts the depiction represented, reinforced concepts that consistently appeared within an atlas' pages. Through those pages, an idea such as the delta arguably emerged as an archetype that could be consistently recalled throughout the narrative. With the gradual adoption of the classificatory registers characteristic of Enlightenment scientific thought, knowledge of deltas, not as individual jurisdictions or specific terrains but as territories apparent only on a map, was formed by analogy. As printed atlases became an increasingly popular means of understanding the world, the qualities of unknown regions such as the Indus and Ganges could be deduced by recalling the characteristics inherent to the Egyptian delta.[9]

If by the beginning of the 19th century the term *delta* had been integrated into the language of geography, the relationship with the river from which it emerged was yet to be definitively established. Describing the way sediment accumulated on the Orinoco's lowlands, Alexander von Humboldt expressed doubts as to the universality of a delta's characteristics. From first-hand observation, the deposition of alluvium could not be ascribed to the same hydrological source. Between "oceanic deltas" formed along the coast and "tributary deltas" created at the confluence of streams, the formation of deltas was equally a question of water flows as it was one of land.[10] Instead of a geographic archetype with multiple variations, for Humboldt the delta referred to multiple overlapping processes of land formation, which while distinct to each individual body of water would eventually merge into the lowlands to become indistinguishable from each other. Shown contained between parallel embankments, the river's water was a substance that created – rather than simply occupied – the background of dry land depicted on the surface of a map.

In the European context, the questions surrounding the mapping of the delta were demonstrated in the cartography of the Camargue in the south of France. With only two access points until the 18th century, this vast region of marshes located at the outflows of the Rhône River experienced frequent floods and was

76   *Liquid Territories*

sparsely inhabited except on the more stable ground along its edges. Hydrologists studying the sequence of the Camargue's historic depictions on maps have pointed out the extensive changes to the locations of sediment and the courses of rivers within relatively short periods of time.[11] As a result, docks, lighthouses and other structures could often end up situated far from their intended coastal location. The reasons for these changes were not always due solely to the forces of nature. Dikes and canals constructed in the saline lowlands and upstream marshes resulted in the diversion of fresh water inflows, allowing salt water to reach the marshes in certain seasons.[12] With most infrastructure in this period constructed by private initiative, canals could therefore become the source of conflict between local power centres, as the changes they induced – improving agricultural land or affecting the rights of existing landowners – could alter the balance of economic and thus political power. To the extent that manmade water infrastructure could isolate or connect topographically distinct extents, the canals and dikes appearing on maps were not just illustrative of water control but, in one sense, also of the Camargue's subdivision into territorial units.

Because the lines denoting the edge of water were only accurate for short spans of time, understanding the phenomenon of land accretions became the focus of concerted scientific study. Georges Pichard's research of the history of the Camargue's geology has pointed out the importance of maps in the formation of scientific theories about the changing condition of the ground.[13] Through observation of the Rhône's mudflats, Virgile de la Bastide theorized that the ground was composed of horizontal layers which he called *créments*. Characterizing *créments* according to their geological qualities and as either salty or sweet, he concluded that the Camargue was once part of the Mediterranean and had been formed by both the sea and river depositing sand and silt. By the end of the 17th century, the engineer Hubert (Henri) Gautier had already attempted to understand the rate of alluvium accumulation. Following the principle that the grains of land had, like Humboldt's oceanic deltas, gradually silted an existing maritime bay, he was able to calculate the ratio of solid (suspended matter) to liquid as one part in 2000 and the geological period of this process as 35,000 years.[14] Viewed through the diachronic lens through which consecutive layers accumulated, the mapped delta made immediate references to the past, the passage of time visible in the permanently displaced lighthouses of the Camargue.

Having conceived of deltas as the areal magnitude of accumulated silt and sand deposits, the use of the term to denote a particular portion of the Mekong's river system appeared in the written accounts of military officers taking part in the colonial occupation of Southeast Asia. For Lieutenant Oswald Taillefer, the entire colony of French Cochinchina was "formed by the delta of the Cambodge [Mekong]".[15] Visualizing the ground in terms of layered *créments*, he described the way sediment deposits produced "real islands of extraordinary fertility".[16] Comparing these islands with the Camargue, Taillefer imagined an agricultural landscape where canals could regulate floods and provide irrigation to make rice production a profitable enterprise. Similarly for Frigate Captain Paulin Vial, the network of waterways carrying people and goods across the Mekong's lowlands recalled the

A Map for Water 77

grandeur of the Nile Delta, the river's outflows covering the entirety of the colony's six administrative provinces.[17] The suggestion that the Mekong's lowlands were comparable with the Nile's and could be characterized in terms of a single geophysical phenomenon resonated with the idea that deltas were conducive to permanent settlement. What a delta on the Mekong River referred to was not so much visible in maps of the terrain's physical characteristics but rather a proposition articulated through the differentiation of French sovereignty from neighbouring kingdoms.

For those growing up in the Vietnam's southern region (Nam Bộ) before colonization, however, the European perspective did not necessarily reflect existing conditions. The Vietnamese linguist and teacher Petrus Ky described the processes associated with sediment accretion at the river's outflows. Written in French for use in colonial schools, Ky's *Petit Cours de Géographie* highlighted how the majority of the territory was formed "by the mud and sand brought by the action of water".[18] The area where these characteristics were concentrated however was not collectively known as a delta. Of all the alluvial soil, the ground encompassed by the delta was located downstream from the town of Vinh-Long where the Mekong's "six mouths" flowed into the sea (**Figure 4.1**).[19] The same region where Taillefer's

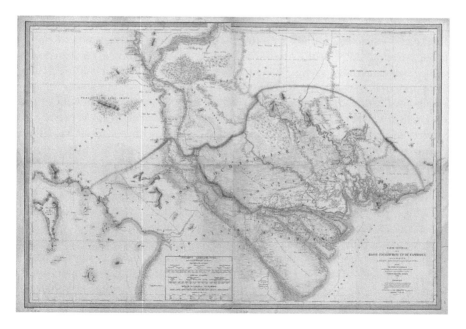

Figure 4.1 **The Mekong's deltas.** Under different lenses, the geographic extent of the Mekong's delta was the majority of the region depicted on this map, the riparian lands up to Phnom Penh or a more limited extent that began at the mainstream's bifurcations at Vinh Long and continued until the coast. L. Manen, F. Vidalin & G. Héraud (1867), *Carte generale de la Basse Cochinchine et du Cambodge*. [*Source:* Université Bordeaux Montaigne-1886. Res 09110803]

78 *Liquid Territories*

"real islands" were located, Ky's roughly triangular delta was known among the Vietnamese as *miệt vườn*, 'garden' lands with highly productive agriculture soils farmed by multiple settlements.[20] Considering Ky did not think it worthwhile to include the term *delta* in his French-Vietnamese dictionary or his translation of geographic terms for the colony's bureaucrats, the importance of the delta was arguably limited, at least in terms of determining a particular dimension for the alluvial soil.[21] Thus, while in theory Ky and the French officers referenced the same geographic concept, the space this notion occupied on the surface of maps was not necessarily equated with a distinct ground condition. If the deployment of the word delta was intended to indicate a terrain formed by the ceaseless accretions of sediment, by correlating human activity with the action of water, the Mekong's delta could be perceived in the cartographic limits of colonial authority or the concentration of cultivated orchards in the 'garden lands'.

Cosmographic Flows

While atlases were clearly tools for developing cognition of the world's geographic and political structure, in the European setting they were not intentionally prepared to support administrative control.[22] In parts of the geographic space named Indo-China, however, collections of maps compiled into books had been a tool of governance since the 15th century. Centred on the embankments of the Red River, the Vietnamese Empire's Lê rulers chose to adopt a visual rather than textual approach to describe the geography of their domain.[23] Having reorganized the empire's bureaucracy to reflect the administrative structure of their Ming dynasty contemporaries to the north, books of maps compiled using Chinese cartographic conventions depicted, across separate spreads, the provinces through which imperial control was exercised. Noting the physical features related to water and the location of settlements, the atlas provided the Court with a way of visualizing an empire that extended beyond the Red River's fertile sediment deposits. The Empire's geography was not solely composed of what could be observed and recorded visually on maps. In the geomantic tradition within which Chinese cartography had evolved, expert geomancers could deduce the "land's principles" and how these principles supported inhabitation of the land. Within this conceptual framework, features of the terrain were underpinned by what Liam Kelley calls "arteries or nodes" of geomantic energy.[24] These energies intersected at the capital Hanoi, which Emperor Thái-tổ had auspiciously relocated to ". . . where the earth lies spacious and flat and high and clear, where the inhabitants are not oppressed by flooding, where the earth is fertile and prosperous . . .".[25] The emperor's control of the geomantic centre allowed food surpluses to be produced, imbuing the territory ruled from Hanoi with political and cultural significance.

Expanding southwards, the emperor's authority eventually encompassed multiple coastal regions created from the riverine accretions of soil. Geographic knowledge of the southernmost provinces conquered by the Vietnamese however was far from complete. As the Nguyen dynasty emerged to challenge the power of the Hanoi-based Trinh rulers, new sets of maps were compiled following an itinerary of travel. Sequentially arranged according to the experience along a specific route, itinerary-style map described journeys that notionally originated within the Nguyens' domain and ended at the Mekong, where Cambodia began. These maps were meant to serve as guides, indicating the days needed to travel between locations and were useful for planning military expeditions or employed by imperial officials who were expected to travel throughout their jurisdictions.[26] Confined within the north-south corridor of land between the Annamite Mountains and the coast, the cross section of geography portrayed on these maps encompassed the lowlands, the rivers and their hinterlands, 'bounded' at the top of the page (west) by the painted silhouettes of ridgelines. At the southern terminus of the itinerary, however, the pictorial combinations of mountain, land and coast ended. Drawn relative to the medieval Khmer Empire's capital at Angkor rather than any mountains, in maps such as the *Binh Nam Đo* (*Maps of the pacification of the south*) from the late 17th century, the lowlands surrounding the Mekong River were portrayed as a frontier between the Vietnamese emperors and the Khmer kings.[27] Located at the 'crossroads' of an economic zone pivoted on trade between Chinese, Vietnamese, Malay, Cham and Cambodian merchants, farmers and technicians, conflict over control of the Mekong's lowlands had pitted Vietnamese armies against Khmer soldiers as well as the Siamese military in separate incidents throughout the 18th century.[28] Having emerged victorious in the civil war against their northern rivals, the Nguyen gradually reasserted control over Nam Bộ, eventually taking over as rulers of the entire Empire in the early 1800s. Relocating the Court to their ancestral home in Huế, the site of the new imperial capital realigned geomantic energies to converge on the coastal lowlands of the Perfume River.

Looking southwards from Huế, imperial map-makers began to see the Mekong's lowlands as the endpoint of Nguyens' dominion. From the perspective of the Cambodian kings, however, the Vietnamese were intruding on the southern edge of the territory inherited from Angkor's mythical "circle of kings". Unlike the Vietnamese, the view of the Cambodians regarding the extent of their ancestral domain was not constructed on the principles of Chinese geography and geomancy. Evidence from Sanskrit inscriptions and the architecture of religious centres has allowed historians of Southeast Asia to argue that the Khmer founders of Angkor adhered to the cosmographic principles developed in India. While no conventional maps of the medieval kingdom have survived, among scholars of the region's cartography, the layout of the temples at Angkor Wat are considered part of Southeast Asia's cartographic corpus.[29] Where Hindu cosmology appears most pertinent for attempting to understand Khmer conceptions of the Mekong's lowlands is the role given to water and rivers in the primordial subdivision of the world. Arranged to mirror the geography of the cosmos, the moat surrounding Angkor Wat appears to represent the encompassing Ocean (**Figure 4.2**).[30] At 250 metres long, the sandstone causeway bridging the width of the moat would have taken minutes for an average person to walk across before entering the temple's grounds. Contemporary analysis of the numerological significance of the moat's width has concluded that relative to other dimensions within the temple, the distance travelled over water symbolized one of the four Hindu time cycles and more specifically the Kali Yuga,

80 *Liquid Territories*

Figure 4.2 **Cosmographic plans.** The painting depicts the key elements of the cosmos shared by Buddhist, Jain and Hindu traditions. Mount Meru is shown in the centre and alternating rings of ocean form the edges of the continents. Linear bands of blue representing rivers connect the waterways to the axis mundi. In medieval Cambodia, the architecture of Angkor Wat is defined by the perimeter moat which is believed to symbolize the cosmic oceans. Unknown painter (1890s), *Manusyaloka, Map of the World of Man, according to Jain Cosmological Traditions*. [*Source:* Library of Congress]

the current and "most decadent age of man".[31] With the moat's cosmic dimensions incorporated in the ceremonial route, water was arguably part of Angkor Wat's ritual space rather than a symbolic separation between opposing notions such as sacred and profane or inside and outside.

The moat was one of several manmade structures used to retain water. Extending nearly 8 kilometres on their longest straight side, the colossal *baray* (reservoirs) flanking the ceremonial centre were not just vast deposits of water. For the French archaeologist Bernard-Philippe Groslier, the *baray* evoked the cosmic seas demonstrating the king's overwhelming command over the elements and the power

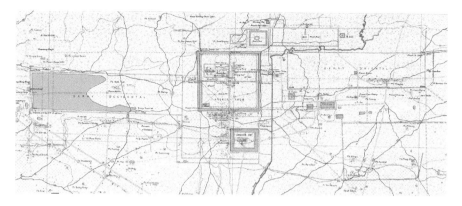

Figure 4.3 **The extents of Angkor.** The map shows Angkor's ceremonial centre including the baray and the temple complexes of Angkor Wat and Angkor Thom. Which collections of buildings constitute the archaeological site of Angkor has changed as excavations have progressed but also as appreciation of what constitutes a single city in the context of medieval Southeast Asia has expanded beyond the ceremonial centre. Service géographique de l'Indochine (1939), *Carte archéologique de la région d'Angkor*. [*Source:* BNF]

to shape "the waters of the primordial Ocean" (**Figure 4.3**).[32] Along with canals, a hydraulic network with symbolic and practical significance collectively defined a *cité hydraulique*. Beyond the ceremonial centre, the hydraulic network that secured biannual rice harvests physically connected settlements possibly much further than 20 kilometres away. Working on the assumption that the water system integrated a terrain composed of inhabited mounds, land routes, natural streams and manmade waterways into a "single operational system", archaeologists have described Angkor as a "low-density city".[33] The conceptualization of the city as a singular entity that is nonetheless inclusive of peripheral settlements is not as old as Angkor. The perception of the relationship between settlement patterns and a selected collection of manmade infrastructure in terms of a singular network stems from 20th-century studies that conceived of cities organized in terms of *metropolitan regions*. The idea that observable phenomena such as employment patterns as well as economic and social relationships were part of the same settlement unit was undoubtedly reinforced by looking at the spatial concentration of these phenomena on maps. The subsequent emergence of metropolitan regions as units of governance reflected the realization that new forms of regulation were needed after massive investment in transport infrastructure had increased geographic mobility and decentralized production. Projected backwards into history, such a model becomes relevant only when the network that theoretically underpinned the locational decisions of individuals was regulated to achieve a particular outcome and controlled with regard to a specific geographic reference. Given the magnitude of Angkor's network revealed by recent mapping, its operation as a single system would have been a complicated effort requiring the mobilization of state resources and the

82 Liquid Territories

administrative organization to coordinate the continued maintenance and operation of the network's multiple parts in service of flood protection, drainage or irrigation. But without the entirety of the network visible on maps, what control was really possible in Angkor? Unfortunately the degree of the state's participation in how the network was managed has not yet been determined.[34] However, the moat's inclusion in Angkor Wat's ritual space, the ceremonial centre's calibration in relation to the *baray* and the deployment of water infrastructure linking the two into a broader network of agricultural settlements suggest a conclusion relevant to cartographic analysis. Along the edge of Tonle Sap's vast floodplain, water diversions could differentiate a particular geographic space from its surroundings without equating water to a boundary that distinguishes between spatial conditions.

A map drawn from the Burmese cartographic tradition provides an insight into the way the depiction of water can structure the cartographic frame without denoting the limits of a particular geographic space.[35] With influences from both China and the Hindu cosmographic tradition, the map displays many features common to Burmese cartographic depictions.[36] Presenting the settlements paying tribute to the leader of Maingnyaung, political boundaries are not depicted but rather described in text in relation to natural landmarks.[37] To the extent that red squares and also red pagodas and red stupas indicate a single domain, the political territory presented on the map is not contingent on rivers for its delineation. Instead, the width of waterways appears to denote the relatively higher importance of the portion of land where the capital is located. Emphasizing the geographic structure of power rather than conveying information about the distance between opposite embankments, the depiction of waterways confers a particular spatial hierarchy to the representation of the terrain that favours the dominant political hierarchy. Apparent similarities between Burmese and the hypothetical Khmer cartography based on Angkor, however, should not suggest a common conceptualization of water's role in shaping territory. Indeed rivers did, in places, act as the border between kingdoms, and thus water was not universally inconceivable as the limit of authority.[38] Even though the gap in cartographic evidence from Cambodia allows only limited speculation of what waterways signified in relation to geographic space, it is possible to conjecture that rivers and more generally waterbodies were not merely the reference in relation to which settlements and social relationships diachronically evolved. Beyond water's cosmographic or geomantic resonance, inundations, floods and droughts were issues that had to be managed, while inland kingdoms remained vulnerable to invaders sailing upstream from the sea. Pictorially by denoting relative importance between places, physically by linking people along a liquid route or operationally by irrigating from a distant dry-season source, the flows of water made discrete, distant locations conceptually dependent on each other. Projected onto the amorphous accumulations of the Mekong River's sediment, the idea that waterways could characterize the terrain is valid less for the floodable extents between two individual waterways and more for the sequence of distinct geographic spaces connected by them. Conceptualized without the areal delineation that would allow direct comparison to the hydrological catchment, the territory denoted by water was not necessarily singular, uniform and perhaps not even contiguous.

Engineering an Imperial Geography

The conceptualization of waterways in the Mekong's lowlands as a single system emerged as the Vietnamese Empire consolidated their military presence in Nam Bộ. With the technical support of the French, the Nguyen dynasty's leaders begun modernizing their army and fortifications according to European principles.[39] Conceived by the military engineer Sébastien Le Prestre de Vauban Vauban, the *pré carré* which structured France's national defence strategy consisted of fortified centres linked by waterways and roads that in the event of attack could mutually support each other.[40] Beginning in 1790 with the fortress in Gia Dinh (Saigon), 32 citadels were constructed throughout Vietnam referencing the "star-shaped" fortresses Vauban designed to defend France. Systematized to a degree that allowed Vietnamese engineers to reconfigure basic elements such as bastions and walls, Vauban's principles were reworked and adapted to the specific conditions of Vietnam's strategic geography (**Figure 4.4**).[41] Part of the military infrastructure centred on the defence of the capital in Huế, seaports, fortresses and garrisoned plantations were collectively intended to consolidate and maintain control over an empire extending several days travel from the centre of power.[42]

Direct contact with the French military also influenced Vietnamese representations of geography. Monique Pelletier notes that French engineers responsible for

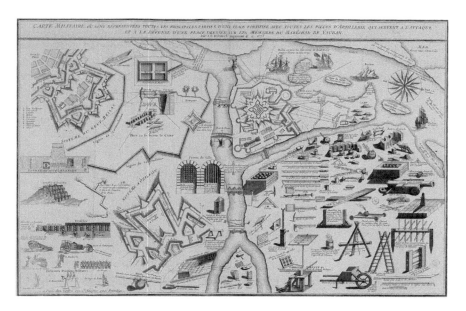

Figure 4.4 **Design principles for fortifications**. Drawn against a hypothetical background, the map presents Vauban's design principles, the main components of fortification and the equipment needed to destroy them. Mantienne claims this map was still available in Vietnam in 1921. J.E. Duhamel (1773), *Carte militaire, ou sont représentées les principales parties d'une place fortifiée.* [*Source:* BNF]

84   *Liquid Territories*

fortifications were among the first group of trained experts who proposed that maps be used as tools for planning.[43] In terms of representation, geographic engineers (*ingenieurs des camps et armees*) prepared maps that paid particular attention to the visual expression of topography using colours and linework to distinguish important features such as the roads and paths accessible to armies and the resources on which soldiers could survive.[44] A corresponding attention to detail is evident in the depiction of Saigon and the surrounding Gia Dinh region by Vietnamese general Trần Văn Học.[45] In the map's planimetric view, the area around the fortress is described with carefully delineated waterways and roads in relation to defensive structures and the building clusters of Saigon and Cholon. Considering the significance of waterways as transport routes for soldiers and invading enemies, the mapped edges of rivers and streams indicated both the terrain's physical qualities and the strategic value of that terrain. Even if the citadel's site fulfilled the main requirements of geomancy, the territory depicted by the map appears to have been considered as a function of control and only incidentally as the mystical convergence of the terrain's vital energies.

The projection of strategic value on the map extended beyond the perception of a single citadel's control over its surroundings. Although the importance of the terrain in planning military strategy was already known to Vietnamese mandarins through the classical texts of Chinese general Sun Tzu, maps allowed the organization of defensive strategy based on the depiction of the terrain. With most densely inhabited settlements accessible via the Mekong's estuary, securing the frontier against outward but also internal threats required adjustment of the military infrastructure to control movement along waterways. Stretching from the coast of the East Sea to the floodplain shared with Cambodia, the Vietnamese established six administrative districts under the authority of military mandarins tasked with organizing defence on behalf of the Empire.[46] A map from the early years of French colonization appears to display the configuration of the military and civic infrastructure deployed by the Vietnamese along the Mekong's waterways (**Figure 4.5**). Drawn across three panels, the map names settlements and their hierarchy within the administrative structure.[47] The map portrays the permanent waterways in a region encompassing Tonle Sap at the top of the first panel, to Saigon at the bottom of the third panel. These are shown in relation to settlements, defensive fortifications, garrisoned plantations (*đồn điền*) and citadels. Without showing the boundaries which differentiated specific royal domains, the drawing displays the geographic organization of defence, structured on the control of particular waterways.[48] Along the Saigon River, sets of defences located on opposite embankments appear to be positioned to monitor traffic along the river and to regulate upstream access to the citadels and naval bases. Together, these fortified centres appear to have regulated access to the territory formed by the delta at the river's "six mouths". Considered collectively, these groups of fortifications, settlements, roads and interstitial streams could be perceived to construct defensive interrelationships pivoted on the access of troops to different locations via the military infrastructure. The maintenance of imperial control described geographic relationships that were based – almost exclusively during the dry season – on the paths prescribed by waterways.

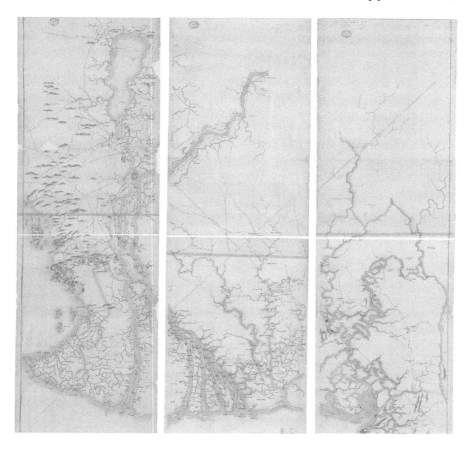

Figure 4.5 **Fortified waterways.** Representing a geographic extent that includes Tonle Sap (top left) and Saigon (bottom right), the map depicts the Vietnamese military infrastructure as understood by the cartographer. The Gulf of Thailand is shown to the left, and the cardinal directions are shown by the diagonal lines crossing all three panels (south is to the bottom left). Citadels, permanent army encampments and settlements are drawn in relation to the region's waterways which are the primary medium connecting these dispersed locations into units of mutual defence. The extents of these defensive units are subtly delineated with colour but a border with the Kingdom of Cambodia is not shown. Unknown cartographer (1861), *Carte de la basse Cochinchine*. [*Source:* BNF]

Dependence on naturally occurring waterways however left particular defensive positions unconnected. Coastal trading towns along the Gulf of Thailand were separated by more than 50 kilometres of water-logged and sometimes hostile terrain from the Bassac River. To provide permanent routes connecting these settlements to the defensive and trading network, the Vietnamese state initiated a concerted infrastructure programme that culminated during the 1820s with the completion of three new waterways.[49] Among them, the 87-kilometre Vinh Tế Canal linked

86 *Liquid Territories*

the citadels of Hà Tiên and Châu Đốc through an interstitial terrain composed of distinct mountain outcrops rising from the lowland plains.[50] Called Thất Sơn, this terrain was considered particularly dangerous by the Vietnamese. For the army, the canal made the journey between the two frontier garrisons possible throughout the year but also allowed soldiers access to the hostile area in between the citadels at any point along the waterway. Access to the interstitial terrain was accompanied by up to 20 new settlements and as the map shows at least six army bases distributed along the canal's western side facing Cambodia.[51] Along with the citadels on either end of the canal, the waterway, settlements and army bases collectively structured a defensive 'line' along which the two opposing sides confronted each other. Rather than a line with two sides, however, the canal did not separate the Cambodian and Vietnamese areas of authority but made the presence of the state permanent and visible in the contested region.

Consolidation of France's holdings in Nam Bộ created a new need to establish European-type boundaries with adjacent kingdoms. Writing only a year before embarking on the exploratory journey to the sources of the Mekong River, Francis Garnier situated the colonial endeavour within the expanse of geographic space he identified as the *Delta du Cambodge*.[52] For Garnier, the toponymic *Delta* extended upstream as far as Phnom Penh, encompassing a terrain that had been controlled by the Cambodian throne before the Vietnamese annexed the southernmost portion.[53] Garnier's assertion that the Mekong Delta was the terrain different parties sought to control, juxtaposed a geographic understanding of the river's sedimentation with a strategic evaluation of the terrain, the overlapping claims over the *Delta du Cambodge* providing the justification for colonial involvement beyond Vietnam's area of authority. Conceived in relation to French political influence in the region, Garnier's *Delta* was only incidentally concerned with the ground conditions formed by the action of water.

The limit of direct French political influence was determined by the colony's provisional boundary. A protectorate of France, the limits of Cambodia's authority were formalized by treaty which saw culturally significant areas for the Khmer such as Angkor and Battambang ceded to Siam. The Cambodian attitude towards the borders with Siam however was diametrically different from that of a boundary with Cochinchina. Shaped to include the Thất Sơn, the border with the colony quickly emerged in Cambodian discourse as a source of dispute. Not only did any boundary across the Mekong's lowlands partition the hereditary Cambodian kingdom, but since the lines were drawn in relation to Vietnamese claims, they obliquely legitimized the violence with which those claims had been imposed.[54] Given that Khmer villages were spread throughout the Thất Sơn, the regularization of colonial borders in 1873 to follow 1,200 metres parallel with the waterway made almost no concessions to the ethnic composition of the region's residents.[55] Instead, with the Vinh Tế acting as a barrier to movement colonial forces could retreat to the canal's defensive line, placing them within shooting distance of the border. The adoption of the canal to form the border favoured the French army's strategic command of the seasonally inundated terrain.

Yet the Vinh Tế did not only act as an edge to territory or just 'funnel' armies, merchants and settlers through a hostile area. It also diverted a proportion of the water that would otherwise have pooled in forested swamps or been gradually discharged through smaller streams. Tasked to plan the improvement of the waterway after years of neglect, the engineer Jacques Rénaud examined the canal within its hydrological context. Noting how the behaviour of water changed according to tides and the annual flood, Rénaud described how the Vinh Tế was annually submerged in a flood which occurred across an "immense horizontal space".[56] The idea that a canal affected and was affected by forces that occurred across different geographic dimensions highlighted the subtle variations of the lowlands' slope that affected soil quality and informed cultivation practices. Thus, while the quantity of deposited sediment per volume of river water may have been more or less equal across a specific extent of the delta, the canal's embankments and capacity to divert water have meant that the distribution of the river's sediment has been transformed in relation to the infrastructure structuring the boundary.[57] If what characterized the *Delta du Cambodge* was a strategic perception of the terrain that aligned with the Mekong's sediment deposits, the Vinh Tế Canal did not just change the way that terrain was controlled. By redefining where these deposits accreted, the cumulative impact of the canal as a barrier, a boundary and a conduit also redefined the nature of the terrain being controlled. Perpetuated by recurring environmental processes linked to the flows of water, the alignment of the limits of authority with a man-made waterway have made the conceptual separation of the delta presented on early maps a tangible reality.

Conclusion

Criticized for reducing the complexity of specific places to the characteristics of the archetype, *nomothetic* comparisons have been condemned by 20th-century geographers for distorting the interpretation of first-hand observation.[58] Considered an 'ideal-type' associated with the geographic space around a river's outflows, the hypothesis expounded by references to the Nile's delta pivoted on the idea that the riparian lands located downstream from the river's bifurcation were conducive to agriculture and settlement. Comparison with the Nile allowed Europeans to conjecture that because of their apparent similarities in relation to the river's 'body', places as far away (and unknown) as the Mekong's lowlands belonged to the same typology of geographic space. Identification of a delta at the Mekong's outflows however had less to do with the geological explanation of layered *créments*, as it did with the range of human activities enabled by the fertility of the soil. The ability to cultivate a delta indicated the potential to support inhabitation on these unknown hinterlands. If the technical control of water through dikes and canals in the Camargue was possible, it was not impossible to imagine that an analogous condition in Southeast Asia could also be the subject of similar water control techniques.

Likewise for the Vietnamese, the inclusion of the Mekong's lowlands into atlases and itinerary maps presented the southernmost parts of their expanding

88 *Liquid Territories*

empire in terms of their distance from the centres of power located along the fertile lowlands of the Red and Perfume rivers. Tasked with depicting this unknown terrain, map-makers in Huế deployed the same cartographic tools to describe a ground condition that resembled the deltas in the distant north. If the presence of Angkor on maps hinted at the overlapping claims of different kings that were unique to the Mekong, the conceptualization of Vietnam's defensive infrastructure in terms of a network of fortified centres not only assigned a strategic value to waterways but also determined a limit to the emperor's control. For the Emperor, the military generals and possibly many of these regions' inhabitants, what made the geography *imperial*, was the military infrastructure underpinning the maintenance of authority regardless of distance from the centre of power. Rather than being simply representations of the terrain on which these strategies were based, maps were also plans – the pictorial elaborations of a specific course of defensive action. Any perceivable 'distortion' of observable facts was therefore not necessarily in the erroneous appreciation of the terrain's physical characteristics. The waterways included within the network of riverine flows could protect from invasion, attribute cosmographic significance or determine habitability. If a delta could therefore be perceived in these maps, it was not in the planimetric differentiation of one ground condition from another. Rather, the delta emerged from the internal coherence alluded to by considering the waterways as defining characteristics of a controlled domain, a network of settlements and a cultivated terrain.

Notes

1 Philip Taylor (2014), Water in the Shaping and Unmaking of Khmer Identity on the Vietnam-Cambodia Frontier. *TRaNS: Trans –Regional and –National Studies of Southeast Asia*, v. 2, n. 1, p. 114.
2 Marine Simon, Alexandra Budke & Frank Schäbitz (2020), The Objectives and Uses of Comparisons in Geography Textbooks: Results of an International Comparative Analysis. *Heliyon*, n. 6, p. 2.
3 According to Celoria, the concept of the triangular Delta was not apparent in the various combinations of Egyptian hieroglyphs which denote the place, and was therefore a notion distinctly Greek. Francis Celoria (1966), Delta as a Geographical Concept in Greek Literature. *Isis*, v. 57, n. 3, p. 385.
4 Celoria points out that one of the earliest mentions for the word delta is attributed to Edward Gibbon, author of the *Rise and Fall of the Roman Empire*, in the late 18th century. *Ibid.*, p. 385.
5 Christine Marie Petto (2007), *When France Was King of Cartography: The Patronage and Production of Maps in Early Modern France.* Lanham, MD: Lexington Books, p. 80.
6 Simon *et al*, *op. cit.*, p. 2.
7 James Akerman (1995), The Structuring of Political Territory in Early Printed Atlases. *Imago Mundi*, v. 47, pp. 138–154.
8 The authors refer specifically to anatomical atlases and not to collections of maps. The principles of compiling knowledge through a sequence of visual images however are immediately relevant to cartographic atlases. Lorraine Daston & Peter Galison (1992), The Image of Objectivity. *Representations*, n. 40, Special Issue: Seeing Science, p. 84.
9 For example, in Malte-Brun's Universal Geography first published in the early years of the 19th century, the Indus "gives off lateral streams as it approaches the sea, it does not form a Delta exactly analogous to that of Egypt" or "the land near the mouth does not

A Map for Water 89

possess the fertility of the Delta of the Nile, or the Ganges". Conrad Malte-Brun (1829), *Universal Geography*. Philadelphia: Anthony Finley, p. 115.

10 Von Humboldt's detailed discussion of deltas unfolds across a significant proportion of his personal narratives from South America in which comparison of similar phenomena is used to interrogate the process of sediment formation rather than the cartographic form resulting from the process.

11 Georges Pichard (2005), La découverte géologique de la Camargue, du XVIe siècle au début du XIXe siècle. *Travaux du Comité français d'Histoire de la Géologie, Comité français d'Histoire de la Géologie*, 3ème série, v. 19, p. 115.

12 R. Mathevet, N.L. Peluso, A. Couespel & P. Robbins (2015), Using Historical Political Ecology to Understand the Present: Water, Reeds, and Biodiversity in the Camargue Biosphere Reserve, Southern France. *Ecology and Society*, v. 20, n. 4, p. 7 and Fig. 3.

13 Pichard, *op. cit.*, p. 113.

14 Following the principle that the grains of land had, like Humboldt's oceanic deltas, gradually silted an existing maritime bay, he calculated the geological period of this process as 35,000 years. Georges Pichard, Mireille Provansal & François Sabatier (2014), Les embouchures du Rhône. *Méditerranée*, n. 122, p. 7.

15 *"La basse Cochinchine est presque entièrement formée par le delta du Cambodge".* Oswald Taillefer (1865), *La Cochinchine: Ce qu'elle est, ce qu'elle sera: Deux ans de séjour dans ce pays de 1863 à 1865*. Perigeaux: Impri. Dupont, p. 45.

16 *"Ces sables se rencontrent partout à des profondeurs variables, et ils atteignent parfois la surface, où ils forment de véritables îlots d'une fertilité extraordinaire".* ibid. Soon after completing his military service Taillefer returned to the colony and formed a company to grow and export rice.

17 *"les six provinces qui forment la Basse-Cochinchine, c'est-à-dire ce delta du grand fleuve, dont les terrains arrosés par les crues régulières du Mékong sont si splendides et si riches qu'après les avoir visités, un amiral écrivait: C'est le delta du Nil, mais bien plus grand et bien plus beau".* Paulin Vial (1874), *Les Premières années de la Cochinchine, colonie française*. Paris: Challamel Aine, p. 285.

18 *"La majeure partie du territoire de cette contrée est un terrain d'alluvion, formé par la vase et le sable apportés par l'action de l'eau, et arrêtés ou retenus par les racines des cây duoc, vet, gîa, ban etc.".* Trương Vĩnh (Petrus) Ký (1875), *Petit cours de géographie de la Basse-Cochinchine*. Saigon: Impri. du Government, p. 12.

19 *"La troisième branche ou fleuve Antérieur . . . forme à Vĩnh-long quatre bras et se jette dans la mer de Chine par six embouchures formant un delta".* ibid., p. 25.

20 In a period in which the colony's educational system was organized to train interpreters and secretaries, the definitions in Ky's textbooks formed part of the material used to train bureaucratic staff during the first 25 years of colonial administration. See Luong Quang Hien (2020), French Educational Reforms in Indochina Peninsula and the Appearance of the Western Intellectual Hierarchy in Vietnam in the Early Twentieth Century. *American Journal of Educational Research*, v. 8, n. 4, p. 210.

21 In his later *Précis de géographie* (1887), Ky translated French geographical terms for use by the colony's Vietnamese bureaucrats; Ky translates the *basin* (*triềng sông*) and the river's *mouths* (*vàm sông*) but omits the word *delta*, a term which is also omitted in his 1884 French-Vietnamese dictionary.

22 Ackerman argues that the way an atlas displayed boundaries in conventional single maps and composed the "mapping unit" (the cartographic frame) were both critical in manipulating political territory. Although individual maps became critical to the governance of European kingdoms, atlases were mostly prepared by private cartographers that were only occasionally employed for state administration. Akerman *op. cit.*, p. 139.

23 Whitmore (1994), *op. cit.*, pp. 481–482.

24 Liam Kelley (2016), From a Reliant Land to a Kingdom in Asia: Premodern Geographic Knowledge and the Emergence of the Geo-Body in Late Imperial Vietnam. *Cross-Currents: East Asian History and Culture Review (E-Journal)*, n. 20, p. 27.

90 *Liquid Territories*

25 Quote attributed to Emperor Thái-tổ that in 1010 moved his capital to the same area where the Tang dynasty's provincial government ruling Vietnam had its base. John Whitmore (2013), Transformations of Thăng Long: Space and Time, Power and Belief. *International Journal of Asian Studies*, v. 10, n. 1, p. 3.

26 Whitmore (1994), *op. cit.*, p. 490.

27 *Ibid.*, p. 494.

28 Attacks focused on overpowering the garrisons of populated centres, such as the port of Ha Tien situated on Gulf of Thailand, that at different times during this period was controlled by Cambodians, Vietnamese and Siamese.

29 Joseph Schwartzberg (1995a), Introduction to Southeast Asian cartography. In *The History of Cartography, v. 2, b. 2, Cartography in the Traditional East and Southeast Asian Societies*. Chicago, IL: University of Chicago Press, pp. 693–696.

30 Common to Buddhist, Jain and Hindu traditions, the cosmic 'axis mundi' was pivoted on mythical Mount Meru located in the Himalayas. Arranged symmetrically in concentric circles around the centre, continents such as Suvarnadvipa – identified with Southeast Asia – appeared separated by oceans.

31 The detailed study on the astronomical and cosmological calibration of Angkor Wat's architecture elaborated on the distance between entrances and gateways along the East-West route through the temple and its surrounding grounds. The enumerated relationship between movement through the temple's space and passage through time was deduced by comparison of absolute measurements with mythical chronology. Robert Stencel, Fred Gifford & Eleanor Morón (1976), Astronomy and Cosmology at Angkor Wat. *Science*, new series, v. 193, n. 4250, p. 285.

32 Bernard-Philippe Groslier (1974), Agriculture et religion dans l'Empire angkorien. *Études rurales*, n. 53–56, p. 99.

33 The identification of raised earthen mounds in close proximity to waterways or pathways has allowed archaeologists to conclude that the settlement extended over more than 1,000 km². The degree to which these areas were of a uniform residential density comparatively lower than the ceremonial centre has not been established. D. Evans, C. Pottier, R. Fletcher, S. Hensley, I. Tapley, A. Milne & M. Barbetti (2007), A Comprehensive Archaeological Map of the World's Largest Preindustrial Settlement Complex at Angkor, Cambodia. *Proceedings of the National Academy of Sciences*, v. 104, n. 36, p. 14279.

34 Roland Fletcher, Christophe Pottier, Damian Evans & Matti Kummu (2008), The Development of the Water Management System of Angkor: A Provisional Model. *Bulletin of the Indo-Pacific Prehistory Association*, The Indo-Pacific Prehistory Association, p. 66.

35 Unknown Cartographer (1860), *Map of the Maingnyaung Region in Upper Burma*. The map is kept at the Cambridge University Library Special Collections and can be viewed online.

36 These common features include the abundant vegetation, the pagodas which serve as visual landmarks and the depiction of settlements as squares. Schwartzberg (1995a), *op. cit.*, p. 689; Joseph Schwartzberg (1995b), Southeast Asian Geographical Maps. In *The History of Cartography, v. 2, b. 2, Cartography in the Traditional East and Southeast Asian Societies*. Chicago, IL: University of Chicago Press, p. 761.

37 In the map, red squares depict settlements paying tribute to the leader of Maingnyaung, the town shown in the centre with four gates. Consequently blue squares show either autonomous settlements or those paying tribute to other leaders. Typical of Burmese maps, boundaries are not depicted but textual notes referring to the identification of boundaries with natural landmarks are shown in blue-outlined rectangular boxes on the four edges of the map. Judging from the way these notes are uncoordinated with the map's geographical background, they were likely drawn last and perhaps as an afterthought. Two separate river systems flow through the map. The bifurcation of the "main" river in the map's centre into two branches of equal width subdivides the cartographic frame into three sections. The central, and the largest, portion is where Maingnyaung and other

landmarks are located. Based on translations of the map's text by scholar Allegra Giovine. https://cudl.lib.cam.ac.uk/view/MS-MAPS-MS-PLANS-R-C-00001/1, accessed 21 October 2021.

38 For example, before the British assumed overlordship of Burma, the boundary between Siam and the Burmese state of Tenasserim was located along rivers and mountain ridgelines. John Prescott, Herold Collier & Dorothy Prescott (1977), *Frontiers of Asia and Southeast Asia*. Melbourne: Melbourne University Press, p. 54.

39 French military officers had supported the Nguyen's campaign to seize power facilitating the acquisition and application of Western military scientific and technical knowledge in the Vietnamese army.

40 Jean-Denis G.G. Lepage (2010), *Vauban and the French Military Under Louis XIV: An Illustrated History of Fortifications and Strategies*. Jefferson, NC & London: McFarland & Co., p. 144.

41 Only the citadels in Saigon and Nha Trang were designed by French military engineers. These proved so successful in their respective military contexts that the imperial stronghold in Huế was also fortified as soon as the Nguyen ascended the throne. Vietnamese adjustments to the French model of fortifications had cultural purposes. Associated with the centres of power in Hue, Hanoi and Saigon, the geometric clarity of the rectangle preferred by Vietnamese geomancers was more predominant in the citadels built in those three cities than the polygonal star-shaped layout. Frédéric Mantienne (2003), The Transfer of Western Military Technology to Vietnam in the Late Eighteenth and Early Nineteenth Centuries: The Case of the Nguyễn. *Journal of Southeast Asian Studies*, v. 34, n. 3, p. 528.

42 Bang Đỗ (2011), *Hệ Thống Phòng Thủ Miền Trung Dưới Triều Nguyễn (Central Defence System Under the Nguyen Dynasty)*. Hanoi: NXB Khoa Học Xã Hội (Social Science Publishing House), p. 12.

43 Monique Pelletier (2007), Representations of Territory by Painters, Engineers, and Land Surveyors in France During the Renaissance. In David Woodward (ed.), *The History of Cartography, v. 3, part 2, Cartography in the European renaissance*, p. 1530.

44 Monique Pelletier (2003), *L'ingénieur militaire et la description du territoire: Du XVIe au XVIIIe siècle, in Cartographie de la France et du monde de la Renaissance au Siècle des lumières* [en ligne]. Paris: Éditions de la Bibliothèque nationale de France, p. 57.

45 As John Whitmore notes, Trần Văn Học had worked with French military engineers on the Gia Dinh fortress and became the main architect for later construction. Whitmore (1994), *op. cit.*, pp. 500–501.

46 The Vietnamese word "dinh" used to name administrative units (such as Gia Dinh where Saigon was located), also meant "army".

47 For example, the map uses the terms *huyen* (town) and *phu* (prefecture) to differentiate what are essentially the same red squares (the cartographic notation for settlements).

48 The map subtly differentiates the terrain using colour according to what subsequent maps would label as the provincial districts annexed by France. While some of these are delineated along the courses of rivers, other limits appear to be less situated in relation to the terrain. Considering this map was a French construction, the district outlines may have been indicated to the cartographer based on oral information collected from local informants.

49 Prior to the 1800s, the most significant waterway improvement in Nam Bộ had been the work carried out on a natural stream connecting the town of Tan An just south of Saigon, with the town of My Tho located on the embankments of the Mekong's mainstream.

50 The canal was constructed by thousands of forcibly conscripted Khmer and Vietnamese labourers, whose treatment was the source of resentment and violent uprisings during and after construction.

51 Vu Duc Liem (2017), Boundary on the Move: Border Making in Vietnamese-Cambodian Frontier, 1802–1847. *Mekong Review*, v. 2, n. 2, p. 4.

52 *"on peut, par des mesures d'ensemble bien combinées et une grande rapidité d'exécution, prendre sans coup férir, tous les points importants du Delta du Cambodge*

92 Liquid Territories

et en prononcer l'annexion à la Cochinchine française". G. Francis (1865), *De la colonisation de la Cochinchine*. Paris: Challamel Aine, p. 13.

53 *"On'sait que tes Annamites eux-mêmes ont toujours considéré les six provinces comme formant un tout indivisible, et que la conquête du territoire de Bien-Oa sur le royaume du Cambodge les a fatalement entraînés à celle de tout le reste du Delta"*. *ibid.*, pp. 7–8.

54 Giving some small degree of consideration to the Cambodian perspective, the 1870 and 1873 agreements between France and Cambodia finalized the exact location of the boundary, reshaping limited parts of the earlier border to fit the ethnic origins of the population's majority. As stated in the treaty *"le Cambodge conservera tout le pays actuellement habité par les Cambodgiens des provinces de Prey Veng, Boni-Fuol, Socthiet. La limite sera tracée ultérieurement, et on réservera pour les possessions françaises la bande de terrain longeant le Vaïco, qui est occupée par les Annamites ou exploitées par eux"*. Bulletin Officiel de la Cochinchine française (1870), *Décision du Gouverneur de la Cochinchine du 9 Juillet 1870 portant délimitation des frontières du Cambodge*, p. 247.

55 *"La frontière entre la Cochinchine française et le Royaume du Cambodge sera marquée par des poteaux numérotés et portant une inscription indiquant leur objet. Le nombre de poteaux sera de 124. Le n° 1 sera placé à l'extrémité Est de la frontière et la graduation sera continuer vers l'ouest dans l'ordre naturel des chiffres jusqu'au poteau 124, placée à 1.200 m environ au nord du canal de Vinh-té et du village annamite Hoa-thanh"*. Convention entre S.M. Norodom et le Gouverneur de la Cochinchine du 15 Juillet 1873 portant détermination de la frontière entre le Cambodge et la Cochinchine française. http://ki-media.blogspot.com/2012/06/border-convention-history-of-cambodia.html, accessed 22 November 2021.

56 *"Les eaux du canal allant du Bassac au bassin du Gien-than doivent traverser cet immense espace horizontal; aux hautes eaux la montée du Bassac de 4 m. 50 cent., le profil en long des eaux ne suit nullement le profil du fond"*. Jacques Rénaud (1880), *Étude d'un projet de canal entre le Vaico et le Cua-Tieu. Excursions et reconnaissances*, n. 3, p. 72.

57 Recent studies of this area's hydrology have indicated that flood flows crossing over the Vinh Te canal from the north contributed around a quarter of total annual flows entering the waterways of the broader floodplain in the year 2000. Hydrological modelling of the Vinh Té have pointed out that the high embankments on the canal's edges limit runoff from Cambodia "causing a significant decrease in maximum water level" compared to the "natural regime". Such a conclusion should be viewed in light of the separate trajectories of agricultural development that have informed the configuration of water infrastructure on either side of the canal and thus the total volume of floodwater flowing from Cambodia southwards through Vietnam's delta area. See Q.T. Vo, D. Roelvink, M. van der Wegen, J. Reyns, H. Kernkamp, V.V. Giap & T.P.L. Vo (2020), Flooding in the Mekong Delta: The Impact of Dyke Systems on Downstream Hydrodynamics. *Hydrology and Earth System Sciences*, v. 24, p. 198; T.V.H. Le, H. Shigeko, H.H. Nguyen & T.C. Cong (2008), Infrastructure Effects on Floods in the Mekong River Delta in Vietnam. *Hydrological Processes*, v. 22, p. 1372.

58 By 1930, the length of primary and secondary canals constructed in the preceding 35 years exceeded 4,000 kilometres. Inspection générale des travaux publics (1930), *Dragages de Cochinchine. Canal Rachgia-Hatien*. Saigon: Gouvernement général de l'Indochine, p. 19.

5 Shaping the Delta

The idea of grouping rural populations, of "centralizing on chosen points the exploitation of the soil" is not new, and the advantages are known . . . cohabitation is tightened by "the need to unite for the development of water, the construction of wells, the maintenance of certain works, the accommodation of an environment favourable to crops". This is how Vidal de la Blache condemned [low density] housing; President Ngo-dinh-Diem is inspired by an identical conception.

Les paysans vietnamiens et la réforme rurale au Sud Viêt-Nam,
Roger Teulieres, 1962

Between the scientific observations of France's eminent geographer and the policies instigated by South Vietnam's post-colonial ruler, the delta which emerged on the outflows of the Mekong River did not simply reflect an existing ground condition. The site of strategic, technical and political considerations before and after the establishment of French Cochinchina, the Mekong Delta has often been discussed as the geographic setting for events. Historical references to the Delta suggest that this particular terrain was diachronically appreciated in relation to the qualities that distinguish a river's coastal lowlands from any other terrain. Even if neither the name nor the extent of the region has remained unchanged across history, to imagine this territory as a delta or part of one is not just to accept that such physical and conceptual distinctions were always possible but also necessary. Correlating this region's identity simply in terms of a natural phenomenon would be to deny that the delta was far from the common perception of the Mekong's lowlands until the beginning of the 20th century. While this argument would appear to privilege the significance of the name over actual events, it is important to consider the archetypal value of the delta was not only its geophysical specificity but also the term's ability to convey meaning about a particular place through its notional resemblance to a larger 'family' of inhabited deltas.

As increasingly more settlers built permanent homes among the Mekong's waterways what was perceived to constitute a continuous region called a delta, also needed to account for how and where people lived. Especially after the first detailed maps of Cochinchina were completed in the 1920s, recurring references to settlement on the lowlands became entwined with geographic discourses.

DOI: 10.4324/9781032706238-8

94 *Liquid Territories*

Promulgated by geographers following the theories of Vidal de la Blache, the correlation between the patterns of inhabitation visible on maps and distinct ground conditions suggested that the extent of any delta was related to groups of people adapting to specific qualities of the terrain. Shaping the delta therefore alludes to two notions. On the one hand, the adaptation of settlement in response to the ground conditions classified by colonial geographers to make a specific delta 'legible' for state administrators, even as new canals redefined the ground conditions responsible for the observed adaptations. On the other hand, the intentional construction and modification of existing settlements by South Vietnam's government responding to a military threat by concentrating people in "agglomerations" and expanding cultivated land around them. Approached from these two perspectives, the chapter asks whether the delta's delineation was a conclusion drawn from observation of the ground or an outcome of theories that imagined settlement as the proxy for the region's limits.

The Extents of Inhabitation

Perhaps the most important changes to ground conditions during French colonial rule was initiated by the construction of new waterways. A means to promote exploitation of Cochinchina's fertile soils by colonial authorities, canalization was effective in extending agriculture into remote terrains.[1] Dimensioned to accommodate French patrol boats, new waterways were excavated in lines that run completely straight for several tens of kilometres, providing access to interstitial lands far from their confluences. Designed primarily to connect between destinations, each individual canal's contribution to the wider system of hydraulic flows appeared to resemble part of a regularly spaced grid of waterways that extended to the limits of the colony's jurisdiction. The cartographic depiction of Cochinchina's waterways would suggest that hydrological knowledge was on the level of the entire colony (**Figure 5.1**). However, the impact of canals had not been fully anticipated by the engineers responsible for their design. Along with the millions of cubic metres of dredged soil stacked alongside their embankments, canals redirected the flows of surface water, transforming what could once have been the edge of a marsh into farmland, or flooding fields that had previously been drained by existing streams. The failure to anticipate the 'side effects' of canalization was attributed to construction problems and the fundamental complexity of the lowlands' hydrology. Despite triggering geophysical processes that gradually transformed the quality of agriculture soils, the regularly spaced intersections between canals became the favoured points for the foundation of new villages and hamlets by tens of thousands of migrants arriving in Cochinchina every year. Following the paths of mechanical dredgers, settlers laid claim and cultivated plots adjacent to manmade waterways, some later discovering that the marshes and forests they had converted into viable agricultural fields with their backbreaking labour was already a landowner's legal property.[2] Those made landless, or losing farms during the years of the Great Depression swelled the number of tenant farmers (*tá điền*) cultivating farms often located several kilometres away from their homes.[3]

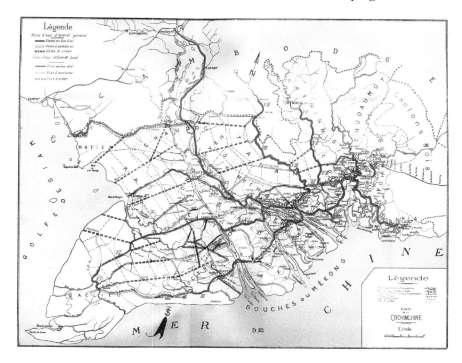

Figure 5.1 **Waterway network.** Drawn by Albert Pouyanne who would subsequently become Chief Engineer of Public Works in the colony, the map shows the relationship between regional and local waterways. Proposed canals (dotted lines) are arranged to intersect at regular intervals and appear to extend to the limits of the colony's jurisdiction. Albert Pouyanne (1911), *Voies d'eau d'Intérêt general*. [*Source:* ODSAS. Object Id: 43757 and 43758]

Equating the limits of discrete settlements with the spatial concentration of buildings was inconsistent with the geographic dispersal of daily activities across a wider, sometimes uninhabited region.

Describing such a settlement near his birthplace, the Vietnamese scholar and writer Sơn Nam related that the village (*làng*) appeared to stretch for 30 kilometres along an even longer waterway and that "when enough numbers were reached, the remote hamlets" on the village's extremes "became new villages".[4] The creation of three new villages through the subdivision of an existing one was not directly contingent on the distance between its farthest buildings. As Sơn Nam pointed out, uncultivated "wasteland" between clusters of buildings could be considered sufficient to initiate the subdivision of an existing settlement into new taxable entities, as was the spatial distribution of markets, educational facilities and spaces for communal gatherings. Taken as the relationship between individual buildings and the focus of a community's social activities, the centrality that was apparent around confluences or in organized villages built on the higher ground was dispersed along kilometres of canals. Popular for his histories of the Mekong's delta, Sơn Nam

96 *Liquid Territories*

grew up on one of the canals designed by French engineers. Rather than a village, he described having spent his early childhood "near the 4th canal" of an area known locally as *miệt thứ*.[5] Composed of numbered canals flowing from the melaleuca forests of U Minh to the Gulf of Thailand, *miệt thứ* was perceived to form a particular region. Built in groups which local residents gradually extended, canals allowed the Khmer farmers and Vietnamese migrants living in dispersed households and small hamlets to trade and communicate with each other. At the same time, by changing surface flows, the canals initiated changes in the habitat areas of snakehead and catfish that were farmed locally and sold for a high price far away.[6] Underpinned by the access provided by such networks of waterways, floating markets, schools and temples were not just features of individual villages. Circumscribed by canals creating a 'local' network of shared amenities, the area reachable by boat collectively described a settlement system encompassing multiple villages including the remote households in between. For different inhabitants the same waterway could form the centre of social activity, function as a fishery, join distant towns, connect individual houses into villages and unify distant villages into settlements encompassing regions. With few exceptions, the extent within which the inhabitants of groups of villages operated did not correspond to the limits of any single pre-existing geophysical condition that could be distinguished on a map.

Specifying the cartographic dimensions of villages was nonetheless an important tool for governance. A measure of population and property, what government officials considered a distinct settlement in the Mekong's lowlands had been critical to Vietnamese administration, where in matters such as taxation and *corvée* labour, the state dealt with the village as an entity rather than with individuals. As the historian Đinh Đâu Nguyễn has observed, the village units entered into cadastral records did not uniformly correspond to the Vietnamese bureaucracy's typical settlement designations such as *xã* (commune) or *thôn* (hamlet).[7] Especially far from towns, where the location of households and farmsteads converged with the embankments of waterways or the edge of topographic depressions, which buildings collectively comprised a specific settlement and which streams or inundated plains constituted the terrain on which they were constructed were deduced by comparison to settlements in the distant north where the empire's bureaucratic codes had been developed.

Typical of the Red River's sedimented lowlands, the socially autonomous villages of Tonkin have been described as "isolated islands" with their own lands, property, justice and customs.[8] These villages were sometimes demarcated by physical structures or bamboo hedges which were symbolic of the emperor's limited control over the village residents. The subsequent abolition of special privileges by the French occupying regime eroded the villages' pre-colonial autonomy while a new population census relating particular extents of either uncultivated or farmed land to the number of inhabitants increased taxation. A financial and geographic operation, determining the areal extent of villages was an important function of new maps. Established with support from the Army's Geographical Service in 1899, the *Service Géographique de l'Indochine* was tasked with mapping the colony's five types of geographic environments.[9] Among plains, plateaus and mountains,

Shaping the Delta 97

deltas occupied a prominent place and being the most heavily populated of all these environments were the focus of extensive surveys. First published in 1909, the *Cartes des Deltas de l'Annam* set a new standard for depictions of the colony's terrain. Instead of the 1 to 100,000 scale used for mountainous areas, maps of French Indochina's coastal lowlands were prepared at the scale of 1 to 25,000 which was considered necessary for planning water infrastructure and the cadastral operations which determined taxation.[10] Depicting a terrain that extended about 40 kilometres inland, a characteristic of this series was the representation of settlements.[11] With individual built structures visible, villages were distinguished from cities, towns and other clusters of buildings and shown to occupy a specific delineated extent. Drawn on a separate layer from the topography by the *Service's* cartographers, the green shaded limits of villages emulated the vegetated clusters of orchards which appeared more like "masses of greenery" rather than agglomerations.[12] Articulating their areal dimension made villages into 'visible' entities subject to specific legal obligations while making their residents wary of cooperation with the Service's mapping operations.[13]

Even with the support of local inhabitants, however, mapping the deltaic lowlands was considered a delicate task. Surveyors needed to account for a terrain whose flatness and lack of vertical landmarks challenged accurate levelling and whose planimetry was "overloaded with details".[14] The topographic homogeneity and dense geodesic canvas made deltas suitable for the deployment of a relatively new cartographic technique. Beginning in the 1920s, the Service introduced the use of aerial photography for surveys throughout the colony.[15] Unlike the detailed surveying of Indochina, the aerial views captured from military airplanes did not require map-makers to access remote or hostile regions. This significantly accelerated the pace of surveys and, by expanding the geographic coverage of maps at the same level of detail, revealed recurring visual relationships between farms, settlements and topographic features. Interpreted as patterns by geographers, the apparent repetition of particular features supported scientific arguments that framed the "region" as a function of the interaction between people and their environment. The most influential French geographer of the period Paul Vidal de la Blache's approach posited that these regions could encompass valleys, coastal plains or entire river basins. Focused on the scientific study of "places", for Vidal the region's "character", which geographic science aimed to explicate, was inseparable from the practices of the people concentrated within that particular region.[16] Based on observations derived from maps, his thesis was particularly attuned to the relationship between human habitats and the qualities of soils that enabled different agricultural techniques. Observing that homogeneous soil conditions propagated the same type of village, he concluded that "the hamlet type and the village type seem to correspond well to geographical differences".[17] The correlation between a group of people and particular features of the cultivated terrain resonated with geographers working in the colonial regions of Indochina.

In his monumental study of the villages in the Tonkin Delta, the Tunisian-born French geographer Pierre Gourou argued for a unity among people, settlements and the surrounding environment that was made apparent through mapping and

98   *Liquid Territories*

aerial imagery. Published in 1936, Gourou's anthropological research was prepared after several years of intensive fieldwork carried out in collaboration with his Vietnamese colleagues at the University of Hanoi. Following the principles of Vidal's geography, the delta's "natural" topographic uniformity was presented as critical to the creation of the "human unity" represented by village communities.[18] The methodological axis of his studies on settlements pivoted on each village's discernible form in relation to the topography. Using photographic reduction techniques and colour tints to distinguish building clusters, Gourou constructed maps on which he claimed even the smallest hamlet was visible. Depicted in solid black, these maps focused attention on the planar arrangement of buildings, which while important, were only one of the characteristics – including communal lands – that defined a *làng xã* as a state-recognized entity. Examining the settlements that appeared together on the maps, he described how the form of the "innumerable multitude of black spots" was underpinned by guidelines that determined different types of villages.[19] Thus, while individual settlements were presented as distinct entities with their own history and customs, the idea that common rules or guidelines could dictate the spatial arrangement of a group of villages redirected emphasis to the collective form of the buildings depicted on the map.

Yet where a planted bamboo hedge or an extent of uncultivated communal land gave villages a discernible areal extent, not all guidelines correlated with the limits and magnitude of building clusters. Especially in agricultural areas where the distance between farmhouses varied considerably and communal land was non-existent, the dikes and canals subdividing the Tonkin Delta conferred a semblance of structure to the disorder and individualism apparent on the map.[20] Called *casiers* by the French, dikes encircling a particular extent of geographic space were a typical feature of the Delta, with each village – rather than the state – responsible for the maintenance of their own flood control structures.[21] While not uniformly distributed throughout the region, the unit of space encompassed by dikes was considered emblematic of North Vietnam's agricultural landscape.[22] Although dikes had altered the hydrological regime by detaining floodwater even after inundation had subsided elsewhere, water infrastructure was associated with a pastoral ideal that was characteristic of Vidalian human geography. The order which was visible on the planar views of settlements, however, was not limited to the impression that waterways simply 'enclosed' clusters of buildings. Rather than considering the village's extent as equivalent to a *casier*'s dikes, as the observable outcome of a process taking place over decades, Gourou's maps suggested that the collective disposition of houses within the *casiers* was also underpinned by particular rules.[23] Groups of buildings confronted with similar conditions, such as a higher ground on a lowland plain or a linear flood-defence structure, appeared to coalesce into distinct areal forms, allowing Gourou to conjecture that waterways and other topographic features were responsible for their arrangement.

The classification of villages into types reflected this notion. Referencing the relationship of a settlement with the topography, the disposition of buildings along river banks or along the edges of hills were classified under different registers.[24] To the degree that village morphology was suitably adapted to the conditions of the

Shaping the Delta 99

deltaic topography, where particular village types were concentrated on the map, also indicated the prevalence of particular topographic conditions. Drawn on maps, the grouping of these "isolated islands" into coherent systems helped explain complicated social phenomena. The areal magnitude of villages in relation to the number of their inhabitants, for example, exhibited population densities that were thought to exceed the capacity of the land to feed its residents. Based on these observations, the cause of poverty in the Tonkin Delta was attributed to "overpopulation" (*surpeuplement*) rather than the economic impact of the Great Depression or the colonial taxation system. These conclusions influenced French officials who began to consider mass migration to Cochinchina as the solution to the "problem" of density.

Applying his cartographic methodology to the lowlands of the Mekong River, Gourou's 1942 study of Cochinchina's rural population was conducted during the colonial Vichy administration. Unlike the years of fieldwork which had contributed to his previous study, however, the Cochinchina he described was based almost exclusively on maps and statistics, of which only relatively few were as detailed as Tonkin's.[25] Arguing that density was the most important factor dictating the difference in conditions between "*Cochinchine deltaique*" and the "*Delta du Tonkin*", the maps accompanying his report divided the colony into subregions that differed primarily in the enumerated spatial concentration of residents.[26] With the "east" appearing far more populated than the "west", and "central" areas having an "optimum" population, the distribution of the region's inhabitants was interpreted as showing the "underpopulated" portions of Cochinchina with the capacity to host migrant resettlement from the north. Prepared using the same mapping technique employed in Tonkin, the Service's map of Cochinchina's villages projected settlements onto a background of fine blue lines representing the embankments of perennial waterways, with the blocks of black ink depicting "villages" displaying the geographic distribution of inhabitation (**Figure 5.2**).[27] Seen through the configuration of ink on paper, the map's striking correlation between settlement and waterways was not of the same fine grain of detail as Gourou's previous study, and at 1 to 250,000 tended to exaggerate the magnitude and continuity of built areas. Articulating village form would therefore have been inconceivable without assuming that just like in Tonkin guidelines underpinned the visible pattern of built areas. Using the map as the guide, Gourou distinguished multiple variations of basic village types and more contextually unique arrangements of buildings. Inasmuch as a settlement's planimetric morphology aligned with the embankments of waterways or clustered behind riparian sediment deposits (*bourrelets*), Gourou believed that as inhabitation adapted to particular topographic conditions villages collectively adopted the *areal form* of natural regions.[28] The fact that mapped villages could be interpreted to signify where certain geophysical relationships began suggests that the geographic space discernible as a distinct region acquired, at least in part, its own cartographic form by the way it was assumed to be inhabited. Considering that on the flatness of the Mekong's lowlands the topographic limits of a swamp or an alluvial depression were only determinable by their subtle differentiation with adjacent areas, for Gourou the cartographic dimension of settlement reflected but also appeared to define the delta's natural geographic limits.

100　*Liquid Territories*

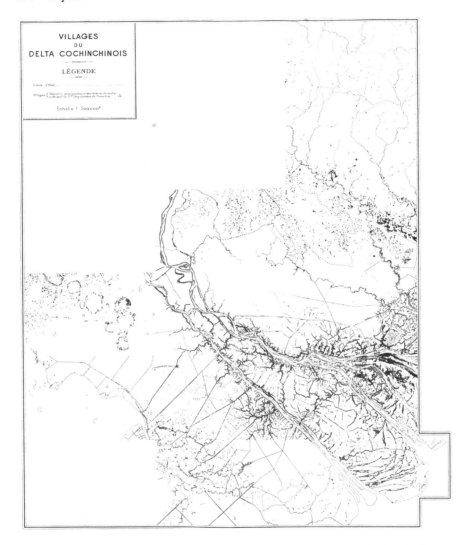

Figure 5.2 **Villages of Cochinchina's Delta.** Coloured black, the map displays built areas in the French colony against a background of perennial waterways depicted with fine blue lines. Although there is considerable exaggeration of the magnitude of built areas due to the techniques employed in the map's preparation, Gourou identified multiple village typologies that appeared to emulate the delta's terrains. Service géographique de l'Indochine (1940), *Villages du Delta Cochinchinois*. [*Source:* Université Bordeaux Montaigne-1886. Res 09110703]

If Gourou's cartographic distinctions between Cochinchina's settlement types implied a correlation between human inhabitation and the different terrains which constituted the delta, this relationship did not account for the countless man-made modifications which underpinned the hydrology and ground conditions

Shaping the Delta 101

experienced by Sơn Nam. New inhabitants burned and cleared forests accelerating the processes initiated by canalization that dried brackish swamps or allowed tides to funnel salt water inland. With demand exceeding the supply of available plots, migrants settled wherever possible requiring the colonial government to reserve the land up to 1 kilometre from canal intersections for civic uses. Gourou's typological classification of villages therefore reflected only part of a settlement's relationship with waterways. By following the logic of Tonkin's self-contained villages, the hypothesis concerning the adaptation of villages to the delta's terrain could not directly account for the fact that the geography itself was also a variable and not the stable background in relation to which groups of people adapted their practices. Yet in suggesting that groups of villages constituted distinct regions, the black blocks of ink representing built areas were able to convey an idea of a specific delta. Even if the apparent configuration of settlement was the consequence of the terrain's characteristics, the ability to alter these characteristics by building and inhabiting new waterways gave inhabitants, but also the state, the agency to also physically construct what constituted a distinct region. The delta apparent on Gourou's map was not the same delta that could be described with reference to sediment accretion, or the boundary with Cambodia. The delta constructed through the geographic discourse on villages and population density appeared less as part of the terrain and more as an areal unit whose magnitude was coterminous with its inhabitants' changing social relations.

Hinged terrains

If the changes in hydrology inadvertently initiated by canal-building made Gourou's thesis redundant as a way to explain the way people adapted to specific qualities of a constantly changing delta, the idea that settlements shaped the terrain around them remained significant. Less than 20 years after Gourou's study was published, the post-colonial regime of South Vietnam incorporated "resettlement" into a new policy of agrarian reform that was conceived as the answer to multiple problems confronted by the newly independent country.[29] Announced in 1957, *Agricultural Development Centers* called Dinh Điền would not only increase the overall land available for cultivation and support diversification of crop production but also contribute to local "self-sufficiency" and more importantly to the national security of a state in an escalating conflict with North Vietnam's communist government.

Closely associated with the personal beliefs of the country's President Diem, the Vietnamese administration's interpretation of self-sufficiency and community development reflected an emerging UN practice for "aided self-help in small communities with modest technical services".[30] Where schemes such as the TVA occupied one extreme of a range of planned modernization processes, the UN, *community development* was considered far more adaptable to the specific requirements and aspirations of local residents. From the perspective of South Vietnam's leader, however, rather than just the government assisting local residents to raise their own standards of living, agricultural communities would also be mobilized to actively contribute to the construction of public projects. Inhabitants of Dinh Điền were tasked not only with clearing unutilized land for farming and building houses

102 *Liquid Territories*

for little or no pay, but in the face of anti-government resistance also with organizing their own security.[31] Due partially to the high proportion of tenant farmers who were considered vulnerable to communist propaganda, the deltaic areas south and west of the capital Saigon were targeted for more than 26 settlements called *khu trù mật* or *agrovilles*. Located along major roads and canals, the *agrovilles* would be positioned to monitor movement through the terrain and serve to expand the extent of agricultural land.[32] Acting as what the Vietnamese called *hinge cities* (*villes charnières*), these settlements were conceived as a "happy compromise" between rural and city life.[33]

In the Mekong's lowlands, what exactly hinged around these "cities" is suggested by the planning of Cái Sắn and the subsequent design of *agrovilles* and *strategic hamlets*. Inaugurated in 1956, the planned settlement at Cái Sắn was situated along either side of a colonial-era canal, in a part of the delta that only a few years earlier had been under the control of the Hòa Hảo sect. According to the information leaflet published by the South Vietnam administration, the rectangular area encompassed by the plan covered about 1,000 km².[34] This area was visible from the air "as clearly as on the map" and bounded by the Bassac River to the north, the Gulf of Siam to the south and existing waterways running between the river and the sea to the east and west (**Figure 5.3**). Maps denoting the geographic space under the control of anti-government militia during the last years of French rule

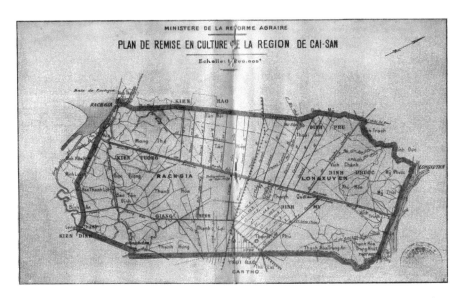

Figure 5.3 **Resettlement plan for the Cái Sắn area.** Encompassing around 1,000 km² the planning area of Cái Sắn is bisected by the Rach Gia-Bassac canal and bounded by existing waterways to the east and west. New canals are named by letters A–H or by numbers 1–5, asserting a technocratic legibility onto the terrain. Ministère de la réforme agraire (1956), *Plan du remise en culture de la región de Cai-San*. [*Source:* Republic of Viet-Nam]

Shaping the Delta 103

in Indochina point out that the canal bisecting the site and the land around it was probably one of the few secure routes for state officials from the Bassac River to the coast. Yet if the sea and river were geographic edges and the main canal a clear central axis, the choice of existing waterways for the planning area's east and west boundaries did not reflect the limits of an existing ground condition. A different map from 1924 shows that to the northeast of the planned area, land had already been subdivided into plots of various sizes: from 1 hectare lots to 30 hectares for large plantations.[35] Drawn a year after the main canal's completion, the property subdivisions that defined the manmade terrain only very rarely appeared to be related to existing streams or even other canals. In this sense, apart for the strategic link from the river to the coast, a significant part of the areal extent on which Cái Sắn was to be planned did not display any specific organizational principle except perhaps for the rationale dictating the surface area of private lots.

Framed in terms of an area requiring overall planning, organizing the configuration of the ground entailed excavation of 200 kilometres of new waterways, with 180 thousand cubic metres of excavated soil deposited alongside the canals.[36] With parts of the colonial plot subdivisions preserved, new waterways were designed to be almost perpendicular or parallel to the main canal and named alphabetically or numerically, structuring a hierarchical sequence of routes that could be understood in relation to each other.[37] Built on 20-metre wide platforms along the canals, houses were grouped into villages and served by clustered amenities such as churches and schools dispersed at waterway intersections. Thus, rather than an isolated 'point' of concentration within a context of diffused building clusters, Cái Sắn was less a city and more a dispersed settlement such as those which the writer Sơn Nam had grown up in. If only metaphorical, references to a *hinge city* indicated the defence of a critical junction within a wider strategic terrain. Distinguished from the adjacent marshland by the regularized recurrence of canal junctions rather than an outer edge or the condition of the ground, Cái Sắn's planning area was not the equivalent of an existing region definable by soil types, vegetation or the behaviour of water.[38] Made "legible" on a map, from the air or even from a boat, the organization of new waterways was a necessary step to transform an undifferentiated part of the sedimented lowlands into a rationalized territory.

Despite being considered an economic and political success, the model of regional settlement demonstrated at Cái Sắn was substantially adapted in subsequent plans for *agrovilles*. Government propaganda portraying happy peasants benefitting from modern facilities and affordable land, however, did not reflect the realities of a bare, treeless terrain which they needed to make arable. By the end of the 1950s, land reform had yielded only a marginal decrease in the proportion of landless households, and by 1959, the security threat perceived by the government had amplified.[39] *Agrovilles* would thereafter intentionally "create densely populated settlement areas" in a countryside where people lived in "such a spread out manner" that it would be impossible for them to avoid the influence of the enemy.[40] If the stated objectives of the *agrovilles* were to improve the life of the rural population, the historical record is full of accounts of the conflicts that occurred between government forces and the thousands violently forced to abandon their homes and

104 *Liquid Territories*

farms, often working without pay to build houses and the infrastructure. The reasoning cited for adopting such an aggressive strategy in the first place revolved around the social and military benefits of "agglomeration". In that part of the Mekong's lowlands administered by South Vietnam, the strategic deployment of "agglomeration zones" was fundamentally different from the planning of Cái Sắn. Where Cái Sắn's clusters of public facilities were dispersed to serve people living along canals, the new *agrovilles* would relocate distant households within relatively close distance from modern schools and medical facilities.[41] Within the new settlements, residents would be theoretically protected by security forces although in reality farmers would still need to travel far outside the settlement's monitored perimeter to work on their old farms.

These contradictions were not just problems arising from planning the configuration of individual settlements. Beginning with the new *agroville* at Vị Thanh, subsequent planned settlements such as those at Đức Huệ and Tân Lược were arranged within a roughly 1 km² area subdivided by a grid of canals or roads with each 'block' apportioned into several household plots. Despite spatial characteristics which appeared odd for the setting, Vị Thanh became the model for subsequent *agrovilles*.[42] Located along the main waterway from the strategically vulnerable region of Cà Mau to the town of Can Tho, Vị Thanh's site had been selected primarily to control movement along the canal rather than the qualities of its soils. Maps from 1960 that show the site of the *agroville* before and after the plan depict the new settlement underpinned by a grid, with the main built area encompassing one side of the main canal and new infrastructure (probably a highway) running parallel to the waterway.[43] On the maps, existing canals are visually subdued or integrated into the outline of roads while significantly, with the *agroville* in place, the terrain surrounding the settlement is no longer depicted as marshland. The regularized subdivision of fields replacing the swamp continues beyond the frame of the map, implying that the new ground condition is a result of the planned settlement and not necessarily confined to a specific area. Considering that less than one-third of the 20,000 peasants recruited to construct Vị Thanh could initially be accommodated within the *agroville*, the purpose of agglomeration was not solely the spatial concentration of the rural population. Instead what is apparent is the aspiration to transform the ground conditions of an area far larger than those where buildings are clustered. If Cái Sắn's plan exemplified the 'rationalization' of the marshland with new waterways, Vị Thanh's appeared to impose order over the adjacent terrain by making the agglomeration zone the point of reference for a vast geographic space.

Seeding Settlement

Recorded in newspaper articles by Vietnamese politicians and in reports by American researchers, the failures of *agrovilles* not only to improve economic conditions but also to halt the spread of counter-insurgency initiated the transition to a new model of fortified settlements. Instead of dealing with the conflict arising from forced resettlement, unpaid labour and the suitability of the terrain to accommodate cultivation, 'tactical hamlets' in areas of strategic importance started to replace *agrovilles*.[44] Named *strategic hamlets* (*ấp chiến lược*), these settlements were intended to articulate the government's vision for a modern country through the grouping of rural inhabitants.[45] Praised by President Diem as the archetype of a cohesive and self-sufficient social unit, the idealized Vietnamese village was promoted as the appropriate model to initiate change.[46] Derived from appreciation of Central and North Vietnam where the peasant village was considered emblematic of the cultivated landscape, the 'model' commune (*xã*) was formed by a "group of inter-dependent hamlets coordinating their efforts along a common scheme".[47] In practice, this vision was to be implemented by fortifying existing settlements and constructing new ones, a process that simultaneously separated government sympathizers from those suspected of having contact with the enemy.

Apart from the implicit references to older Vietnamese modes of colonizing hostile terrains epitomized by the *đồn điền*, British colonial policy in Malaya was also cited as the source of the newer model.[48] To prevent the resupply of communist guerrillas following the end of the Second World War, the British administration had moved dispersed landholders into identical houses clustered in groups, where their movements could be monitored.[49] In South Vietnam, the goal of disrupting communication with the enemy materialized in the construction of physical barriers. Peripheral fortifications made of barb-wire, bamboo posts and trenches controlled inhabitants' movements through guarded openings and restricted their access to the settlements' supplies by insurgents. A technique suitable for protecting buildings clustered on land rather than along a waterway's embankments, the construction of these fences was the subject of communist propaganda that cast the hamlets as incarceration or concentration camps. Especially for those used to living along the region's waterways, the fenced perimeter of an individual hamlet ruptured the relationship between farmers and cultivated land and removed people from proximity to ancestral graves and ceremonial centres. Referring to the strategic hamlets, James Scott has described how their fences produced "concentrated state spaces", where direct control and discipline over people were more important than the appropriation of the geographic extent which the boundary enclosed.[50] From the perspective of the thousands displaced in the name of national security, this conclusion would reflect the armed surveillance experienced within these settlements. The spatial disposition of these "points" of concentration however suggests a different way to perceive what terrain "agglomeration" appropriated.

How individual hamlets were perceived to form groups with other settlements and their adjacent terrain was critical to their spatial arrangement. Published in 1963, the same year the programme was terminated, the government's official brochure on strategic hamlets declared that the benefits of the "rural revolution" instigated by the hamlets would strengthen solidarity between the region's dispersed inhabitants and the state. To achieve this, individual settlements were transformed into hamlets and, along with new hamlets wherever required, collectively formed a village with elected leadership. What conditions triggered the requirement for a new hamlet to be erected is suggested by another goal of the programme. The widespread infiltration of existing villages by an enemy hiding "in the forest or among the population", required a "frontline" to be produced.[51] To this end, the hamlets would become a "human wall" along the country's vulnerable frontiers, where the inhabitants would theoretically

106 *Liquid Territories*

also benefit by accessing "untapped" resources.[52] The disposition of new in relation to existing hamlets would therefore need to simultaneously contribute to two groupings of settlement: one collectively forming a *village* and another forming a 'visible', if not necessarily linear, frontier. However, with more than 4,000 hamlets housing a third of the region's population planned for the Mekong's lowlands, this "frontline" alone would not form the limit of a controlled terrain.[53] If the pattern of model villages further north was defined by the geographic proximity between distinct settlements, the hamlets would need to be positioned at relatively regular intervals throughout the terrain. Considering that most homes in the Mekong's countryside were dispersed along a waterway's embankments rather than clustered around a centre or confined to a peripheral barrier, the distribution of hamlets would have to contend with conditions that challenged the proposed concentration of settlement.

A 1965 US Army map presenting the topography of South Vietnam's delta region illustrates the contradiction between ideas of agglomeration and local settlement organization (**Figure 5.4**). Although by no means typical of the programme's

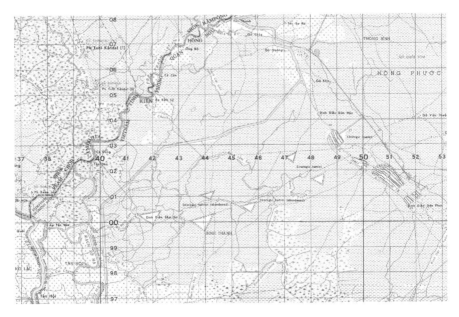

Figure 5.4 **Strategic delta.** An excerpt from a larger map of the region east of Hong Nu, the drawing shows a number of strategic hamlets and *dinh điền* arranged across 10 kilometres of marshland. The largest of the triangular hamlets is about 800 metres on its longest side. A levee wall appears to stretch from the Mekong River across the entire map. Constructed on mounds typical of this part of the marshes (*xứ gò*), Sa Rài village is located a few hundred metres from the canalized Rạch Sa Rài and is not typical of the region's waterway settlements which are shown closer to the River (left). Defense Mapping Agency (1966), *Hong Ngu Vietnam; Cambodia, (Sheet 6030 I), Series L7014*. [*Source:* University of Texas Libraries, The University of Texas at Austin]

Shaping the Delta   107

implementation elsewhere, the map appears to present six strategic hamlets and *dinh điền* situated in the marshes close to the boundary with Cambodia. Rather than reinforcing an existing settlement, these consistently adopt the triangular planimetric form of the Plei Me Special Forces (Delta Force) camp. Separated rather than joined with each other by waterways, these are arranged along a 10-kilometre notional line roughly parallel to a dike. The "levee wall" which is also several kilometres long would have presumably contained the floodwater flowing overland across the border, as well as block movement across a terrain where "travel by small boat is unrestricted and concealment easy" for several months of the year.[54] With some hamlets labelled "abandoned" and others presumably still inhabited, their reference to a military base and the insistence on a continuous state presence *across* this particular stretch of uninhabited marshland suggest that these would collectively form a third "wall" behind the geopolitical boundary and the dike. Prepared by the US military and shared with their Vietnamese allies, such topographic maps at 1 to 50,000 were more useful for providing an overview over a particular area rather than for navigating through the terrain.[55] If recent remote imagery shows no trace of these hamlets, revealing the position of these tactical bases on a map would have been inconsistent with their strategic value as a defensible "frontline" along a sensitive frontier. Thus, even if these hamlets were never constructed, much less abandoned, their appearance on the map was arguably deliberate and served a different purpose than merely depicting an existing condition. Considering the "levee wall" – if ever planned – was never built, to conclude that these possibly 'phantom' hamlets and infrastructure were drawn to intentionally show these frontiers as secure would also imply that such a distant and inaccessible border area first needed to become 'visible' in order for it to become controlled. For an audience of military and government officials, the cartographic figures of hamlets suggested the geographic limit of a 'state space' constructed by the planning of settlements and dikes rather than adherence to geopolitical boundaries.

Cited as one of the more important reasons leading to the hamlet programme's failure, the "traditional settlement pattern in the Delta region" was regarded as antithetical to policies of population concentration.[56] Existing settlement patterns were too "spread out" to oversee effectively, and overly concentrated along the existing waterways to monitor movement across the interstitial inundated plains. Planning the configuration of settlement would act as an 'antidote' to a ground condition considered favourable to concealment and infiltration, but also – by providing modern social facilities – to the destitution and isolation of the rural population. Among the many things they can be interpreted as representing, the planning of Cái Sắn, *agrovilles,* such as Vị Thanh, and strategic hamlets also presented three different approaches to establish what constituted a particular settlement unit. Although impossible to separate from the threat of violence which underpinned the choice of approach, what Scott calls the "radical simplification" of planned settlement patterns was considered necessary to deliver services, and the enforced "villagization" a way to reorganize social units "in order to make them better objects of political control".[57] Yet if all three aimed to make the inhabited terrain *legible* to agents of the state, the construction of legibility under each approach was notably different. The choice of dispersal along a new sequence of waterways, concentration within

108 *Liquid Territories*

a grid of infrastructure or isolation inside a fence was not just a matter of reducing the project's scale to increase the speed at which it could be completed.[58] At Cái Sắn and Vị Thanh, the new and existing waterways were pivotal in circumscribing the building clusters constituting villages, establishing these canals as references for a wider area that also encompassed farms, uncultivated land and uninhabited ground. The fencing of settlements into hamlets, and the grouping of hamlets into villages on the other hand, sought to replace the dispersed clusters of homes along waterways with delineated social units that adhered to the spatial order of the idealized commune further north. While it is not possible to characterize these agglomerations as 'urban', the programmes confirmed that what could be considered *rural* in the context of the Mekong's delta encompassed a geographic area whose extents could be designed by the planning of settlement.

Conclusion

From different perspectives, Vidal's geographic theories underpinned Gourou's analysis of the delta's villages, and President Ngo's subsequent approach to 'resettlement'. On the one hand, Gourou's conviction that "rural density" was the result of people's "perfect" adaptation to the *milieu* allowed the colonial geographer to assume that the areal form of villages in Cochinchina reflected the limits of the various terrains constituting the delta. On the other hand, President Ngo's belief that concentrating the population of dispersed, canal-side settlements into 'hinge cities' would enable a new social order to emerge was equally an implicit reference to Vidal's observations regarding the benefits of "centralizing on chosen points the exploitation of the soil", as well as driven by the need to create safe routes between government-controlled parts of the terrain.[59] Both approaches developed their theses by idealizing aspects of the traditional northern Vietnamese village into 'models' whose principles were applicable to settlement on the Mekong's lowlands. For Gourou, the mapped relationship between cultivated land and Tonkin's villages provided the baseline to assess conditions in Cochinchina's delta. Even if the geographer appreciated that the condition of the ground influenced settlement, on a map on which building clusters were drawn only in relationship to perennial waterways, the flood-prone, unproductive soils characterizing the 'underpopulated' parts of the Mekong's lowlands were simply areas available for human inhabitation.

Recognizing the strategic value of these available locations, South Vietnam's resettlement of refugees in *agrovilles* positioned along navigable canals and the arrangement of strategic hamlets structured a defensible 'state space' on the Mekong's sediment deposits. Conceivably, the frontier formed by President Ngo's "human wall" could have been imagined in other ways. On the US Army topographic map it manifested in distinct military settlements arranged adjacent to each other and parallel to the boundary with Cambodia, their presence *on the map* reinforced the government's projection of authority within the fourth tactical military zone which encompassed the Mekong Delta. On maps, settlements were not simply layers of information on top of a 'stable' delta that described how the terrain was

Shaping the Delta 109

inhabited. The cartographic arrangement of villages proposed particular ways to either 'see' the relationship of human activity with the condition of the ground or to project a specific 'reality' onto that ground. These propositions were instrumental in decisions of which terrain would be the site for resettlement and how – in the form of agglomerations – settlement would be implemented. An outcome of the way human activity was made legible on maps through the areal form of villages, the delta described in relation to settlement conditions, was also the cause for a particular set of responses that set out to regulate human activity as a function of the delta's entirety. What prescribed that 'whole' was not the hydrological catchment area nor the edge created by the boundary with Cambodia. Instead, the delta was constituted by the presence or absence of settlement on the map.

Notes

1 By 1930, the length of primary and secondary canals constructed in the preceding 35 years exceeded 4,000 kilometres. Inspection générale des travaux publics (1930), *Dragages de Cochinchine. Canal Rachgia-Hatien*. Saigon: Gouvernement général de l'Indochine, p. 19.
2 Pierre Brocheux (1995), *The Mekong Delta: Ecology, Economy, and Revolution, 1860–1960*. Madison, WI: Center for Southeast Asian Studies, pp. 122–123.
3 According to Pierre Gourou, up to four-fifths of all agricultural land was cultivated by landless peasants. See Trần Hữu Quang & Nghị Nguyễn (2016), Reframing the 'Traditional' Vietnamese Village: From Peasant to Farmer Society in the Mekong Delta. *Moussons*, v. 28, p. 68.
4 *"In case the village is too large like Dong Thai village which was 30 km long, when enough population numbers were reached, the remote hamlets were separated and three more villages established, Dong Hung, Dong Hoa and Dong Thanh in 1914"*. (*Trường hợp làng quá rộng như làng Đông Thái dài 30 cây số, dân đến cư ngụ lần hồi, khi đủ số thì những ấp ở xa trở thành làng mới, tách ra lập thêm ba làng là Đông Hưng, Đông Hòa và Đông Thạnh từ năm 1914.*) Sơn Nam (1973), *Lịch Sử Khẩn Hoang Miền Nam (A History of Settlement in the South)*. NXB Chưa Cập Nhật. Born in 1926 as Phạm Minh Tày, Sơn Nam spent his childhood in the far south of Cochinchina. He published many books on the đồng bằng sông Cửu Long – the Vietnamese name for the Mekong Delta – collecting observations of the terrain, oral histories and linguistic nuances of the local dialect into historical accounts and popular adventure novels.
5 Pascal Bourdeaux (2014), Sơn Nam ou la dualité d'une oeuvre. Évocations poétiques et ethnographiques du Viêt Nam meridional. *Moussons*, n. 24, para. 41.
6 Nam, *op. cit.*, p. 79.
7 The most comprehensive survey of *Nam Bộ* prior to French colonization recorded over 1,600 separate settlements and information regarding individual plots such as boundaries, land quality, crops and property rights. Nguyễn mentions multiple examples of settlements whose origins were farms (*trai*), corporate villages (*phuông*) or formed by navy veterans known as *thuyên* (boat). He concludes that *"Si l'on traduisait xã en commune et thôn en hameau, cela ne cadrerait pas avec la réalité"*. Đinh Đâu Nguyễn (1991), Remarques préliminaires sur les registres cadastraux (địa bạ) des six provinces de la Cochinchine (Nam Kỳ Lục Tỉnh). *Bulletin de l'École française d'Extrême-Orient*, v. 78, pp. 275, 280.
8 Trần & Nguyễn, *op. cit.*, p. 65.
9 Les Armées Françaises D'outre-Mer (1931), *La Carte de l'Empire Colonial Français, Exposition Coloniale Internationale*. Paris: Impri. Georges Lang, p. 100.

110 *Liquid Territories*

10 Gouvernement Général de l'Indochine (1931), *Service géographique de l'Indochine: Son organisation, ses méthodes, ses travaux, Exposition Coloniale Internationale.* Hanoi: Impri. d'extrême-Orient, p. 14.

11 Including the maps of Cochinchina and the Tonkin Delta, a total of 277 maps are reported to have been prepared at a scale of 1:25000. Les Armées Françaises D'outre-Mer, *op. cit.*, p. 118.

12 *"Service Géographique de l'Indochine attribue un vert spécial aux surfaces occupées par les villages parce que ceux-ci apparaissent dans le paysage beaucoup plus comme des masses de verdure que comme des agglomérations de maisons. Mais lorsque les jardins disparaissent le vert village disparaît également ce qui pour résultat de diminuer sur nos cartes importance de emprise humaine".* Pierre Gourou (1942), La population rurale de la Cochinchine. *Annales de Géographie*, v. 51, n. 285, note 1, p. 23.

13 Gavin Bowd & Daniel Clayton (2003), Fieldwork and Tropicality in French Indochina: Reflections on Pierre Gourou's Les Paysans Du Delta Tonkinois, 1936. *Singapore Journal of Tropical Geography*, v. 24, n. 2, p. 161.

14 Les Armées Françaises D'outre-Mer, *op. cit.*, p. 104.

15 Taken at scales similar to the desirable level of cartographic detail, photographic proofs would be sent to the Service's specialist laboratory in Hanoi where technicians would confirm their location in relation to geodetic reference points and trace over identified features with a pencil. Gouvernement Général de l'Indochine, *op. cit.*, p. 23.

16 Richard Hartshorne (1951), *The Nature of Geography: A Critical Survey of Current Thought in the Light of the Past.* Lancaster, PA: The Association of American Geographers, pp. 161, 200.

17 *"L'habitat dispersé et l'habitat aggloméré, le type hameau et le type village y semblent bien correspondre à des différences géographiques".* Paul Vidal de la Blache (2015), *Principes de géographie humaine: Publiés d'après les manuscrits de l'auteur par Emmanuel de Martonne.* Paris: ENS Éditions.

18 *"Dans ce pays pétri d'humanité, où l'homme a créé partout le paysage tel que nous le voyons, cette unité de la population paysanne est un puissant facteur d'uniformité; et l'uniformité naturelle d'un pays deltaïque n'a pas peu contribué à créer cette unité humaine. uniformité naturelle et unité humaine, en s'aidant l'une l'autre, ont cree un pays remarquablement homogène et une nation parfaitement cohérente".* Pierre Gourou (1936), *Les Paysans Du Delta Tonkinois. Etude de Géographie Humaine.* Paris: EFEO, pp. 14–15.

19 *"l'on est au premier regard frappé par l'innombrable multitude des taches noires qui représentent les villages et par la surface très importante qu'elles occupant sur la carte. Il semble tout d'abord que ces taches sont jetées avec désordre, comme tracées au hasard par un insecte qui aurait trempé ses pattes dans l'encre. Mais très rapidement des lignes directrices apparaissent; l'étude de l'habitat consistera à mettre en valeur ces lignes directrices et à déterminer les différents types de villages".* *ibid.*, pp. 237–238.

20 *"les lignes directrices sont les mêmes, constituées par des digues parallèles aux rivages et des canaux perpendiculaires aux digues, maisles villages sont faits d'éléments dispersés . . . qui révèlent plus de désordre et d'individualisme".* *ibid.*, p. 246.

21 David Biggs (2011), Aerial Photography and Colonial Discourse on the Agricultural Crisis in Late-Colonial Indochina, 1930–1945. In C.F. Ax, N. Brimnes, N.T. Jensen & K. Oslund (eds.), *Cultivating the Colonies: Colonial States and Their Environmental Legacies.* Athens: Ohio University Press, p. 116.

22 As David Biggs explains, for Gourou and indeed many other colonial scientists, the hydraulic compartmentalization of the Delta's topographic "uniformity" and the labour required to build and maintain a village's *casiers* reflected the heroism of the hardworking Tonkin peasant.

23 The way "guidelines" could have affected the accretion of buildings into villages was described by the Japanese architect Fumihiko Maki three decades later. Analyzing what

Shaping the Delta 111

he called "group form", Maki examined villages as a general settlement type whose configuration emerged from certain "generative elements". Rather than a "skeleton" of physical infrastructure in relation to which buildings clustered, what made a settlement into a coherent group that could be discerned as a village was the repeated use of certain physical features such as walls or gates in the sequential accretion of houses. According to Maki, the geographic concentration of these basic elements defined an "environmental space" which could be added to (or presumably subtracted from) "without changing the basic structure of the village". Fumihiko Maki & Masato Ohtaka (1964), *Investigations in Collective Form*, Special publication, n. 2. St Louis: Washington University School of Architecture, pp. 14–19.

24 Gourou's three main categories of "relief villages" located settlements according to river banks, the edges of hills and coastlines.

25 The 1:25,000 maps of Cochinchina were initially limited to the most densely inhabited parts of the colony. With the introduction of aerial photography, approximately 30,000 km^2 were recorded in images and from 1928 onwards, photo-topography was also applied to the cadastre. Les Armées Françaises D'outre-Mer, *op. cit.*, p. 115.

26 *"la Cochinchine et le Delta tonkinois présentent des conditions tout fait différentes puisque les parties deltaïques de la Cochinchine ont une population rurale de 100 par km2 tandis au Tonkin la population rurale atteint une densité moyenne de 430 par km2"*. Gourou, *op. cit.*, p. 17.

27 The specific technique involved printing the green plates which the Service géographique used as a coloured overlay to demarcate villages on their 1:100,000 maps of the region. The map's scale was then accurately reduced with photographic prints to obtain a map with the built area overlain on a background of the region's waterways.

28 *"Le village ou plutôt ensemble des villages épousé la forme même du plateau et arrête á ses limites"*. ibid., p. 25.

29 Although French engineers and planners had proposed several plans for moving 'surplus' people from the overpopulated villages of Tonkin to the underpopulated areas of the Mekong Delta, these were only partially implemented.

30 United Nations Educational, Scientific and Cultural Organization (UNESCO) (1956), *The Definition of Community Development*. Working Paper n. 3, p. 1. For South Vietnam's viewpoint, see Edward Miller (2013), *Misalliance: Ngo Dinh Diem, the United States, and the Fate of South Vietnam*. Cambridge, MA: Harvard University Press, p. 164.

31 *"to create Agricultural Centers and find land that is agreeable, to organize their own defense, to clear the land by means they already possess, and to erect houses so that gradually their families may join them"*. President Diem quoted from Joseph J. Zasloff (1962), *Rural Resettlement in Vietnam: An Agroville in Development.* Washington, DC: Agency for International Development, p. 1.

32 Roger Teulières (1962), Les paysans vietnamiens et la réforme rurale au Sud Viêt-Nam. *Cahiers d'outre-mer*, n. 57–15e année, pp. 47–84.

33 Zasloff, *op. cit.*, p. 2.

34 Republic of Viet-Nam (1956), *The Dramatic Story of Resettlement and Land Reform in the 'Rice Bowl' of the Republic of Viet-Na.* Saigon: Secretariat of State for Information, Republic of Viet-Nam, p. 23.

35 See Victor Duvernoy (1924), *Monographie de la province de Longauyen (Cochinchine).* Hanoi: Gouvernment de Cochinchine.

36 Republic of Viet-Nam (1956), *op. cit.*, p. 8.

37 Planned for 120,000 future inhabitants, 20,000 existing residents were relocated along the primary canal, sometimes too far from their existing farms, while 50,000 refugees were given three hectare plots along the secondary waterways. At 120 people/km^2 the anticipated residential density of Cái Sắn would have been considered high in relation to Gourou's density maps. Zasloff, *op. cit.*, p. 9.

112 *Liquid Territories*

38 David Biggs mentions Cái Sắn's design included an encircling dike such as those in the casiers of the Red River Delta (See Biggs, *op. cit.*, p. 162). The government's information leaflet mentions that to the north of the site, farmers cultivated "floating rice" on floodwater which would be contradictory to the idea of an outer perimeter of flood protection. In addition, considering an outer flood barrier would have been an important achievement for the government's engineers, it is not mentioned in the leaflet.

39 Trần & Nguyễn, *op. cit.*, p. 68.

40 Zasloff, *op. cit.*, pp. 1–2.

41 *Ibid.*, p. 30.

42 Vị Thanh was designed as a showcase for similar projects, with the central facilities and shopping area planned by the prominent architect Ngô Việt Thu who would later design Saigon's Independence Palace. It was nonetheless described by American officials as akin to a suburban mall, with the significant distance between the centre and the closest houses seen as equal to the mall's asphalted parking lots.

43 These two maps are published on the website of the Journal of the Institute of Vietnamese Studies without a source or a specific date. They appear to use mapping conventions common in military maps of the 1960s. Lạp Chúc Nguyễn Huy, *Chính sách nông thôn thời Việt Nam Cộng Hòa (Rural Policy: Republic of Vietnam Period).* Institute of Vietnamese Studies [online edition]. http://viethocjournal.com/2018/10/chinh-sach-nong-thon-thoi-vnch-lap-chuc-nguyen-huy/, accessed 19 February 2022.

44 Milton Osborne (1965), *Strategic Hamlets in South Viet-Nam.* Ithaca, NY: Cornell Southeast Asia Program Publications, note 25, p. 24.

45 Teulières, *op. cit.*, p. 64.

46 *"The Commune, made up of one or several hamlets (Ap) was conceived in itself to be a moral being with the right to the full exercise of civil rights, with the powers of purchase and with free access to justice".* Republic of Viet-Nam (1956), *op. cit.*, p. 22. Catton makes the argument that South Vietnam's ruling family (President Ngo Dinh Diem and his brother Ngo Dinh Nhu), which had grown up in Central Vietnam, idealized the Vietnamese village as symbolic of a "native" type of government organization that preceded colonization. Philip E. Catton (1999), Counter-Insurgency and Nation Building: The Strategic Hamlet Programme in South Vietnam, 1961–1963. *The International History Review*, v. 21, n. 4, p. 936.

47 Republic of Viet-Nam (1963), *Viet Nam's Strategic Hamlets.* Saigon: Directorate General of Information, p. 6.

48 Adapted from the Chinese military agricultural settlement *tuntian* (屯田), what Bigg's calls "garrisoned plantations", known as *đồn điền*, had preceded the establishment of new civilian villages (*dinh điền*) by Vietnamese migrants during the pre-colonial period. These outposts of imperial power were manned by soldiers or civilians trained to serve as soldiers and were organized for farming and defence. The *đồn điền* were among the various types of settlement recorded in the pre-colonial census of the region which, along with communal rice fields (*công diên*), placed up to 15% of cultivable surface areas of Nam Bộ under the direct ownership of the state.

49 James Scott (1999), *Seeing Like a State: How Certain Schemes to Improve the Human Condition Have Failed.* New Haven, CT: Yale University Press, p. 188.

50 *Ibid.*, p. 188.

51 Catton, *op. cit.*, p. 920; Republic of Viet-Nam (1963), *op. cit.*, p. 5. References to the creation of a "frontline" are mentioned numerous times in the government brochure.

52 Miller, *op. cit.*, p. 163.

53 Republic of Viet-Nam (1963), *op. cit.*, p. 22. 11 of the region's 13 administrative provinces are cumulatively listed as having a resident population of around 5 million of which about 2 million are listed as residents of strategic hamlets. Moreover, nearly half of Saigon's 1,275,000 residents also appear to be residents of these settlements.

54 Osborne, *op. cit.*, p. 5.

Shaping the Delta   113

55 The army's topographic maps are annotated in Vietnamese, French and English, indicating that the audience was not just American. Although army maps printed at 1: 25,000 were also available, their coverage of the same extents as the 1:50,000 is not certain. However, since the 1:50,000 maps do not indicate bathymetry along any waterway, it is not unreasonable to assume that maps at other scales would also have been available for consultation.

56 Osborne, *op. cit.*, p. 5.

57 Scott, *op. cit.*, p. 224.

58 Even if the provision of modern facilities was a consistent objective of all these projects, conceivably these could have been provided where inhabitants were already concentrated rather than relocating entire settlements.

59 *"Une coopération réglant les dates des actes de la vie agricole, fixant certains procédés d'exploitation, s'impose comme avantageuse à tous. La nécessité de s'unir pour l'aménagement des eaux, la construction de puits, l'entretien de certains travaux, l'accommodation d'un milieu favorable aux cultures, resserre la cohabitation. Le village est un organisme bien défini, distinct, ayant sa vie propre et une personnalité qui s'exprime dans le paysage".* Vidal de la Blache, *op. cit.*, p. 186.

6 The Metropolis' Hinterland

> *. . . the Mekong Delta and Ho Chi Minh City accounts for more than 60% of the national GDP. However, the role of the Mekong Delta, Ho Chi Minh City and Ho Chi Minh City region in the whole country is not simply reflected in the proportion of that contribution . . . investment and support for the Mekong Delta means investment in Ho Chi Minh City itself. This is an interactive and interrelated relationship.*
>
> *Closing speech by the Prime Minister*,
> Prime Minister Nguyễn Xuan Phuc, 2019

If today the "interactive" relationship between Vietnam's largest metropolis and the intensively cultivated deltaic lands to its south appear to present a *de facto* economic reality, the cartographic lines reinforcing the state's view of a delta on the Mekong River also suggest a deliberate strategy. Conspicuous for its presence on nearly all maps of the Mekong Delta, post-colonial Saigon's importance as the centre of the South Vietnam's political, military and administrative power was equalled only by its significance to the national economy. Inexorably linked to rice production, South Vietnam's economic system was described as equivalent to a "Mekong Delta economy" centred on Saigon.[1] Renamed Ho Chi Minh City (HCMC) following Vietnam's unification, the spatial and economic relationship between the city and the delta initially unfolded in *five-year plans* framed through the state ideology of "deurbanization" and the practical need to feed a growing population. The subject of separate planning efforts since the early 1990s, the articulation of an 'urban' agglomeration and a 'rural' countryside has set the scope for state investment in water and transportation infrastructure and the construction of new urban areas (NUAs) by private developers. If the notions of city and countryside are conceptually distinct in Vietnamese culture, today HCMC's metropolitan area extends over 30,000 km^2.[2] With almost a quarter of this area overlapping with the contemporary delineation of the Mekong Delta, the relationship between the city and the delta has been framed as two parts of the same economic region, adjoining planning entities or intersecting areas of government administration. The cartographic manipulation of the delta's catchment to align with the state's vision of economic growth, environmental protection and urbanization has set the stage

DOI: 10.4324/9781032706238-9

for the most recent incarnation of resettlement policies aimed at confronting the impending climate crisis.

Alternating the focus of the cartographic frame between the city and the delta, this chapter examines the Mekong Delta that emerges in relation to the urban agglomeration to its northeast. Taking into account recent plans by Dutch consultants emphasizing a hierarchy of densely populated centres, the aspirational Delta qualified in numerous planning studies and government documents contradict actual conditions on the ground and stress the spatial distinction with HCMC. If the alignment of the term delta with a particular geographic space no longer refers to a particular behaviour of the river's flows, the chapter asks what the Mekong Delta's region denotes: the city's rural hinterland, an autonomous rice-growing economy or the territory that emerges from the process of urbanization.

The Area of Agglomeration

The most extensive agglomeration in post-colonial South Vietnam, Saigon's population increased dramatically with the arrival of refugees from the north and migration from rural settlements further south.[3] With the majority of residents and services such as healthcare and education overwhelmingly concentrated in the urban centre, Saigon's infrastructure was considered inadequate for the people it was intended to serve. Confronted with deteriorating housing conditions and insufficient utility supplies, urban and regional planning became necessary to organize the new country's capital city. The goal of geographically redistributing people and activities would first entail the determination of an outer limit for Saigon. Plans from 1958 onwards calibrated the areal extent of the city in relation to the spatial requirements of a projected future population. With demographic prognoses ranging from three million residents in the Ministry of Urban Planning's *Grande Saigon* and nine million in Doxiadis Associates' *Metropolitan Saigon*, the 1967 "post-conflict" planning scenario by the Joint Development Group (JDG) addressed the city's regional dimensions. Headed by the Vietnamese economist Vũ Quốc Thúc and the TVA's former chairman David Lilienthal, the JDG eschewed the type of comprehensive planning which frequently led "to paralysis of action".[4] The JDG's report nonetheless noted the challenges of any planned expansion surrounding the urban centre. Not only did the deep clay of the deltaic soils make construction technically and financially challenging, but the "disconnection" between Saigon and surrounding areas was further augmented by the military infrastructure controlling access to the urban centre.[5] From the JDG's perspective, a meaningful relationship with the city's "rural hinterlands" did not already exist and would need to be defined by the state before Saigon and its surrounding provinces could one day constitute a "unified region".[6]

The difficulty of constituting a regional Saigon was briefly considered in a new "Metropolitan Plan" proposed in the early 1970s. Presented in a report for the USAID by the American urban planner James Bogle,[7] Saigon's metropolitan limits would place the colonial-era core at the centre of a region that included outlying villages and agricultural lands. The rationale for selecting these particular set of

116   *Liquid Territories*

limits diverged from contemporary ideas of the metropolis. The basis for delineating metropolitan regions had been described a decade earlier in Jean Gottman's analysis of settlement patterns on the East Coast of the United States.[8] For the noted French geographer Jean Gottman, the pattern of "loose urbanization" beyond city centres was less important than the administrative subdivisions which could be used to identify a statistically observable set of economic relationships between distinct agglomerations. Gottman's analysis drew on the US Census Bureau's categorization of areal units, where the designation of a *standard metropolitan area* included "urban centers together with all adjoining territory that has been demonstrated to be closely linked with the central cities".[9] Similarly, for influential planners such as Jane Jacobs, metropolitan areas indicated the observable, physical expansion of distinct cities beyond their formal, political boundaries, to coalesce "with other, formerly separate, cities".[10] Rather than indicate a particular urban form or the extent of a specific place, the configuration of the metropolis' region attempted to explicate economic, social or physical conditions that unfolded across multiple jurisdictions.

Saigon's metropolitan area (SMA) however was not configured to reflect a set of existing conditions. Almost entirely situated on the lowlands formed by the sediments of the Saigon and Vaico Rivers, the population and economic activity in Saigon's rural hinterlands were unevenly distributed. Agriculture and undeveloped land occupied almost three quarters of the SMA's total surface area, with any 'urban' characteristics limited to the compact settlement adjacent to the Saigon River. If the metropolitan boundary did not represent the limits of any specific natural or manmade phenomenon, from Bogle's perspective, a "natural metropolitan area for the city" could be constituted by combining separate administrative subdivisions closer to the urban centre. Considered adequate to house the residents of the densely populated urban areas and more than a million people already living in surrounding administrative districts, the denoted area would 'contain' projected future residents and prescribe the location of infrastructure for urban services.[11] Since district units were used for data collection by the South Vietnamese government, the area's 'content' of resources and people could be directly scrutinized using existing statistical categories. Unlike the JDG's assumption that Saigon could extend to the boundary of South Vietnam's 4th tactical Corps, Bogle's SMA terminated at Long An Province which straddled the interstitial space between the two Vaico Rivers. If the social, economic or geographic relationships necessary to distinguish the city's region were not apparent in the existing context, the cartographic construction of the SMA suggested that such a region could be created by determining where the future city "ended" and therefore where the Mekong's "rural hinterlands" began.

The Dimensions of the 'Rural'

While plans for a metropolitan Saigon were formulated only to remain on paper, the JDG's *Program for Mekong Delta Development* defined its planning area as "the sixteen southern provinces, lying south of the West Vaico River".[12] Published in 1967, the JDG's Mekong Delta excluded the sedimented lowlands within Long

An Province which were considered part of the 'fragmented' region centred on Saigon. Instead, development focused on "the long-term future of that area which is producing enormous amounts of rice".[13] A significant part of the economic system that had emerged since independence began with the Delta's farmers and revolved around Saigon's rice brokers. The sequence of processes involving paddy producers, agents, processors and intermediaries before rice – either as grain or as flour – finally reached consumers, was described in detail by the USAID analyst V.L. Elliott. According to Elliott, the entire process was effectively controlled by 10–12 firms based in Saigon that also owned the majority of mills located in the Delta provinces, processed and then shipped rice to Saigon via the system of waterways.[14] Leveraging the value of future rice production, these brokers could raise large amounts of capital to finance the import of consumer goods, thus regulating access to foreign exchange and the market information critical for setting the price of crops. For paddy farmers selling exclusively to agents within "specific, protected buying areas", this situation amounted to local monopolists setting unfavourable prices for their crops which in turn reduced the incentive to produce surpluses large enough for trade.[15] To the extent that the cultivation, processing and distribution of rice were seen as part of a single system, Elliott's reference to a "Saigon-centered Mekong Delta economy" did not just indicate the dependence of farmers on the decisions of brokers in the city. It also defined an agricultural region that included the Mekong's sedimented lowlands, parts of Cambodia, as well as cities much further north where other agricultural goods were produced (**Figure 6.1**).[16]

Confronted with levels of rice cultivation below the optimal production capacity of the existing agricultural land, the JDG proposed extending farming to areas where maps indicated soil types suitable for agriculture. In an environment in which farmers had to deal with either "too much or too little rainfall during critical periods of growth", capital-intensive drainage and flood control infrastructure would be needed to extend the growing season to allow the intensive cultivation of new rice varieties.[17] To achieve this ambitious goal, a Mekong Delta Development Authority (MDDA) would be established. Much like the TVA, within its area of operations the MDDA would investigate, plan and construct projects and programmes related to the control of water resources for the purposes of agriculture and transportation.[18] Responsibility for implementation of these projects would be Local Development Associations conceived as groupings of existing villages which would construct, operate and maintain the infrastructure needed to drain "excess" rainfall and irrigate individual farms within their area of responsibility.[19] The idea of groups of settlements collectively responsible for the management of their own infrastructure within a broader framework provided by the state strongly suggests an organization reminiscent of Powell's self-regulating, hydrologically determined *irrigation districts*. Nonetheless, where individual irrigation districts in America's West were – at least imagined as – natural subdivisions of a larger river basin, the larger catchment area of the Delta would be modified in relation to each individual Association's control of water.

The catchment area constructed by combining individual Associations is demonstrated in the conceptualization of the Delta's flood protection system. For the

118 *Liquid Territories*

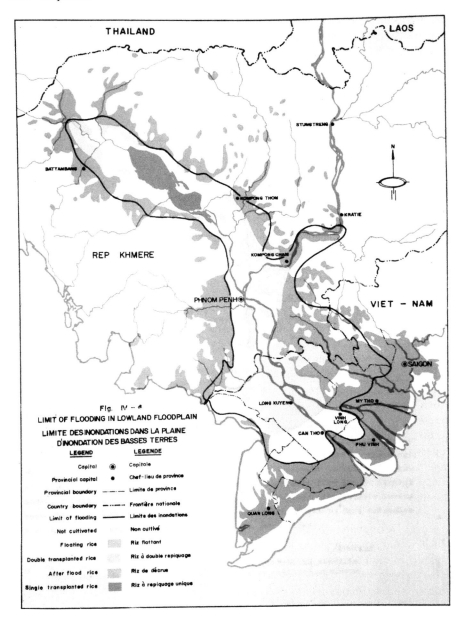

Figure 6.1 **Rice cultivation in the Mekong's lowlands.** Rice cultivation in the 1960s covered an extent that included Saigon, with areas of intensive cultivation (double annual crops) in darker grey mostly situated south of the Bassac River. Whereas these cultivation areas were not distinct regions in themselves, their economic interdependence with rice brokers in the city suggested these constituted parts of a Saigon-centred Mekong Delta economic region. Mekong Committee (1970), *Limit of Flooding in Lowland Floodplain*. [*Source:* United Nations]

The Metropolis' Hinterland   119

Mekong Committee's engineers, the delta's irrigation and flood control requirements could only be met with "substantial upstream storage and regulation" provided by the Pa Mong and Stung Treng projects.[20] Framed within the context of the Lower Mekong Basin, cost–benefit assessments showing the benefits of flood protection to downstream agricultural yields made these distant projects in Thailand and Cambodia appear advantageous to South Vietnam.[21] Using computer modelling to investigate flood defence, the JDG's hydrologists concluded that although upstream reservoirs would eventually be necessary for dry season irrigation, these projects would have negligible impact on floods in South Vietnam's Delta.[22] Although they would take decades to complete, construction of levees and by-pass canals would be sufficient to control inundations from the Mekong's overflow and heavy monsoon rains. Once completed, the state could subsequently regulate water within the extent of its sovereignty, if not independently from conditions further upstream, then at least by assuming that those conditions would remain stable over the foreseeable future. The technical capacity to direct surface water flows effectively allowed the Delta's water control network to be considered as a catchment separate from the larger basin.[23] Designed to stimulate the production of agricultural goods, the configuration of water infrastructure organized a 'rural' region calibrated to serve the country's Saigon-centred economy.[24]

Nonetheless, the northeast limit of the Delta did not indicate the southwest edge of a future 'urban' Saigon. As evidenced by the use of administrative subdivisions but also the adoption of either the East or West Vaico rivers to indicate the city's region or the Delta's limits, attempts to articulate a "natural" boundary for Saigon or the delta cannot be attributed to any single set of spatial relationships such as the concentration of building clusters, soil types or water flows. More a projection of possible future land uses than a map of existing conditions, the territory prescribed by the outlines of the Delta or of Saigon was too vast to have any immediate relevance for the lives of existing inhabitants. Without policies and infrastructure investment consistent with these geographic units, knowledge of their areal magnitude had little value except perhaps to reinforce the boundaries of existing geographic subdivisions. From an economic perspective, however, the land considered part of the Delta was significant. The mapped Delta articulated which portion of all the sedimented lowlands would need to become productive over subsequent decades to satisfy rice consumption for the Delta's and Saigon's projected population. In this sense, the relationship between 'rural' and 'urban' was one in which the former would be developed to feed the latter's prospective growth. If Saigon's "natural" extent included the areas peripheral to the colonial core, by considering the Mekong's cultivated lowlands as essential to the city's future, the 'rural' Delta outlined on the map signified the metropolis' agricultural hinterland.

The Hinterland's Metropolis

Although none of these plans were systematically implemented, the differentiation between 'urban' and 'rural' gained new significance after the victory of North Vietnam in 1975. Already by the mid-1950s, North Vietnam's government had

120   *Liquid Territories*

adopted the scientific economic and urban planning principles more common in the USSR, China and Eastern European countries.[25] Beginning with Vietnam's unification in 1976, new principles of regional and urban planning were introduced. Controlling development with consecutive policy documents called "Five-Year Plans", administrative and political power became concentrated in the capital city of Hanoi which was promoted as an example of "true Vietnamese values". In comparison, southern cities such as HCMC, were identified by economist Dao Van Tap with overcrowded conditions and a "distorted, pattern of development" reflecting Western "consumer-society".[26] Confronted with a significant reduction in rice production in the years following unification, Vietnam's socialist government sought to "deurbanize" HCMC by moving residents to new agricultural settlements and industrial towns strategically positioned to complement food production. In the belief that a rational redistribution of population was possible without the extreme violence employed by the Khmer Rouge, deurbanization aimed at instituting communal farming following the same model practiced in the North.[27] Perhaps unsurprisingly, government programmes to collectivize agricultural production met with limited success among farmers who continued to value individual production and private ownership.[28] The failure of these programmes and persistent food shortages led to a new attempt to revitalize rural resettlement with the third Five-Year Plan (1981–1985). Faced with an economic downturn, the introduction of market-oriented economic policies in 1986 brought an end to the relatively short period of socialist planning in the country's south.

A consequence of these economic reforms, HCMC's industrial output, overseas trade and foreign investment accelerated, attracting increasing numbers of migrants from villages and hamlets. Classified as 'urban' within the limits of 'inner-city' districts (*quận*) rather than the 'outer city' districts (*huyện*), the task of enumerating the city's urban population was not a clear-cut process. Despite having been resettled there by the state to cultivate food for the city's population, the 1989 census, for example, excluded residents of HCMC's green belts from the total.[29] The frequent reorganization of administrative districts, including the municipal boundaries of Vietnam's cities, made the characterization of land as *urban*, an exercise conducted on maps. As the geographer Terry McGee has pointed out, reshaping the geographic extent of Vietnamese cities by the state was intended to reflect demographic changes as – presumably – rural areas assumed "more urban characteristics".[30] Yet with urban environments specified by population thresholds in relation to a state-delineated geographic area, the Vietnamese city's cartographic limits did not necessarily enclose one specific condition that could be uniformly characterized as urban, or extend far enough to include all the interrelated activities that supported a distinct settlement's economy. Moreover, the cartographic differentiation between urban and rural was not permanent and subsequent changes to the delineation of city regions soon rendered existing spatial divisions obsolete (**Figure 6.2**). Even on the surface of maps, the differentiation between urban and rural was not a distinction between conceptual opposites. Woven together within the outlines of the city, densely clustered housing, dispersed households, agricultural land, public services and infrastructure formed geographic entities that deliberately staked out a projected condition that was yet to manifest.

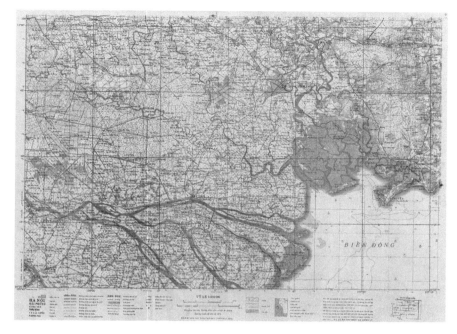

Figure 6.2 **Ho Chi Minh City's southern periphery.** Published in 1982 and based on a 1972 map by the US Defense Mapping Agency, this Vietnamese map shows the topography south and east of HCMC's urban areas. HCMC is represented by a roughly triangular area in a darker shade. Considering the differentiation between the colours indicating the condition of the ground, the area extending immediately south of the city to the Mekong's mainstream appears to be distinguished from the floodplain further west and agricultural areas to the north and the forested areas to the east (green shades). Gov. Vietnam (1982), *NC 48–7*. [*Source:* Virtual Saigon]

From this perspective, the 1993 spatial "master plans" for the country's two largest cities should be seen as attempts to consolidate the 'content' encompassed within the fluid outlines of administrative subdivisions. For the capital Hanoi, the master plan was prepared by architects and engineers as an "urban design" based on centralized decision-making.[31] For HCMC on the other hand, the plan granted the city's government the right to allocate land for export processing zones and for the development of New Urban Areas (NUAs) by private developers. HCMC's master plan was nonetheless considered ineffective, not least because the population projections its planners adopted were soon superseded.[32] Especially beyond the boundaries of designated Urban Areas, the state's limited appetite to enforce planning regulations coupled with the widespread practice for self-organized housing structured a 'disorderly' settlement pattern. Although nominally classified as 'rural', the area surrounding HCMC was not exclusively agricultural. Clustered along transportation corridors heading north to Bien Hoa and south towards the major settlements in the Mekong Delta, commercial and small-scale manufacturing

122 *Liquid Territories*

activities were located alongside houses, orchards and rice paddy. But the apparent 'sprawl'-like unplanned development in these zones was not solely a result of spontaneous bottom-up processes. Used as a tool by the state to control development, 'satellite' NUAs on the periphery of HCMC established new residential neighbourhoods within driving distance of the existing urban centre making the land surrounding interstitial transport routes valuable for some types of activities. Moreover, in the early 2000s new privately operated manufacturing clusters began to be constructed within the marshland drained by the Xang Canal, west of the centre. Located along the administrative boundary between HCMC and Long An Province, these industrial areas benefited from their proximity to the city while remaining within the planning jurisdiction of Long An's provincial government.[33] Spatially separated from the city's built areas by flooded agricultural lands, the relatively new industrial zones appeared to reinforce the model of a geographically distributed regional economy, with a spatially distinct HCMC in the centre.

Even as the new master plan for HCMC was approved by the city's government, the first regional plan for the Delta under conditions of national economic growth was published in 1993. With the opportunity for Vietnam's government to access international funding for water infrastructure from the UN and World Bank, a Dutch consortium – that included Vietnamese engineers and planners – formulated the "first multi-purpose and multi-sector planning document for the delta".[34] The plan reframed the Mekong Delta within the basin-wide hydrological regime arguing that full flood protection was inadvisable due to the adverse effects on Cambodia's lowlands. Such concern for the environmental impact of projects funded through multilateral organizations had been carefully outlined six years earlier in a UN report entitled *Our Common Future*. Introducing the new notion of "sustainable development" of shared resources in a wider "global commons", the report became an important point of reference for the new plan.[35] Apart from proposals for water infrastructure and agricultural production, the plan also introduced principles of environmental management and conservation that were novel concepts in Vietnam's typically goal-oriented planning discussions. As some of the plan's proposals were gradually constructed over the following decade, a precedent was established for transferring a specific type of technical knowledge to Vietnam. If the areal magnitude of the Delta had changed little from previous iterations, the coordinated planning of water resources was perceived to produce greater value than the separate planning of the same area's individual parts. Divided into distinct types of sedimented ground each requiring a different approach in their planning, the idea that these terrains could be controlled collectively allowed the Delta to be perceived as a single geographic unit with a specific surface area positioned immediately south of HCMC.

The state's ability to produce and implement master plans for an entire region proved effective in attracting foreign investment and meeting development targets. Yet the situation on the ground was far from regulated. Following the Dutch plan, the construction of flood-protected irrigation and drainage schemes in the Delta had unforeseen and increasingly observable adverse impacts on biodiversity, the distribution of floodwater and river bank erosion. Simultaneously, the commodification of land accelerated by economic reforms and foreign investment required that planning institutions formulate strict land use controls.[36] In response, major cities, including the Mekong Delta's largest urban area Cần Thơ, were given special status and directly administered by the central government following the paradigm of Chinese state planning. The dominance of urban centres in the national planning hierarchy is best illustrated in the adoption of metropolitan designations for Hanoi and HCMC (**Figure 6.3**). Approved in government decrees after 2008, the metropolitan conceptualization of these cities was a shift from previous policies emphasizing the containment of urban growth and the development of smaller settlements.[37] For HCMC, the metropolitan area encompassed more than 30 km^2, recentring around 20 km^2 of predominantly agricultural land on the tree-shaded boulevards of colonial Saigon. Redefining the hierarchy between existing settlements, the metropolitan plan called for urban and industrial development to be consolidated within 30 kilometres of the city centre and "counter-balanced" by developing existing urban centres in adjacent provinces. Even though these centres have been described as little more than "provincial crossroad towns", in the plan these are imagined as critical components of a regional spatial structure, which extends radially outwards from the city along specific transportation routes.[38] Adopting specific targets for the conversion of 'rural' land into other land uses, the geographic space classified as "urban" equates to the sum of the city's projected economic needs.[39]

As with other planning endeavours on this scale, however, the metropolitan plan does not appear to propose a new spatial configuration. Instead, it consolidates multiple existing plans at different scales and administrative hierarchies such as provinces and districts which produce their own five-year plans. In the discourse of Southeast Asia's urbanization, the geographic area reconfigured by the imposition of this hierarchy has sometimes been understood as a "Mega Urban Region" (MUR). Seen through the MUR model, various activities and land uses that can be found as far away as 200 kilometres from the city core are conceived to be part of the same system of economic, if not social, relationships.[40] If the lower-density rice-growing areas in the floodplain are included in HCMC's metropolitan area, their cohesion into an MUR is not because these particular farms contribute more than other rice-growing areas to the city's economy but because they are located within the designated metropolitan region. Given that historically HCMC has been the only major city in Vietnam's south, the MUR is not observable in the phenomenon of "formerly separate cities" merging into a singular metropolis, but rather in the geographical imagination of policy-makers that relates distance from the city centre with the control of economic activity.[41]

Planning the Mekong's Delta

In relation to the Mekong Delta, what metropolis is being constructed on the map is especially important. The most recently completed strategic planning effort for the Mekong Delta however appears to eschew the regional centrality of HCMC. Prepared in 2013 by a team led by the Dutch engineering consultancy Royal Haskoning, the *Mekong Delta Plan* (MDP) was the result of a concerted effort by the Netherlands' government to sell Dutch water management as a global water

124 *Liquid Territories*

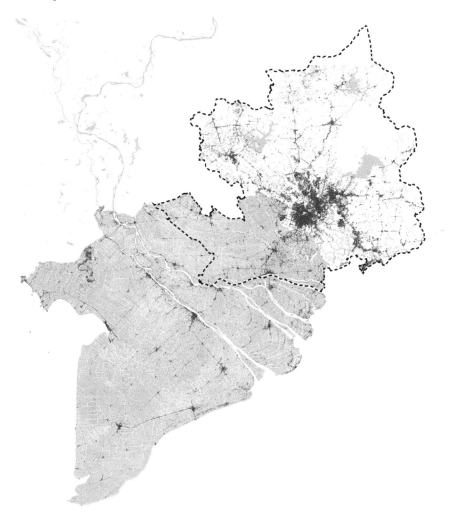

Figure 6.3 **HCMC metropolitan region.** The map depicts the land covered by manmade structures such as infrastructure and buildings (dark grey) in relation to the metropolitan boundary (dotted line) and the Mekong Delta region (grey shaded surface). From the land cover arrangement it is possible to discern the location of concentrated building clusters and buildings arranged along the linear routes of roads and waterways. The majority of the land included within the provincial outlines used to delineate the metropolitan area is primarily agricultural. [*Source:* Author]

solution.[42] In many ways similar to America's marketing of the TVA after the Second World War, the MDP was an opportunity for the Dutch government to "export" the cumulative technical knowledge from decades of water infrastructure planning to Vietnam.[43] To market Dutch engineering expertise as the global paradigm of best practices in water management, the Netherlands as a whole was presented as a "safe and liveable delta".[44] Despite the inclusion of riparian lands unrelated to the accretion of sediment deposits in the context of the Netherlands, the value of the Dutch approach to Vietnam's lowland economy was accentuated in an alarming report prepared by the engineering consultancy Deltares.[45] Highlighting that the Mekong Delta is almost equal in surface area to the Netherlands, the report presented the impact from rising sea levels and inundation for the Mekong Delta's agricultural economy, noting that the 1993 Dutch scheme would be ineffective in meeting the challenges of climate change. The implication that a new plan was now necessary also suggested that Dutch delta planning approaches conceived in the European setting and underpinned by decades of public consultation and community cooperation in the context of the Netherlands would be the most appropriate model for future development in south Vietnam's monsoon environment.[46]

Aiming to develop the Delta into a "safe, prosperous and sustainable region", the Dutch planning process sought to shift focus from enumerated economic objectives to building consensus around long-term measures involving new infrastructure and the diversification of agricultural crops.[47] Adhering to the Adaptive Delta Management approach, the preparation of alternative development scenarios was supported by the subdivision of the Delta into distinct "hydrological zones" (**Figure 6.4**). Grouping parts of the floodplain within Vietnam into an "Upper Delta" and coastal areas affected by tides and salinization into a "Coastal Delta", Dutch planners delineated a new "Middle Delta" encompassing the industrial periphery of HCMC and the densely populated 'corridor' of unplanned activities situated along the highway connecting to Cần Thơ. Unlike the upper and coastal delta which appeared to signify specific behaviours of water, the Middle Delta grouped multiple hydrological regimes, causes and problems into one zone. The significance of the catchment framed by the Middle Delta surfaced in the MDP's future development scenarios. According to one of the four development trajectories, the current concentration of industrial activities along the north-south highway was anticipated to evolve into "an industrialised metropolis in a highly fertile and flood-prone area and a rural hinterland struggling to keep up pace".[48] Conflating a broadly conceived urban "metropolis" with the hydrological maps illustrating different development scenarios, the plan drew attention to existing urban centres rather than the terrain. Presented with the choice, Vietnamese decision-makers showed their preference for the more geographically distributed "agro-industrial" scenario that appeared to highlight the importance of provincial administrative centres. In this development trajectory, Cần Thơ would eventually emerge as a complementary second "node" to HCMC (**Figure 6.5**). Given the city's special status within Vietnam's structure of centrally administered cities, Cần Thơ would function as the 'capital' of the Mekong Delta region to become the centre for a network of urban areas connected by road infrastructure. On the MDP maps, the extent occupied by the Delta's urban network is deliberately differentiated from HCMC.[49] However, with emphasis given to creating an "agro-business", the water-related planning which made Dutch expertise relevant to Vietnam in the first place was given far less attention than socioeconomic "adaptation". As a result of the focus on agriculture, the

126 *Liquid Territories*

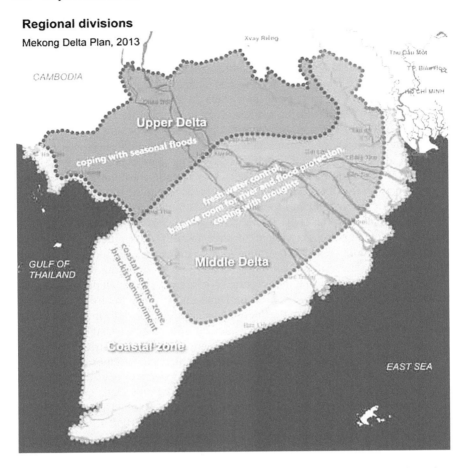

Figure 6.4 **Hydrology of the urban Delta.** The map shows the Mekong Delta Plan's three "hydrological zones". These regions are underpinned by generalized problems (coping with flooding or coastal defence) rather than the specific condition of the ground or the action of water. The Middle Delta's delineation corresponds with the "corridor" of urbanization along the highway from HCMC to Cần Thơ.
[*Source:* Mekong Delta Plan, 2013]

more general problems of fresh water supply, subsidence and salinization are seen through the lens of cultivation, and therefore problems of policy. Delivered as a reference document for revising spatial planning rather than as a set technical recommendations surrounding water management, the Delta presented in the MDP was geographically if not functionally distinct from HCMC.

Since the MDP's publication, the planning principles which emerged from the process have been incorporated into legislation and the World Bank-financed project initiated in 2016. The three "hydrological" zones expressed in the MDP became four zones in World Bank documents and the basis for considering long-term

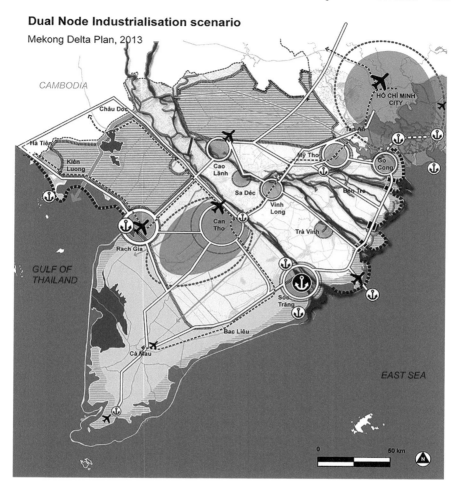

Figure 6.5 **Planning scenarios for the Mekong Delta Plan.** Seeking to repair the undesirable conditions identified with the "corridor" development outlined by the Middle Delta, this map of the "dual-node" scenario shows the preferred planning direction, where Cần Thơ is presented as a complementary urban centre to HCMC. At the geographic centre of the Mekong Delta, Cần Thơ dominates a hierarchy of smaller centres. The area surrounding the Delta's "capital" city appears as an agricultural "hinterland", distinct from adjacent ground conditions. [*Source:* Mekong Delta Plan, 2013]

"sustainable" planning interventions. In legislation, the four hydrological zones became six "agroecological zones" similar to those already identified in the 1960s, with government resolutions setting out these zones as the new geographic references for agricultural development and industrial investment.[50] These have been accompanied by policy statements to "develop the morphology of rural residential space" according to the characteristics of each sub-region.[51] Either raised on

128   *Liquid Territories*

stilts, grounded on the soil or floating above the tidal plain depending on their location, encouraging local people to live on water or to move to higher elevations during the flood season recalls older government policies for "living with the flood". Initiated in the 1990s to reflect the state's inability to control floods with infrastructure, the hands-off approach to "living with the flood" was substantially revised to "protect urban areas".[52] In the new policy documents, the reorganization of settlement patterns will aim for "compact" population clusters and eliminate "continuous urbanization in deep floodplains" as well as "between deltaic and coastal" areas.[53] Moreover, calls to limit construction in areas adjacent to rivers, canals and high-risk areas appear to draw inspiration from the regulatory context of the Netherlands where certain land uses can be excluded from riparian zones to make "room for the river".[54] In the context of the delta's settlement however, such policies appear contradictory. Although residents' preference for waterfront housing is gradually diminishing – especially closer to larger towns – many of the Delta's inhabitants continue to reside in close proximity to the continuous network of waterways.[55] Reducing the risks associated with floods or the inadequate water supply for rice cultivation by reorganizing settlement, the 'sustainable' Delta emerging from these planning endeavours does not so much ignore the context, as seek to transform current conditions to conform to a pan-delta model of urbanization applicable anywhere.

Arguably government resolutions only define the broad policy direction rather than providing a plan for physical change. However, the discrepancy between the government's approach and the conditions where millions of people live suggests an almost abstract preoccupation with settlement morphology framed on the scale of the entire region. In this conceptualization, what constitutes the *urban* is just as important as what constitutes the region. The view that urbanization is a major component of economic development has been embraced by Vietnam's government in an attempt to frame economic regions such as the Mekong Delta as competitive 'global spaces' geared towards attracting investment.[56] Despite the obvious contradictions inherent in this approach, such ideas are supported by technical experts based in Europe. According to the most recent World Bank-funded plan for the Mekong Delta (also prepared by Royal Haskoning), the government will "further develop the system of existing urban areas".[57] But with their expansion deliberately constrained, urban areas will be developed with support from new integrated agro-industrial hubs.[58] Restrictions on building outside a designated 'urban area' will concentrate high-value economic production inside these controlled development zones reinforcing the differentiation with the surrounding countryside, perhaps inadvertently recalling failed proposals for agro-industrial centres already proposed in the 1980s. Rather than the threat to national security from the 1960s or the ideologically driven deurbanization of the post-unification period, the promotion of compact settlements is cast as supporting "sustainability", providing an answer to the impending impact of climate change and resource depletion. In its current iteration, population concentration would conceivably allow planners to focus flood protection infrastructure on particular settlements rather than the entire network of waterway houses. To imagine such operations affecting the entire region however appears to ignore the fact that market forces have been far more influential than state planning in shaping the urban environment of a major city such as HCMC, let alone the multiple urban and rural areas encompassed by the Mekong Delta.[59] Evaluated in relation to the resettlement of thousands of people into "compact" urban areas, such an endeavour would take decades to achieve and its impact on flood risk reduction or agricultural production would most likely require a critical mass to be implemented and monitored before the benefits could be validated and the inevitable adverse impacts recorded. Perhaps deliberately, these plans and policies are more theoretical than realistic in that they project an idealized climate-resilient and sustainable territory onto the Delta. Shaped by the overlap of best-practice regulations and enumerated key performance indicators generated on spreadsheets, the catchment that emerges in these fictional plans resembles the service area of urban transit stations rather than an area of water.

Conclusion

Outlining the conceptual contradictions of defining a particular area as *urban* in relation to Southeast Asia's rice-growing regions, Stephen Cairns has framed the explanation of this unplanned configuration of diverse activities by suggesting the agency of a "pre-existing rurality".[60] Yet while this would imply that a 'rural rationality' would be a better way to understand the pattern of land uses observable on maps and aerial imagery, the cartographic differentiation of land as either *urban* or *rural* is not always intended to represent an existing condition. From the perspective of the state, land classified as urban has a higher value for the region's economy than agricultural areas. Although in many ways speculative, the controlled conversion of rural into urban land uses signals that, despite the difficulty of articulating the difference between urban and rural in areas where farms adjoin industrial parks or the residents of agricultural settlements receive an income from non-farming activities, non-city settlement conditions are, in the end, "urban in intent or destiny".[61] The inclusion of parts of the Mekong Delta into HCMC's metropolitan designation but also the identification of the urbanized Middle Delta in Dutch plans are part of a deliberate effort to delineate such an urban condition, even if the majority of residents continue to be involved in the cultivation of rice or other crops.[62] Evident in the MDP, the Delta formed on the planners' maps is organized according to the presence of distinct urban centres of various magnitudes. The amplification of the importance of existing urban areas and their collective organization into a network of agro-industrial production centres suggests that urbanization is not just a process that arises through the unplanned activities but also a purposeful strategy to redefine the Delta's relationship with the country's economy. In this equation the management of water continues to be critical for the state and local people. But it is clear that even though the total surface area has remained the same, what the delineation of the Mekong Delta denotes today is fundamentally different from a hydrological catchment within the extents of Vietnam's sovereignty. The Delta's significance as the geographic unit for resolving problems

130 *Liquid Territories*

through planning now equally aligns with social and economic considerations as much as a group of the river's flows. As such, it is tempting to think of the Mekong Delta presented on maps as the anthropocentric manifestation of a pre-existing hydrological condition, modified by calibrating the extent of the *rural* with the proposed hierarchy of flood-protected urban centres that complement HCMC's. From an extent created by sediment deposits to the projected area of control over land, the delineation of the Delta on maps suggests the construction of a new geography based less on the river's surface flows as on an anticipated condition of settlement that may never emerge.

Notes

1 Elliott's definition of the Mekong Delta encompasses the geographic extent of colonial Cochinchina but also parts of Cambodia where transplant rice was grown. The study for the USAID presented the economic system of this region from rice paddy to retailer in detail. V.L. Elliott (1973), *Development Problems in Viet Nam: A Discussion and Definition of the South Viet Nam (Mekong Delta) Economic Region*. Washington, DC: USAID, p. 4.
2 Socialist Republic of Vietnam (2008), *Decision No. 589/QD-TTg Dated May 20, 2008 of the Prime Minister Approving the Master Plan on Construction of the Ho Chi Minh City Region up to 2020, with a Vision Toward 2050*. Hanoi: Government of Vietnam, pp. 1–4.
3 The built area identified as Saigon was the home of around a million residents by the end of WW2, to which around 700,000 people were added during the Indochina War. Du Huynh (2015), The Misuse of Urban Planning in Ho Chi Minh City. *Habitat International*, n. 48, p. 12.
4 Joint Development Group (1969), *The Postwar Development of the Republic of Vietnam: Policies and Programs, v. 1*. Saigon & New York: Postwar Planning Group & Development and Resources Corporation, p. 505.
5 *Ibid.*, p. 499.
6 *ibid.*
7 Bogle's earlier planning work in Southeast Asia had seen him involved in the Jengka Triangle for the Federal Land Development Authority in peninsular Malaysia. In regional plans which included the resettlement of farmers in relation to vast new palm tree plantations, the Jengka Triangle included 23 new settlement centres dispersed over 400 km².
8 Jean Gottmann (1964), *Megalopolis: The Urbanized Northeastern Seaboard of the United States*. Cambridge, MA: The MIT Press, p. 21.
9 Bureau of the Census (1950), *Population of Standard Metropolitan Areas: April 1, 1950, Census of Population, Preliminary Counts*. Series PC-3, n. 3. Washington, DC: US Department of Commerce, p. 1.
10 "Metropolitan Area – Economically, it means the same as 'city'. Politically, it means a city that has physically expanded beyond its formal boundaries, in the process engulfing former towns and, in some instances, coalescing with other, formerly separate, cities". Jane Jacobs (1969), *The Economy of Cities*. New York: Random House, p. 258, quoted in J.E. Bogle, Republic of Vietnam, Daniel Mann Johnson & Mendenhall (DMJM) & William C. Rasmussen and Associates (1972), *Dialectics of Urban Proposals for the Saigon Metropolitan Area*. Washington, DC: United States Agency for International Development (USAID), p. 22.
11 *Ibid.*, p. 22.
12 Joint Development Group, *op. cit.*, p. 505.

The Metropolis' Hinterland   131

13 Quote attributed to David Lilienthal. Franklin Huddle (1972), *The Mekong Project: Opportunities and Problems of Regionalism*. Science, Technology, and American Diplomacy. Washington, DC: U.S. Government Printing Office, p. 47.
14 Elliott, *op. cit.*, p. 8.
15 Elliott makes the point that another disincentive for farmers to produce surpluses was Viet Minh "taxation" in areas not controlled by government forces.
16 Elliott mentions the highland towns of Dalat and Bao Loc where vegetables and tea were the main products. Elliott, *op. cit.*, p. 1.
17 Joint Development Group, *op. cit.*, p. 520.
18 *Ibid.*, p. 526.
19 *Ibid.*, p. 525.
20 Committee for Coordination of Investigations of the Lower Mekong Basin (1970), *Report on Indicative Basin Plan: A Proposed Framework for the Development of Water and Related Resources of the Lower Mekong Basin (E/CN.ll/WRD/MKG/L.340)*. Bangkok: United Nations, pp. I–15.
21 Cost–benefit calculations for individual projects were included in the Committee's Basin Plan. As regards to the benefits of flood protection, these were calculated on the basis that increased agricultural production would offset the damage caused. *Ibid.*, pp. IV–63.
22 "The analyses revealed that none of the assumed upstream reservoir capacities will result in full control of flooding in the Delta, although the larger amounts would theoretically permit a reduction in the magnitude of Delta flood protection works. These larger amounts, however, are probably at the upper limits of possible development at the two sites". *ibid.*
23 The divergence in the different plans for water was partially reconciled in a new study commissioned by the Committee from a team of Dutch engineers which upheld the JDG's conclusions on the value of upstream dams for flooding.
24 Compared to 1960, the number of residents living in South Vietnam's "urban" areas had doubled to around 6.3 million by 1970. Of the 10 largest urban areas in the country, 3 were situated in the Mekong Delta. Nonetheless their combined population totalled to around 5% of the Delta area's estimated 6 million residents. See Bogle *et al*, *op. cit.*, p. 68; and Joint Development Group, *op. cit.*, p. 508.
25 William Logan (2009), Hanoi, Vietnam. *City*, v. 13, n. 1, p. 88.
26 Dao Van Tap (1980), On the Transformation and New Distribution of Population Centres in the Socialist Republic of Vietnam. *International Journal of Urban and Regional Research*, v. 4, p. 504.
27 For the country's fertile delta regions, the socialist government's "agro-industrial" strategy was planned on the basis of geographic units called New Economic Zones (NEZ). Organized into districts encompassing up to 120 km^2 and reaching 150,000 residents, NEZs were located on both virgin and fallow land in marginal parts of the Mekong Delta. Within these administrative units, existing hamlets would be regrouped into agricultural communities of up to 20,000 inhabitants, while new villages would be constructed for every 5,000 persons resettled from urban areas. *Ibid.*, p. 54.
28 The differences between villages in the North and the South have been examined by Tran & Nguyen, identifying the former with a 'corporate' and the latter with an 'open' structure. Following unification, party leaders strongly criticized villagers in the South for 'individual farming', 'fragmented landholding', 'unequal development' and the influence of capitalism. See Trung Dang (2018), *Vietnam's Post-1975 Agrarian Reforms: How Local Politics Derailed Socialist Agriculture in Southern Vietnam*. ANU Press, pp. 32–43. See also Tran & Nguyen, *op. cit.*, p. 68.
29 Judith Banister (1993), *Vietnam Population Dynamics and Prospects*. Institute of East Asian Studies. Berkeley, CA: University of California, pp. 40, 54.
30 Terry McGee (2009), Interrogating the Production of Urban Space in China and Vietnam Under Market Socialism. *Asia Pacific Viewpoint*, v. 50, n. 2, p. 238.
31 Logan, *op. cit.*, p. 88.

132 *Liquid Territories*

32 According to Du, the 1993 plan was intended to serve five million people until the year 2010 – a number that would avoid high population density and cater for security and defense concerns. However, even by the end of 1990s, population estimates were already higher and by 2010 had reached around 7.4 million or 9.6 million if the 'floating' migrant population was included. Du, *op. cit.*, p. 14.

33 World Bank data from 2011 show that between 1999 and 2009, 22 new industrial zones were created in Long An Province, by far the highest number nationally. World Bank (2011), *Vietnam Urbanization Review: Technical Assistance Report*. Hanoi: World Bank, p. 49.

34 Although the rate of annual increase in rice production accelerated after economic liberalization, planning of water resources in the Delta remained under the purview of what Simon Benedikter describes as self-serving "elite networks" of engineers from North Vietnam. As such, the engagement of Dutch consultants to plan the Delta broke from an established planning system, most likely due to the availability of funds available through multilateral institutions. Simon Benedikter (2014), Extending the Hydraulic Paradigm: Reunification, State Consolidation, and Water Control in the Vietnamese Mekong Delta After 1975. *Southeast Asian Studies*, v. 3, n. 3, pp. 579–580.

35 M.F. Van Staveren, J.P.M. van Tatenhove & J.F. Warner (2018), The Tenth Dragon: Controlled Seasonal Flooding in Long-Term Policy Plans for the Vietnamese Mekong Delta. *Journal of Environmental Policy & Planning*, v. 20, n. 3, p. 274.

36 T.H.L. Pham (2010), The Legislative Framework for Urban Design and Planning in Vietnam. In K. Shannon, B. De Meulder, D. Derden, T.H.L. Pham & D.T. Pho (eds.), *Urban Planning & Design in an Era of Dynamic Development Innovative and Relevant Practices for Vietnam*. Hanoi: Ministry of Construction, pp. 19–21.

37 World Bank, *op. cit.*, p. 3.

38 Erik Harms (2019), Megalopolitan Megalomania: Ho Chi Minh City, Vietnam's Southeastern Region and the Speculative Growth Machine. *International Planning Studies*, v. 24, n. 1, p. 60.

39 With a 2050 horizon, projected areas for the city's key economic land uses total 340,000 hectares (240,000 hectares for urban construction and 70,000 hectares for industrial uses). In the updated decree from 2017, the same quota for "urban" construction is expected to be fulfilled by 2030. Socialist Republic of Vietnam, *op. cit.*, p. 2.

40 For HCMC, in particular, see D.N. Anh (2008), The Mega-Urban Transformations of HCMC in the Era of Doi Moi Renovation. In G.W. Jones & M. Douglas (eds.), *Mega-Urban Regions in Pacific Asia: Urban Dynamics in a Global Era*. Singapore: National University of Singapore Press, pp. 196–197. See, for example, the "Zonal Model of Southeast Asian Mega-Urban Region C2000", which places the urban core as the conceptual centre of a collection of different land uses including a peripheral 'desakota' zone 150 kilometres wide. See T. McGee & I. Shaharudin (2016), Reimagining the "Peri-Urban" in the Mega-Urban Regions of Southeast Asia. In B. Maheshwari, B. Thoradeniya & V.P. Singh (eds.), *Balanced Urban Development: Options and Strategies for Liveable Cities*. Water Science and Technology Library, v. 72. Cham: Springer, pp. 502–503.

41 Harms, *op. cit.*, p. 55.

42 N. Laeni, M.A. van den Brink, E.M. Trell & E.J.M.M. Arts (2021), Going Dutch in the Mekong Delta: A Framing Perspective on Water Policy Translation. *Journal of Environmental Policy & Planning*, v. 23, n. 1, p. 17. For Dutch Delta practices as an "international brand" see Ellen Minkman & Arwin van Buuren (2019), Branding in Policy Translation: How the Dutch Delta Approach Became an International Brand. *Environmental Science and Policy*, n. 96.

43 S. Hasan, J. Evers, A. Zegwaard & M. Zwarteveen (2019), Making Waves in the Mekong Delta: Recognizing the Work and the Actors Behind the Transfer of Dutch Delta Planning Expertise. *Journal of Environmental Planning and Management*, v. 62, n. 9, p. 1584.

44 *Ibid.*

The Metropolis' Hinterland 133

45 The particular areas of concern for the Dutch Delta Programme are laid out in a map. These include the riparian lands of the Maas River until the international boundary which has little to do with the sedimented lowlands indicated by the geographic term "delta". The Delta Commission (2008), *Working Together with Water, Findings of the Deltacommissie 2008*, p. 16.

46 *Ibid.*

47 Government of the Netherlands & Government of Vietnam (2013), *Mekong Delta Plan.* Consortium Royal Haskoning DHV, WUR, Deltares, Rebel, p. 46.

48 *Ibid.*, p. 39. Except for generalized warnings that particular scenarios would lead to unnecessarily high costs to achieve adequate water supply, the issue of water appears to be considered as the background for economic planning.

49 Maps and government decrees present the Mekong Delta as equivalent to the limits of provincial administrative units. On the MDP maps, the boundary of the Delta with HCMC does not follow the outline of Long An Province and shows the city extending to the interstitial area between the two Vaico rivers.

50 Socialist Republic of Vietnam (2018), *Decision No. 68/QD-TTg: On Approving the Revision of the Construction Plan of the Mekong Delta Region by 2030 with Vision Towards 2050*. Hanoi: Govt. of Vietnam, p. 3.

51 "Develop the morphology of rural residential space according to the characteristics of each sub-region: In the deeply flooded sub-region, form concentrated population clusters with the form of houses on piles; in the sub-region in the middle of the delta, to develop concentrated residential areas towards modernization and increase in density; In the coastal sub-region, concentrated residential areas will be formed in the form of clusters of floating projects associated with the mangrove landscape and aquaculture space". *(Phát triển hình thái không gian dân cư nông thôn theo đặc trưng của từng tiểu vùng: Tại tiểu vùng ngập sâu, hình thành các cụm dân cư tập trung với hình thái nhà trên cọc; tại tiểu vùng giữa đồng bằng phát triển các khu dân cư tập trung theo hướng hiện đại hóa và tăng mật độ; tại tiểu vùng ven biển hình thành các khu dân cư tập trung theo hình thức các cụm công trình nổi gắn kết với cảnh quan rừng ngập mặn và không gian nuôi trồng thủy hải sản.) ibid.*, p. 7.

52 Chu Thai Hoanh, Diana Suhardiman & Le Tuan Anh (2014), Irrigation Development in the Vietnamese Mekong Delta: Towards Polycentric Water Governance? *International Journal of Water Governance*, v. 2, p. 74.

53 "limiting large-scale concentrated urban development and expansion; do not form urbanized areas, continuous urbanization bands in deeply flooded areas, between plains and coastal areas". *(... hạn chế mở rộng, phát triển đô thị tập trung quy mô lớn và trên diện rộng; không hình thành các vùng đô thị hóa, các dải đô thị hóa liên tục tại các khu vực ngập sâu, giữa đồng bằng và ven biển.)* Socialist Republic of Vietnam, *op. cit.*, p. 3.

54 Initiated in 2007 by the Government of the Netherlands, *Room for the River* (Ruimte voor de Rivie) was an infrastucture programme to increase the capacity of the country's floodplains to retain water. As a result, further development in certain areas would be limited. The proposed *Room for the River* concept in relation to the Mekong Delta was presented by Deltares researcher Marcel Marchand using the interstitial area between the Mekong and Bassac Rivers to retain floodwater. See M. Marchand, D. Pham & T. Le (2014), Mekong Delta: Living with Water, But for How Long? *Built Environment*, v. 40, n. 2, pp. 230–243.

55 Thi Hong Hanh Vu & Viet Duong (2018), *Morphology of Water-Based Housing in Mekong Delta, Vietnam*. MATEC Web of Conferences, n. 193, 04005, p. 2.

56 McGee, *op. cit.*, pp. 236, 242.

57 Rather than quoting directly, the text of the consultancy report appears to imitate the language in government decrees. Royal Haskoning & Deutsche Gesellschaft fur Internationale Zusammenarbeit (GIZ) (2020), *Mekong Delta Integrated Regional Plan MDIRP-RHD-D4-XX-RP-Z-0007*, p. 153.

58 *Ibid.*

134 *Liquid Territories*

59 Du, *op. cit.*, p. 18.
60 Stephen Cairns (2018), Debilitating City-Centricity. In Rita Padawangi (ed.), *Routledge Handbook of Urbanization in Southeast Asia*. Abingdon, Oxon & New York, NY: Routledge, p. 120.
61 *Ibid.*, p. 116. Cairns argues for the fallacy of assuming Southeast Asia's high-density rice-growing areas as a rural condition whose inevitable outcome is to become "urban". Based on the observation of the mix of land uses in areas far outside HCMC's densely populated centre, it is indeed difficult to imagine such a transition, if the designation "urban" is intended to indicate a city-like environment rather than just sporadic clusters of non-agricultural activities.
62 Based on the results of the 2019 census, 1, 417, 050 people out of Long An's 1, 688, 547 total population continue to be classified as residents of "rural" areas. See General Statistics Office (2020), *Completed Results of the 2019 Viet Nam Population and Housing Census*. Hanoi: Statistical Publishing House, p. 36.

Part C

Floodplain

Divided into seasons of heavy rainfall (wet) and intense sunshine (dry), the tropical year in Southeast Asia alternates between periods of abundant water and drought. When the accumulated wet season rains cause rivers to overflow beyond their cartographically prescribed limits, a particular extent of ground can be submerged for weeks or even months. Referred to as 'floodplains', the geographic spaces where water briefly erases most terrestrial landmarks can be technically understood as any "land area susceptible to being inundated by water from any source".[1] In the Mekong's lowlands, floods are not only the result of the river's annual pulse but also the outcome of floodwaters distributed by manmade waterways, extreme local precipitation events and, closer to the coast, by high tides during storms.[2] If a single flood's occurrence cannot be assigned to only one of these factors, when drawn on a map, this seasonal process occupies an area that suggests a specific geographic space. Cartographically delineated, the allusion to a 'stable' ground onto which water periodically invades contradicts not only the interannual variability of inundated zones but also the succession of ground conditions which range from waterlogged to patches of dryness. The ambiguity inherent in the conceptualization of the flood as a specific space and an event is reflected in the way the extent of inundation is recorded. In a phenomenon unique to the Mekong's geography, a proportion of the wet season river water reaching Cambodia is detained in a topographic 'bowl' centred on Tonle Sap, thereby increasing the lake's surface area sixfold.[3] Of the vast volumes of floodwater that continue flowing southwards along the mainstream, those overflowing south and west of the river can reach as far as the coast of the Gulf of Thailand. To the mainstream's east and north however they are retained within a shallow geological depression where they merge with the flows of the Vaico River submerging a terrestrial surface nearly 10,000 km² that belongs to different river basins. In places a perennial marsh and in others a productive agricultural ground, this submerged area is known today as Đồng Tháp Mười by the Vietnamese and has been historically associated with the different dangers that stem from the impact of inundation. Also known as the *Plaine des Joncs* or *Plain of Reeds* by Europeans and Americans, the cartographic delineation of this specific section of the entire floodplain has been the subject of maps and plans seeking to define where water is absent or present.

DOI: 10.4324/9781032706238-10

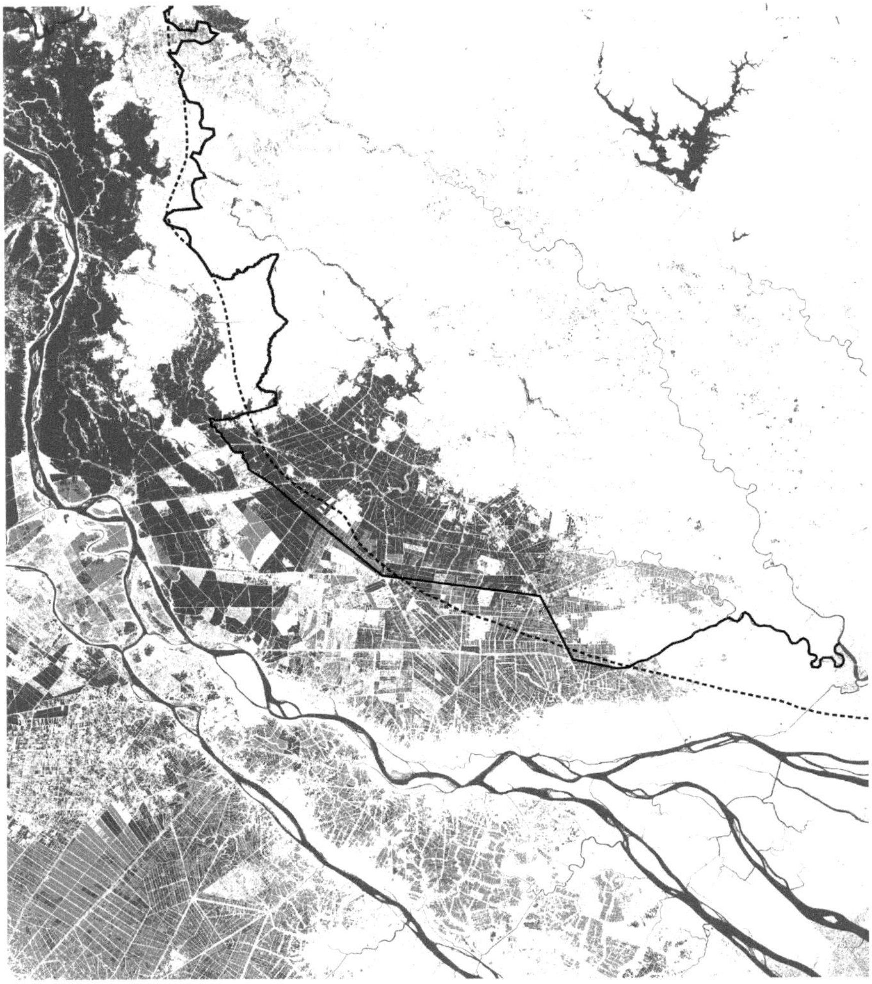

136 *Liquid Territories*

Figure C.1 **The floodplain's catchments.** The map shows satellite-detected surface water in the Plain of Reeds during two key moments of annual flood – the middle of the wet season in late August 2018 (black) and the end of the wet season in early November 2017 (grey). The Mekong's basin (black dashed line) and the catchment area delineated by the units of water management (black line) appear to divide the flooded areas into two parts. The majority of the "dry" areas produced by dikes is visibly concentrated south of the catchment/basin limit. [*Source:* Author]

If today, infrastructure has significantly altered the way floodwater is diverted in comparison to the 1970s, the question of what the outline of the floodplain represents remains relevant, especially as the total volume of floodwater reaching the Plain of Reeds becomes increasingly harder to predict.

Notes

1 Federal Emergency Management Agency (FEMA), *National Flood Insurance Program Terminology Index*. www.fema.gov/flood-insurance/terminology-index, accessed 10 October 2020.

2 Claudia Kuenzer, Huadong Guo, Juliane Huth, Patrick Leinenkugel, Xinwu Li & Stefan Dech (2013), Flood Mapping and Flood Dynamics of the Mekong Delta: ENVISAT-ASAR-WSM Based Time Series Analyses. *Remote Sensing*, n. 5, pp. 691–692.

3 Avijit Gupta (2009), Geology and Landforms of the Mekong Basin. In Ian Campbell (ed.), *The Mekong: Biophysical Environment of an International River Basin*. New York, NY: Academic Press, pp. 44–45.

7 A Section in Water

These are immense quagmires on which grow rushes, aquatic plants and forests of a thorny tree, with white bark, with rare foliage which is called the Tram. These unproductive plains are designated under the generic name of Plains of rushes.
Les Premières années de la Cochinchine, Colonie française,
Pauline Vial, 1875

Formed by the sediment deposits that also define a delta, the floodplain is scientifically considered more a riverine process rather than a specific landform. Determined through the observation of an existing condition, by records of historical high-water events or by the qualities of a specific topography, the extent of the floodplain has a different significance for a farmer benefitting from the river's waterborne nutrients and for the inhabitant of an urban settlement threatened by invading water. Described as a "territory of risk" by Nathalie Pottier, the delineation of the floodplain's limits are not solely related to the determination of the threat posed by the seasonal action of water on property and people's livelihoods.[1] Within one part of the 50,000 km^2 floodplain stretching to Cambodia, the temporary "disappearance" of political boundaries in the Plain of Reeds or the stagnant pools of water left behind as the floodwaters drain have associated the areas where land is periodically submerged with the dangers of disease or with the lack of military control by the state. Identifying what risks the floodplain is drawn to denote can therefore also suggest a way to perceive what on a map would otherwise be considered the representation of a temporary shoreline. Based on colonial-era maps, this chapter examines how a distinct territory was constructed from a section of the floodplain to denote an uninhabitable and uncivilizable terrain, far from the control of the colonial state.

Pathologies of an Empty Map

The notion that part of the geographic space encompassed by the Mekong's flows could also be described by a relationship with inundation was perhaps first suggested in Tang-dynasty Chinese annals. Sent as ambassadors to Angkor, 7th-century

DOI: 10.4324/9781032706238-11

140   *Liquid Territories*

Chinese chroniclers described the kingdom of "Water Chenla", which contemporary scholars situate within the flood-prone south part of Cambodia.[2] Studying the historical record, Oliver Wolters has argued that the division of Chenla into separate polities of Land and Water was geographic, and most likely related to the ambassadors' observations of local floods rather than reflecting a specific extent of political authority.[3] A name the Vietnamese later associated with the Khmer kingdom, Chenla and its kings' hereditary jurisdiction over the Mekong's lowlands was a key reason for the establishment of the Nguyen dynasty's military fortifications in Nam Bộ. Annexed by the Vietnamese from Cambodia, Nam Bộ's administrative subdivision into six districts took into account the movement of troops across particular sections of the terrain. While Vietnamese canals created new perennial water routes through impassable wetlands, these water-logged areas were not solely the result of the Mekong's flood. Torrential monsoon rains combined with daily tides made the presence of water on the ground ubiquitous throughout the wet season and the division of the region according to the extent of the river's overflow relevant only for very few.

Prepared by naval hydrographers, early maps of the colony concentrated on articulating the main branches of the Mekong, which connected existing densely clustered riparian settlements. Between the main waterways, however, depictions of the interstitial, inundated areas were devoid of geographic detail. Introduced almost a century earlier by the French cartographer JBB d'Anville, the deployment of pictorial voids on maps was a reaction to the practice of depicting uncharted regions with imaginary creatures or terrains. Rather than considering these areas featureless, such blank spaces indicated a lack of verifiable topographic knowledge about the physical geography of these terrains.[4] But in a region where the ground continuously fluctuated between states of wetness and dryness, mapping the ground was itself a challenge. The use of typical cartographic notations that differentiated land from water, such as coast lines or embankments, only represented a momentary glimpse of a monsoonal region where water was everywhere, in numerous forms, throughout the year.

A local perspective on the relationship between the flood and the ground was captured by the Vietnamese writer and educator Petrus Ky who presented the action of water (*l'action de l'eau*) as the critical factor underpinning the colony's geography. But rather than water acting on an existing stable surface, the allusion to a land formed incrementally by alluvium deposits suggests a condition inseparable from the behaviour of floodwater.[5] With water creating the colony's ground, the triangular delta which Ky located downstream from Vinh Long, was only a small part of the total land formed by the river's sediment. References to localized topographic conditions appear common in the regional Vietnamese dialect. In what contemporary scholars call the 'language of the river region' (*ngôn ngữ miền sông nước*), the spatial and seasonal differentiation of moisture content on the ground subsoil and atmosphere has been conveyed in specialized expressions for fresh and saline water. Used to describe the liquid's multiple distinct states (such as still, slow or fast), such expressions implicitly or directly reference the location of such regularly occurring micro-topographic conditions.[6] Thus, rather than the geographic magnitude of periodic inundation, the toponymy of discrete terrains addressed permanent or recurring topographic characteristics such as mountains or water-logged areas.[7]

The contradiction between the seasonal influence of water and the stillness of maps, also surfaced in French accounts of the Mekong's geography. Discussing the emergence of "*real* islands of extraordinary fertility", Oswald Taillefer identified these relatively drier areas as most suitable for the location of settlements and intensive rice cultivation.[8] The *reality* he recognized was produced by the replenishment of land by the Mekong's annual sediment deposits, which gave the delta's 'garden lands' (*miệt vườn*) the appearance of permanence and durability. Beyond such naturally occurring havens from the invading waters, however, the perpetually soaked ground of the floodplains was considered part of a separate domain. The wetness of the vast inundated floodplains and brackish coastal marshes of the Mekong was directly implicated by Dr Jules Harmand as responsible for the spread of tropical infections. Pointing to these nameless places on the map, Harmand's commentary associated the intangible threat of disease with the physical condition of the ground, suggesting that the terrain itself was suffering from the constant presence of water.[9] Siobhan Carroll called these natural regions which remained blank on colonial maps *atopias* or non-places in the sense that their intangibility, inhospitality or inaccessibility did not allow them to be converted into spaces of inhabitation.[10] In colonial Cochinchina, these *atopias* manifested around areas of 'excessive' wetness where the action of water inhibited the formation of firm land.

The pathologies of the maps' empty spaces overlapped on the Mekong's floodplains. Flat, wet and covered in more than a metre of floodwater for months, these areas were in every way the ontological opposite to Taillefer's dry, fertile islands. On early colonial maps, the geographic space annotated as "plaine inondée couverte d'herbes" or "plaine d'herbes couverte d'eau" extended from Cambodia to the western doorstep of the French administrative capital in Saigon. Cartographic zones of the colony alluding to particular characteristics of the terrain, presented the extent encompassed by the "Plaine des Joncs" as equivalent to the water-logged ground on either side of the Mekong (**Figure 7.1**). However, the chosen name did not describe a grass-covered extent. While today trees are a rare sight, historical botanic research describes a region covered with clusters of melaleuca forest – a species of myrtle – with only limited areas of grass.[11] Rather as naval captain Pauline Vial noted, colonial references to vegetated plains indicated a generic 'overgrown' and unproductive region, an *atopia* centred on the "deep depressions in the ground occupied by marshes".[12] The perceived disorder of these peripheral landscapes was further compounded by the absence of solid ground to pursue those resisting colonial rule. Citing the area known as "la plaine de joncs" the colony's official newspaper described the hiding place of "agitators" such as Võ Duy Dương whose stronghold was located in the ruins of Tháp Mười, north of the river. Surrounded by swamps, pursuing armies needed to laboriously wade through the stagnant water, making the exercise of military control almost impossible and the wet condition of the ground tantamount to a state of lawlessness. From the viewpoint

142 *Liquid Territories*

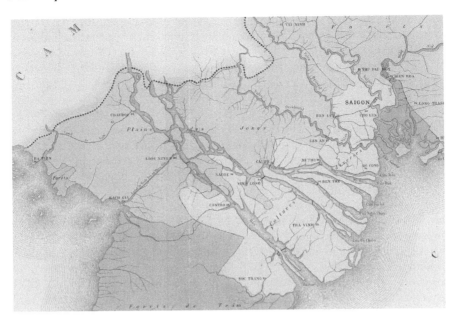

Figure 7.1 **Wetland hinterlands.** Extending on both sides of the Mekong, the grey-shaded area on the map represents a geographic space annotated as *Plaine des Joncs*. Rather than describing the extent of a grass-covered ground, this zone encompasses the uncultivated, inundated wetlands adjacent to the more populated areas described by "diverse cultivations" rather than any particular geophysical characteristic. M. Bertaux (1882), *Carte de la Cochinchine francaise divisee en quatre zones*. [*Source:* BNF]

of the newspaper's journalist, the plain was located as far from colonial authority as if it was beyond the colony's frontiers.[13]

When later these frontiers were finalized along the Vinh Tế canal, they delivered a new geographic focus for cartographers and administrators which required depictions of the terrain to adopt new toponyms and subdivisions. On these maps, the annotation *Plaine des Joncs* was used to signify only the inundated land within the boundaries of French Cochinchine and north of the Mekong.[14] Yet in relation to the entire extent covered by floodwater, the area that could be identified as constituting the floodplain was not immediately evident. The observable and thus recordable condition of the ground during wet season rains was not a phenomenon limited to a particular type of landscape or a single distinguishable terrain. Working with reference to Cochinchina's colonial boundaries rather than any notion of the Mekong's delta, for the Algerian-born engineer Albert Pouyanne the limits of inundation appeared to cover the majority of the colony's surface area.[15] In maps published in 1910, Pouyanne's outline of the floodplain differentiated a particular area from what he considered a single immense plain with only minor topographic undulations (**Figure 7.2**).[16] The planimetric depiction of the flood's

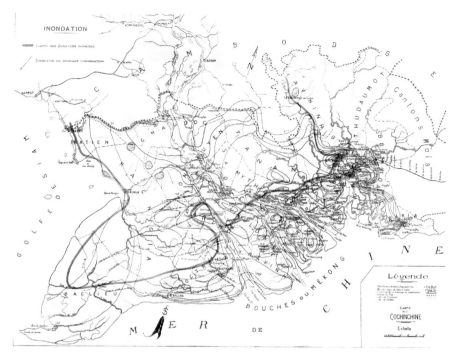

Figure 7.2 **Inundation in French Cochinchina.** Encompassing a significant proportion of the entire colony, the thick dark (green) line on the map displays the limits of the land covered by floodwater during the wet season. Albert Pouyanne (1911), *Inondation.* [*Source:* ODSAS, Object Id: 43769 and 43770]

maximum extent however did not just differentiate between areas of seasonal wetness and dryness. Within the cartographic limits of inundation, regions with notable topographic, historical or cultural differences were all presented as unified by the impact of a single phenomenon. This apparent unity however was only temporary and contradicted the different rates at which particular areas became flooded or drained. For an engineer like Pouyanne the delineated area experiencing inundation was not just the record of a particular condition. Later appointed colonial Inspector of Public Works for all Indochina, he identified the problems related to flooding in the Red River Delta as the focus of the colony's public works projects. Referencing the dangers to agriculture and villagers' lives from floods, the mapped outline of inundated land clarified the colonial engineer's primary *area of operations*.[17] Significantly, on Pouyanne's maps of Cochinchina's hydrology, the entire collection of waterways within the colony was presented as part of a single system that could be designed concurrently. Allowing uninterrupted navigation between the Mekong and Vaico rivers, new canals such as the Duperré or Lagrange acted as both connections within the hydraulic network and waterways linking two river basins.

144 *Liquid Territories*

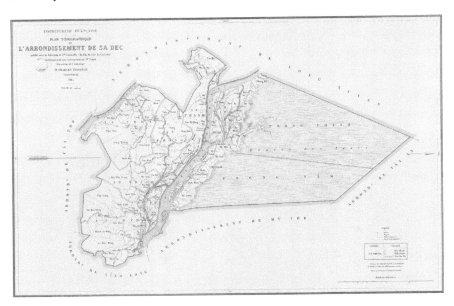

Figure 7.3 **Flooded *atopia*.** The map shows the Province of Sa Dec. Settlements are located adjacent to the *Fleuve Antérieure* (Mekong River). Depicted neither as dry land nor as the same water flowing through rivers, the Plaine des Joncs is shown as a homogeneous surface permanently covered by inundation. Camouilly & Boisson (1885), *Plan topographique de l'arrondissement de Sa Dec*. [*Source:* BNF]

If areal depictions of the flood alluded to a particular geographic space confronted with similar problems, new administrative subdivisions appeared to fragment the floodplain. As the French consolidated power in Cochinchina, districts (*arrondissments*) used to qualify the extent of subregional governance subsumed control of the Plaine des Joncs' amorphous ground within a regional hierarchy that privileged the drier, higher landforms around rivers. With the notional centre of the map focused on the banks of the Mekong where settlements were overwhelmingly located, on maps the Plain appeared as a permanently submerged hinterland on the margins of civilization (**Figure 7.3**). By the first decade of the 20th century, however, the area's marginal relationship to the colony's social and economic life had begun to change. Hundreds of kilometres of canals had been excavated around the southern and eastern edges of the swamp, enabling army gunboats to patrol throughout the year and new agricultural land to be farmed. To construct the canals, slow mechanical dredgers sliced through the compact clay soils in continuous straight lines that paid little attention to topographic nuances. These public works became a key feature of colonial maps, on which their colossal scale seemed to rival the length and importance of many natural waterways. Crossing the empty spaces of the map, the solid blue lines representing the canals, filled the void with the man-made geometry of water. By appearing to restrict the presence of water in the landscape only to the canals and rivers, later maps also suggested that the ground around these manmade waterways was, if not totally dry, then at least in some way modified to manage wetness.

The Archaeology of Limits

As new routes were cut through the swamps to permanently change the floodplain's hydrology, the production of not only geographic but also historical knowledge of the region was promoted in new colonial institutions. Founded in Hanoi at the turn of the century, the *École française d'Extrême-Orient* (EFEO) concentrated its researchers' attention on knowledge of "oriental" cultures. Especially after 1930, colonial scholars at the EFEO addressed Indochina's growing social and economic problems, such as the movement of thousands of migrants from Tonkin to Cochinchina, which geographers examined in relation to the natural setting in which these problems appeared.[18] As part of the EFEO's scope, historical studies presented the colony's distant past as a function of Southeast Asia's mutual influence from India and China. Facilitated by the inclusion of both Cambodia and Cochinchina within French Indochina, cross-border historical research published in the EFEO's bulletin examined new and available archaeological evidence in relation to the topography of the Mekong's monsoonal lowlands.

Translated by the EFEO's most eminent archaeologist Georges Coedès, an inscribed stela found in the Plaine des Joncs revealed the royal lineage of a religious "domain conquered on the mud".[19] The vivid reference to the condition of the ground in relation to a controlled domain suggested not only the relative autonomy of the region's *mandala* polities but also the sense that qualities of the topography were critical to understanding the location and perhaps the dimension of that control. Conjectured to be part of the prehistoric "kingdom" of Funan noted in Chinese annals, the archaeological remains of Tháp Mười (or Prasat Pream Loven in Khmer), where the stela had been discovered, were given a new geographic dimension with the advent of aerial photography. The assemblage of aerial images taken in the late 1920s, allowed provincial administrator and amateur archaeologist Pierre Paris to identify older canals connecting distant locations of the Mekong's lowlands.[20] Although parts of these structures were already known from ground-level observations, on the map the routes of ancient waterways appeared to converge on the inhabited mounds of Tháp Mười to the north and the hill of Ba Thê further south. Close to the hill, an archaeological expedition funded by the EFEO in the 1940s uncovered the ruins of a major urban settlement. In the eyes of the expedition's leader Louis Malleret, the canals had enabled a regional trade network to develop but would also have drained floodwater seawards removing the toxic levels of acid sulphate from the soil that inhibited the cultivation of rice.[21] Drawn in relation to the limits of inundation, archaeological sites on Paris' map appeared to be strategically situated on the edge of the floodplain. With the canals' location framed within the outline of the seasonal

146 *Liquid Territories*

movement of surface water, the map presented a prehistoric domain associated with the flood's coverage.

The significance of these discoveries to the region's geography was pointed out by Pierre Gourou. Writing as France's post-war hold on Indochina disintegrated, a short article published in the *Annales de Géographie* discussed the historical succession of landscapes in Cochinchina. Framing current conditions as a continuity with the distant past, the article pointed out that "today [1950] the sites occupied by these cities are almost uninhabitable".[22] Based on Malleret's thesis, Gourou claimed that it was the "large hydraulic organization" that had made civilization on such a scale possible in the inundated terrain. In this scenario, the flood's seasonal sediment deposits also required the canals to be regularly maintained and, Gourou conjectured, this lack of regular maintenance – caused by political unrest – was the reason these canals and their associated settlements had been abandoned more than 1,000 years ago.[23] For Gourou, the societal value of these ancient structures was therefore comparable to the benefits of the hydraulic organization inaugurated by the French, implicitly associating the flood with the potential for civil unrest and the canals with the colonial 'order'. Specified as the context for historical discourse, the floodplain was framed as a distinct landscape in which modern canals were just the latest iteration of a long lineage of infrastructure works considered necessary for inhabitation.

Yet the experience on the ground was quite different. Excavation of the canals in the Plaine des Joncs had indeed accelerated the rate at which the floodplain drained. However, the patchwork of new dry zones that appeared in the upstream areas was not uniformly distributed.[24] Although *alum* (acid sulphate) was indeed the result of the naturally occurring ferrous soils, the oxidization producing toxic levels was exacerbated by the canals' construction which exposed the excavated subsoils to the atmosphere during the dry season before being carried away by the rising water. Thus, rather than 'repairing' a natural condition threatening the stability of the colony, the impact of modern canal building on the floodplain was far from uniformly beneficial for local farmers, and only incidentally comparable with the transformation of the inundated *atopia* of the past into a habitable terrain. From this perspective, the areal extent constituted by the limits of the flood was not just the context on which prehistoric settlers and migrant farmers struggled to grow crops. It also framed the threat of armed conflict and political unrest that followed the Second World War and which colonial governance theoretically prevented rather than generated.

Conclusion

If the floodplain's seasonal submersion could indicate the inhospitability of flood-prone areas or a refuge for rebels, it would also not be enough to imagine a basic hydrological concept onto which social, technical and political ideas were grafted. As part of the entirety of flooded areas encompassed in an archaeological landscape or an engineer's area of operations, the Plaine des Joncs supported claims regarding a singular terrain threatened by impending danger. Positioned as the Mekong's north floodplain, the uninhabitable swamp or the distant hinterland of riverine settlement was presented as a separate domain. Unlike the "sublime" wasteland which David Cronon has identified with the unexplored American wilderness, however, the plain's pathologies were not considered immediately redeemable. While 'amputation' would be an exaggerated way to describe the notional separation between the Plaine and the rest of the colony, the discursive marginalization of this *atopia* was consequential in supporting different ideas referring to the same geographic extent. Although the planar surface area covered by water could be visually equated with the floodplain's extent as it appeared on a map, the succession of ground conditions that followed inundation ranged from waterlogged to relatively dry, until the next rainy season restarted the process. In this sense, the delineation of the floodplain's magnitude was fundamentally different to the inclined ground defining the basin or the accretion of sediment describing the delta which changed according to the rhythms of earth's geology. The mapped limit of both a specific space and an annual phenomenon, the floodplain's outline referred to the temporary accumulation of water rather than an extent of land. This accumulation could be understood in terms of the annual sequence of human activities, such as agriculture, that were contingent on the changeable condition of the ground. From the perspective of the immense human labour involved in cultivating, inhabiting or domesticating any part of the inundated areas, the floodplain's delineation reflected an intimately anthropocentric conceptualization of the Mekong's riparian areas. The improbability of ever defining an indisputable limit to the floodplain made the accuracy of the mapped outline secondary to the conviction of the arguments which made its visual presence on the map necessary in the first place.

Notes

1 Nathalie Pottier (2000), Risque d'inondation, réglementation et territoires. *Hommes et Terres du Nord, Hydrosystèmes, paysages et territoires*, pp. 94–95.
2 Michael Vickery (1994), *What and Where Was Chenla?* Paris: Recherches nouvelles sur le Cambodge, École française d'Extrême-Orient, p. 16.
3 O.W. Wolters (1974), North-Western Cambodia in the Seventh Century. *Bulletin of the School of Oriental and African Studies, University of London*, v. 37, n. 2. pp. 369–370.
4 Lucy Chester (2000), The Mapping of Empire: French and British Cartographies of India in the Late Eighteenth Century. *Portugese Studies*, v. 16, p. 257.
5 Trương Vĩnh (Petrus) Ký (1875), *Petit cours de géographie de la Basse-Cochinchine*. Saigon: Impri. du Government, p. 12.
6 Pascal Bourdeaux (2014), Sơn Nam ou la dualité d'une oeuvre: Évocations poétiques et ethnographiques du Viêt Nam meridional. *Moussons*, n. 24, para. 89. Among the regionally unique phrases recorded by the Vietnamese author Sơn Nam to describe water in the Mekong's delta region: High water, poor water, upwelling water, slump water, shockwaters, crawling water, running water, standing water etc. See also Nguyễn Văn Nở (2014), Tìm hiểu cách vân dụng thành ngữ, tục ngữ trong tác phẩm Sơn Nam (Study on the Use of Locutions and Proverbs in the Work of Son Nam). In Dao Huu Vinh & Pham Duc Binh (eds.), *Ngôn ngữ Miền sông nước (Language of the River Region)*. Hanoi: Nxb Chính trị quốc gia, pp. 90–118.

148 *Liquid Territories*

7 Topographic features such as hills (Thất Sơn – Seven Mountains) or swamps (Cà Mau – Black Swamp) were part of the region's geographic nomenclature prior to colonization.

8 Italics added. *"Ces sables se rencontrent partout à des profondeurs variables, et ils atteignent parfois la surface, où ils forment de véritables îlots d'une fertilité extraordinaire"*. Taillefer (1865), *La Cochinchine: Ce qu'elle est, ce qu'elle sera: Deux ans de séjour dans ce pays de 1863 à 1865*. Perigeaux: Impri. Dupont, p. 45.

9 *"Si l'on jette les yeux sur une Carte de Cochinchine, on verra des espaces immenses, presque sans nom de villages, et portant la mention: Marais incultes, plaine de joncs"*. Jules Harmand (1874), *Aperçu pathologique sur la Cochinchine*. Versailles: Impri. Aubert, p. 14.

10 Siobhan Carroll (2015), *An Empire of Air and Water: Uncolonizable Space in the British Imagination, 1750–1850*. Philadelphia, PA: University of Pennsylvania Press, p. 6.

11 Le Cong Kiet (1993), Dong Thap Muoi: Restoring the Mystery Forest of the Plain of Reeds. *Restoration & Management Notes*, v. 11, n. 2, pp. 102–103.

12 *"Entre les différents bras des fleuves existent de profondes dépressions du sol occupées par des marais. . . . Ce sont d'immenses fondrières sur lesquels poussent des joncs, des plantes aquatiques et des forêts d'un arbre épineux, à l'écorce blanche, au feuillage rare que l'on nomme le Tram. On désigne ces plaines improductives sous le nom générique de Plaines des joncs"*. Paulin Vial (1874), *Les Premières années de la Cochinchine, Colonie française*. Paris: Challamel Ainé, p. 31.

13 *"Quand toutes les préoccupations des habitants se portent vers le commerce et l'industrie, les excitations des agitateurs qui se sont réfugiés dans les bois et la plaine de joncs ou qui se cachent au delà de nos frontières ne sont plus que des menaces vaines et puériles"*. *Partie non officielle (Saigon, 5 novembre 1865)*, Courrier de Saigon (1865), *Journal officiel de la Cochinchine Francaise*, n. 21, November 5, p. 2.

14 In his collection of local folklore, the Vietnamese historian Nguyễn Hữu Hiếu points out that parts of the flat, annually flooded region north of the Mekong, were known by different names prior to French colonization. Nguyễn Hữu Hiếu (2018), *Văn hóa dân gian vùng Đồng Tháp Mười (Folklore in the Dong Thap Muoi region)*. Nhà xuất bản: Văn hóa – Văn nghệ.

15 In his 1910 *Atlas Cochinchine*, Pouyanne does not mention the delta as the site of the hydrological phenomena which his maps and plans depict. While it is certain that the future Inspector of Public Works would have been aware of the term, the absence of any mention of the river's delta in the context of Cochinchina suggests that this was either an important hydrological factor or, at the time of writing, a widely used reference for parts of the colony.

16 *"Toute la basse Cochinchine, don't la superficie attaint environ 4 million d'hectares, constitue une immense plaine qui presente de tres faibles ondulations"* A.A. Pouyanne (1926), *Inspection générale des travaux publics*. Hanoi: Impr. d'Extrême-Orient, p. 98.

17 *"La question des inondations et des crues du Fleuve Rouge et celle des travaux de défense contre les inondations sont d'une importance primordiale pour le pays"*. *Ibid.*, p. 130. Pouyanne noted the disasters caused by breaches in the casier flood defences of Tonkin and the importance of inundation for agriculture.

18 David Biggs (2011), Aerial Photography and Colonial Discourse on the Agricultural Crisis in Late-Colonial Indochina, 1930–1945. In C.F. Ax, N. Brimnes, N.T. Jensen & K. Oslund (eds.), *Cultivating the Colonies: Colonial States and Their Environmental Legacies*. Athens: Ohio University Press, p. 105.

19 *"Tout ce que l'on peut tirer du texte, c'est que le roi père de Gunavarman était de la race de Kaundinya, et qu'il avait mis son fils à la tête d'un domaine « conquis sur la boue », c'est-à-dire évidemment récupéré par drainage et assèchement sur les alluvions du Mékong qui constituent l'actuelle Plaine des Joncs"*. Georges Coedès (1931), Etudes cambodgiennes. XXV, Deux inscriptions sanskrites du Fou-nan. XXVI, La date de Kôh

Ker. XXVII, La date du Bàphûonm. *Bulletin de l'Ecole française d'Extrême-Orient*, v. 31, p. 2.

20 Pierre Paris (1941), Autres canaux reconnus à l'Est du Mékong par examen d'autres photographies aériennes (provinces de Châudôc et de Long-xuyên). *Bulletin de l'Ecole française d'Extrême-Orient*, v. 41.

21 Louis Malleret (1951), Les fouilles d'Oc-èo. Rapport préliminaire. *Bulletin de l'Ecole française d'Extrême-Orient*, v. 45, n. 1, pp. 80, 88.

22 Gourou Pierre (1950), La succession des paysages humains en Cochinchine occidentale. *Annales de Géographie*, v. 59, n. 313, p. 79.

23 *"Des troubles politiques – qui ont peut-être coïncidé avec la fin du Fou Nan – ont dû provoquer l'abandon des travaux d'entretien; les hommes ont été chasses par l'inondation croissante".* *ibid.*, p. 80.

24 Olivier Husson (1998), *Spatio-Temporal Variability of Acid Sulphate Soils in the Plain of Reeds, Vietnam: Impact of Soil Properties, Water Management and Crop Husbandry on the Growth and Yield of Rice in Relation to Microtopography.* Unpublished PhD thesis, Delft University of Technology, p. 80.

8 Articulating Inundation

The designation "Plain of Reeds" is widely used but general agreement as to the limits of the area encompassed is lacking ... because of a lack of uniformity it should not be considered as an entity but as separate geographic areas.
Accelerated Development in the Plain of Reeds,
Engineer Agency for Resources Inventories, 1968

Although the risks associated with the Mekong's floodplain pervaded colonial references to the phenomenon of wet-season inundation, the geography encompassed by floods on Plain of Reeds evaded straightforward definition. Even as cartographers of the Engineer Agency of Resources Inventories (EARI) sought to unify "separate geographic areas" into a discrete region, the reality they observed suggested that floods were not a problem everywhere. Differentiated from the *mùa lũ* (flood season) associated with natural disaster in the Red River Delta, *mùa nước nổi* (the water-rising season) in the Mekong Delta typically heralds the arrival of fertile sediment deposits critical for agriculture. As colonial atlases from the turn of the century show, topographic conditions and the annual variability of floodwater volumes meant that some areas were affected more often and for longer than others (**Figure 8.1**). Yet even in those geological depressions where floodwaters receded more slowly, conditions varied. The floodwaters which appeared to extend Tonle Sap's size during the wet season also created the conditions for fish to spawn, supplying local residents with food for the entire year. In the Plaine des Joncs on the other hand, wet season inundation sustained expansive marshlands which were widely considered inhospitable for human habitation. Thus, if the mapped limits of floodwater defined the extent of geographic space subject to the threat of inundation, they also suggested the delineation of particular regions which could presumably also be characterized by the activities of a group of people taking place within the floodplain.

In the Plain of Reeds, however, submerged surfaces did not necessarily equate with one single type of terrain or a particular group of people. Not only did Vietnamese and Khmer residents of the Plain live on both sides of Cambodia's border with Cochinchina but melaleuca forests, stagnant pools of giant lotus, mounds of

DOI: 10.4324/9781032706238-12

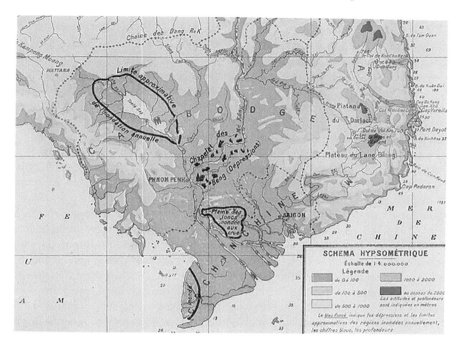

Figure 8.1 **Submerged lands.** Extracted from a colonial atlas published in 1914, the map shows the topography of French Indochina and identifies the geological depressions (dark outline) affected annually by inundation. The denotation *Plaine des Joncs* is restricted to the area encompassed by the flood. Note that inundation in the southwest corner of Cochinchine is caused by tidal fluctuations and precipitation but not by the Mekong's flood. Henri Brenier (1914), *Schema Hypsometrique*. [*Source:* Cirad]

accumulated sediment and concentrations of toxic acid sulphate soils also created diverse ground conditions that enabled or constrained human activities. For French and American cartographers, recording these characteristics was not just a matter of documenting their location and extent. Underpinned by maps that assigned a specific magnitude to the floodplain's catchment area, the answer to the question of where flood phenomena occurred was critical to establish the *site* for new development as well as control surface water. Occurring 40 years apart and unfolding under significantly different political contexts, the chapter examines two attempts to delineate the Plain of Reeds. Drawing on maps from the PhD thesis of military officer Victor Delahaye and the US Army's EARI plan for polders in the Plain of Reeds, the chapter asks what the cartographic articulation of wet and dry areas denoted. Did they specify a course of action aimed at correcting a perceived imbalance in the natural, political and social equilibrium? Or did they set out to redeem the marginal *atopia* from the underlying threats posed by inundation by controlling the flows of people and floodwater.

152   *Liquid Territories*

Challenging Flatness

Having consolidated their colonial empire in Southeast Asia at the end of the 19th century, the work of mapping French Indochina was undertaken by the *Service géographique d'Indochine*. Beginning with Tonkin and the Red River Delta in the first decade of the 20th century, new surveys expanded the scope of cartographic knowledge southwards, reaching Cochinchina in the early 1920s.[1] For many colonial geographers, the *Service's* cartographic representations were critical to understanding the qualities of the landscape (*paysage*).[2] The importance of *paysage* for the study of social relationships was framed in the geographic discourse of Paul Vidal de la Blache. Characterized by the rejection of political boundaries as the spatial extent of geographic study, Vidal's 'regionalist' approach viewed the landscape as the product of a process of adaptation by a group of people to particular features of their natural surroundings (*milieu*). Using large-scale topographic or geological maps, Vidal and his students believed that the science of geography could deduce the "human dimension" of the *milieu* and identify the restrictions imposed by the *milieu* on that group of people.[3] Although Vidal warned that cartography could not fully explain all the facts, for those geographers seeking to define the different relationships between people and the colony's ground, the Service's new maps were important documents that could provide insights into existing social conditions.[4]

In this context, the most well-known studies of Indochina's geography began to appear towards the end of the 1920s. Following the principles of 'Vidalian' geography, both Charles Robequain's investigation of the Thanh Hoa delta (1929) and Pierre Gourou's research on the Red River's delta (1936) were significant for applying a "French science into a landscape hitherto unstudied in France".[5] But while these studies focused on the historically densely populated deltas in the north of Indochina, the geographic research of Victor Delahaye focused more specifically on the sparsely inhabited ground of the Mekong River's floodplain. Entitled *La Plaine des Joncs et sa mise en valeur*, Delahaye's doctoral thesis was published in 1928, and it was one of the few studies on colonial geography conducted by a French military officer.[6] Stationed in the Plaine des Joncs, his examination of this "very distinct and original small region" was based on personal observations and first-hand experience of the annual flood. Similar to Robequain and Gourou, the study of the region was accompanied by photographs, planimetric sketches and the classification of local villages into types. Yet unlike those other studies, Delahaye's goal was not merely to describe an existing condition. Narrating his experience during the flood of 1923, he noted how farmers remained in their homes until finally, overwhelmed by the force of the current, they were forced to flee in despair. Proposing specific interventions that would 'arrest' the primordial flows of the flood at the "origin of evil", Delahaye chose to focus his research on the cartography of the floodplain in order to formulate and verify the technical feasibility of his plans.[7]

Imagining the view from an airplane, Delahaye's introductory description noted the flat "reed-covered" lowlands, the "silver ribbons" of waterways, plantations and the clusters of melaleuca forest that characterized the topography of the "particularly depressed and very humid zone, which the floods of the Mekong inundate every year".[8] To explain the flood regime he had witnessed, Delahaye turned to a study by the colony's Chief Engineer LMJ Bénabenq. Less than a decade earlier, Bénabenq had noted that the rise of floodwaters along the Mekong corresponded to an equal rise along the Vaico two days later, while the waters receded almost simultaneously across the same area.[9] He had also noticed that particularly in east-west canals, flotsam on the surface and the sediment below water would render many waterways almost unnavigable. Conceptualizing the floodplain's catchment area lying between the Mekong and West Vaico rivers, Bénabenq hypothesized the existence of an 'outer' tidal zone where nearly all agriculture was located, and an 'inner' flooded area that gradually drained towards the middle of the floodplain. On a terrain that was generally perceived as "absolutely flat" and marshy, the subtle changes in elevation determined the effectiveness of canals to drain floodwater or to act as transport routes. Knowledge of the floodplain's gradient was therefore important in understanding the way floodwater moved (or remained still) over the terrestrial surface but also critical if Delahaye's proposals were to accomplish the goal of draining the Plaine des Joncs and removing the threat of periodic flooding.[10]

The distant perspective which allowed Delahaye to compare the vegetated floodplain with a billiard-table cloth, contrasted with his experience of mapping the ground. A captain in the colonial army, Delahaye's posting in Cochinchina had taken him on cartographic missions throughout colony including the Mekong's deltaic lowlands. To challenge the perceived flatness of the floodplain, Delahaye highlighted the significance of levelling (*nivellement*). He argued that knowledge of the height of the ground above a notional datum was more valuable than topographic features to understand the flood regime and therefore essential for the region's future development.[11] Acknowledging the efforts of surveying officers, he was nonetheless highly critical of the *Service geographique's* attempts to record elevations in the Plaine des Joncs. He pointed out that the pylons used to triangulate location were sometimes invisible from other surveying stations and were also moved after monsoonal storms. Individually minor, the cumulative impact of these errors compromised the accuracy of maps, suggesting that these were unreliable tools for planning infrastructure on the floodplain. In response to his own critique, a new contour map was extrapolated from elevation measurements taken nearly 20 years earlier (**Figure 8.2**). Considering the extensive 'gaps' of reliable information between survey points, Delahaye's pursuit of levelling suggests that this map was not drawn to accurately represent the ground.[12] Symbolized by the distance between individual 1-metre contours, the terrain's gradient framed a relationship between water and ground that appeared to unfold across more than 100 kilometres. The subtle slope rendered visible by the map defined the geographic magnitude of the *inaction* of stagnant water which perpetuated the widely accepted idea of an 'uncivilisable' *atopia*. Equated with the 'site' of Delahaye's proposals, the extent of hydrological phenomena embodied by the contours did not so much identify the observable "human dimension" of the floodplain espoused by Vidalian geography as calibrate the configuration of water infrastructure in relation to the floodplain's catchment.[13]

154 *Liquid Territories*

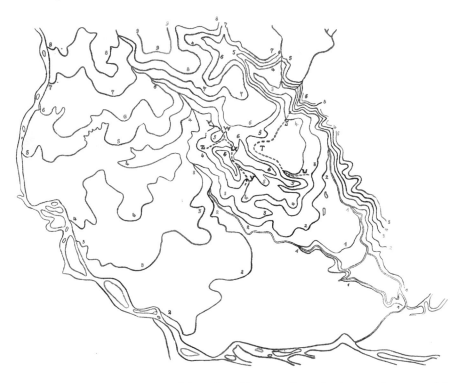

Figure 8.2 **Levelling the terrestrial surface.** The map shows the topography assumed to affect the flows of floodwater. The contour lines are extrapolated from an older survey of spot elevations with significant distances between measuring points. Despite such gaps in information, the contours span the breadth of the region, providing knowledge of the entire floodplain. Victor Delahaye (1928), *Topographie*. [*Source:* Koninklijke Bibliotheek]

In a period in which the length of waterways increased every year, Delahaye's proposed water infrastructure did not just aim to "dry" the floodplain. During the time he had spent on surveys, Delahaye had observed that the arrangement of small canals excavated by Vietnamese farmers had washed away the toxic acid sulphate soils which prevented cultivation of nearly four-fifths of this flood-prone region.[14] By deploying a flood barrier (*digue*) along the natural waterways, all three canals in his development plan were extended southwards from the meanders of natural waterways. By reinforcing the canals with high embankments, these waterways would be converted into monumental drainage channels that collectively evacuated all the floodwater to the sea. Where excavation was required, new waterways would follow the slope of the terrain shown on his own map and, with the information provided by levelling, maximize the height difference between the canal's two ends. Adherence to the 'reality' presented by the gradient on his map was particularly emphasized for Canal No. 2. Following the route of a proposed waterway that had originally appeared on a cadastral map of Cochinchina, the "Dinh-Ha to Mytho

Canal" was incorporated into the plan.[15] Extending southeast in the same direction as a natural drainage channel, No. 2 joined the flows of the Tam-Ly River at the boundary with Cambodia with the Lagrange and Grande canals. Positioned in the middle of the floodplain – approximately where Bénabenq had previously hypothesized that floodwaters converged – the embankments of the canal were designed to prevent the diverted floodwaters from overflowing into adjacent areas. Considering that No. 2 bisected the geographic space between the Mekong and West Vaico rivers, the new water infrastructure would also divide the floodplain into discrete segments and maintain the relative dryness that would follow.

Haven from Threat

If only conceptual, Delahaye's thesis prefigured discussions on the settlement of the floodplain that would culminate in the next two decades. Increasing pressure to resolve the problem of overpopulation in Tonkin presented the French administration with an incentive to examine the planned resettlement of villagers from the north to the sparsely populated areas of the Mekong's floodplain. The historian David Biggs distinguishes between two approaches favoured by colonial engineers:[16] On the one hand, the monumental infrastructure works that would remove floodwater across the entirety of the catchment and on the other hand, the construction of dikes to protect the farms and settlements situated on the floodplain. Spearheaded by the left-wing Popular Front government of France (1936–1938), the latter approach sought to apply water control techniques from the Red River Delta to the Mekong's delta. Called "*casiers*" by the French, the dikes encircling an extent of geographic space were a typical feature of Tonkin's countryside. Technically synonymous with the polders constructed in the inundated lowlands of the Netherlands, the land enclosed by *casiers* allowed water within the dikes to be controlled independently from the surrounding hydrological regime.[17] For Pierre Gourou and other colonial scientists and observers, these structures were not just important for controlling hydrological phenomena. With each village – rather than the state – responsible for the construction and maintenance of their own flood control structures, the geographic unit encompassed by dikes was considered emblematic of North Vietnam's agricultural landscape. Thus, although dikes altered the hydrological regime by detaining floodwater even after water levels had subsided elsewhere, *casiers* became associated with the 'natural' adaptation of a group of people to local topographic conditions that was characteristic of Vidalian human geography.[18]

Whereas Tonkin's villagers were praised for their "stubborn" subdivision of the Red River Delta into "an infinity of casiers", the apparent order visible in the patterns of dikes and settlements on aerial photographs contrasted sharply with the extensive, uncultivated tracts of land in Cochinchina's floodplain.[19] For the colonial administrators dealing with the problem of overpopulation, the construction of *casiers* on the Mekong's lowlands was seen as a model for resettlement that could also increase the total land used for agricultural production. Planned as a grid of canals surrounding an existing manmade waterway, the *casier tonkinois* was dredged by colonial engineers in 1943 and soon became the home for 750

156 *Liquid Territories*

migrant families from the north.[20] To the degree that the movement of water could be controlled in the Mekong's southern floodplain, the *casier's* outer perimeter of dikes acted as a barrier to the rising floodwaters while canals within the perimeter would irrigate (or drain) the agricultural land between them. However, the separate hydrological regime created within the dikes was soon plagued by severe water shortages that undermined the control over floodwater promised by the design and had made this part of the floodplain viable for settlement and agriculture in the first place.[21] Despite such apparent failures, the *casier* model continued to be promoted by French agricultural engineers of the *Service du génie rural* and the colony's Vietnamese politicians, who saw the paid construction jobs and potential improvements in crop yields as an antidote to destitution and the rising influence of communist agitators.[22] If only implicitly, the geographic space defined by dikes suggested a haven from the perpetual threat of inundation, a condition that would not have been apparent in the dispersed waterside settlements elsewhere on the floodplain. Finite and theoretically controllable, the enclosed protected area of the *casier* was the conceptual opposite to the natural and manmade waterways that disappeared on the flat horizon of the Mekong's lowlands.

As the only example of a *casier* planned and constructed prior to the collapse of colonial rule, the *casier tonkinois* was arguably the reference for the planning of Cái Sắn more than a decade later. Located between parts of the floodplain that were still controlled by political and religious groups hostile to the government, Cái Sắn was planned to accommodate mainly Catholic refugees fleeing from communist-controlled Tonkin. Yet where both projects focused on the resettlement of migrants along a group of new waterways, the canals and natural rivers forming the edges of Cái Sắn's rectilinear planning area are unlikely to have constituted a single protective flood barrier for the entire 1,000 km^2 area. The separation from the floodplain's hydrological regime occurred along the new canals where "the rich clay soil" excavated during their construction was "piled into dikes along the banks".[23] Although each of the many dike-defined enclosures could be considered a distinct polder, the absence of an outer perimeter of flood defences suggests that the similarity to Tonkin's *casiers* was not in the creation of a cohesive haven from inundation. Framed as the solution to the problem of claiming the land abandoned during the conflict of the Indochina War, Cái Sắn's planning was also aimed at installing a permanent government presence on a disputed terrain. Rather than a dike, the visual clarity of Cái Sắn's rectilinear perimeter on maps indicated the limits of a state-controlled 'shelter' in which residents would be defended from "natural and social hazards" by a benevolent government.[24] The association between *casiers* and an extent of protected land recast the multiple issues related with security – against inundation, hunger, hostility or even long-term tenancy – as an integrated problem resolvable within the manmade boundaries of a group of waterways.

Articulating Inundation

As regional conflict in Southeast Asia intensified after the mid-1960s, the use of polders to structure the flows of water within vast swathes of the floodplain was described by the Joint Development Group's (JDG) *Program for Mekong Delta*

Development. Prepared in 1967, plans by the JDG and David Lilienthal's Development and Resources Corporation conceived of polders creating six separate geographic units. Presented in a report for the US Agency for International Development (USAID), the polders aligned with the existing and proposed waterways, controlling inundation in order to improve agricultural yields. The escalation of regional military conflict however did not allow these monumental plans to be further elaborated. Especially after the surprise attack during 1968's Tết celebrations, efforts to reclaim the floodplain's "abandoned land" were severely hindered by the loss of government control over significant extents of the Mekong Delta. Subsequent planning and economic studies were set within an imagined "post-conflict" condition that allowed planners to focus on the technical rather than political issues of developing the floodplain. Instead of acknowledging the fragmentation into different areas of military control, the Delta's geographic space was presented as essentially contiguous within the extents of a catchment area that extended from South Vietnam to Cambodia's Tonle Sap. Within this context, the deployment of polders for agricultural production introduced a new scale of geographic compartmentalization that was not solely intended to control water.

Published in 1968 and 1969, two planning reports by the US Army's Engineer Agency of Resources Inventories (EARI) demonstrate the way water infrastructure was conceived in the flood-prone border areas of South Vietnam. Founded in 1963 with the intention of providing the USAID with the technical services of the US Army Corps of Engineers, the EARI was staffed with geographers, geologists, cartographers and engineers.[25] Geographically focused on the Mekong's floodplains, the EARI's studies aimed to resolve the problem of the "uneven distribution of water" which restricted the Mekong Delta's "tremendous economic potential".[26] The suggestion that there was "*too* much water in the wet season" reflected a particular understanding of the total extent within which such a perceived excess was recorded.[27] Presented as the area where the overland flows from three rivers merged, the defined outline of the Plain of Reeds on hydrological maps appeared in contrast to the dashed "indefinite" extents of drainage basins (**Figure 8.3**). Adopting the boundaries used by Delahaye 40 years earlier, the delineation of the floodplain's catchment enabled engineers to estimate that, constrained by the volume of water flowing through the hydrological catchment in both Cambodia and Vietnam, only a small proportion of the terrain could be exploited for cultivation. Even on this small proportion of the floodplain, however, the feasibility of agriculture was uncertain. Considering that the coverage of acid sulphate soils had not been previously mapped in sufficient detail, the effectiveness of the extensive drainage infrastructure required to "flush" the acidic water could not be guaranteed. Despite calls from the Mekong Committee for both Cambodia and South Vietnam to jointly focus on solving the economic and social problems of the Plain of Reeds, the costly infrastructure and limited benefits to agriculture meant that development of the floodplain remained a low priority for the state.[28]

However, it was another cartographic feature of the floodplain that became increasingly significant as armed regional conflict escalated. Appearing to straddle the geopolitical jurisdictions of both South Vietnam and Cambodia, the EARI

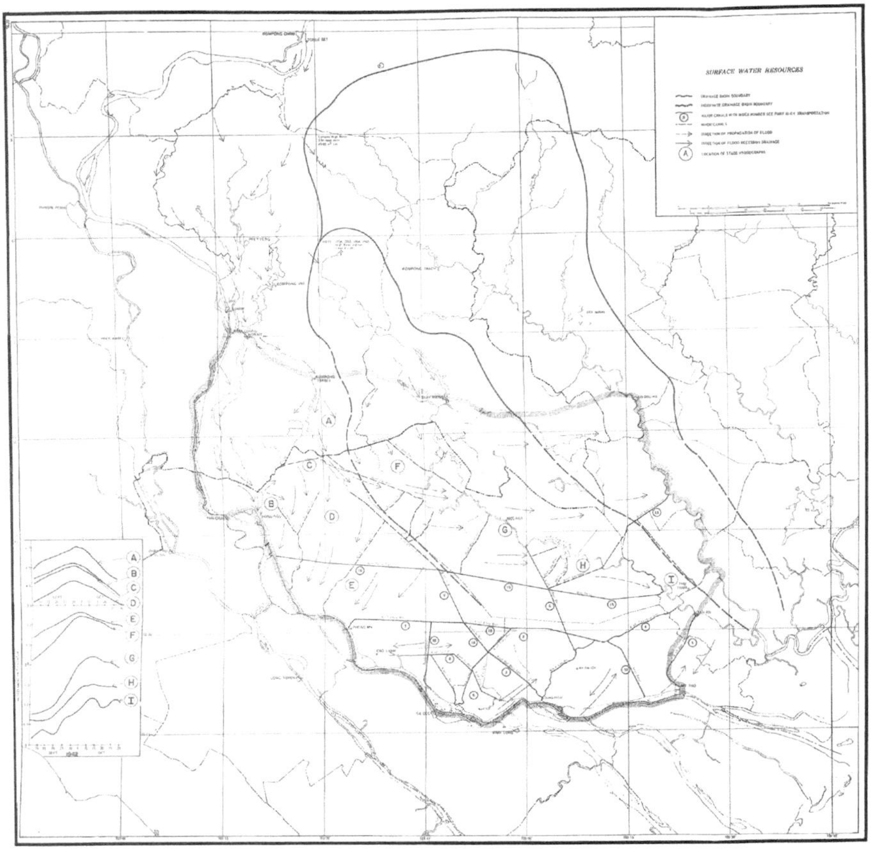

158 *Liquid Territories*

Figure 8.3 **Hydrology of the Plain of Reeds.** On the map, the hydrological extent of the Plain of Reeds (grey outline) is presented against the boundaries of "drainage basins" (darker lines). These boundaries become dashed when crossing into the Plain from the north, suggesting an "indefinite" watershed between the Mekong and the East and West Vaico rivers that contrasts with the "definite" extent of the floodplain's delineated catchment. Engineer Agency of Resources Inventories (1968), *Surface water resources.* [*Source:* Google Books]

considered the Plain of Reeds a "natural reservoir" without which "flooding would make the Mekong Delta virtually untenable".[29] During the wet season, a significant proportion of the floodwaters covering the Plain flowed southwards from Cambodia. Reaching around 2 metres in depth, the rising flood overtopped the rivers that acted as the dry-season marker for the national boundary with South Vietnam.[30] The border's temporary disappearance under seasonal floodwaters and the perennially wet condition of the ground facilitated the illicit movement of people, weapons and supplies between Cambodia and South Vietnam's communist-controlled areas.[31] The absence of settlements in many parts of the Plain exacerbated the perception that the flooded border area was a vulnerable frontier. Thus, from the perspective of the security situation "the high costs of reclamation could conceivably be accepted" if they eliminated a strategic risk that maps portrayed as lying on the western "doorstep" of Saigon.[32] Conflating the movement of water with the movement of people, the EARI's planning report stated that constructing water barriers parallel to the border as part of the development programme would also "provide barriers to infiltration".[33] With "infiltration" referring to the penetration of enemy troops rather than the absorption of floodwater into the ground, the perceived threat from inundation was not confined to the damage caused directly by water. Promoted as the answer to these multiple concerns, the planning of "large-scale polder development involving extensive dikes and levees" did not allude to traditional *casiers*.[34] Instead, they referenced the modern techniques and equipment that would overcome the terrain's susceptibility to the inundation which inhibited growth. Cast as technical solutions, the spatial magnitude of polders was determined by the relationship between available water resources and financial costs. Using the Delta's 62,000 km^2 catchment area to estimate average annual flows, only a small fraction of the total could be irrigated and up to 20 optimally sized polders – 100 km^2 each – would be feasible.[35] However, the possibility that the upstream infrastructure could be constructed in the future allowed far larger sizes to be considered. With individual polders reaching extremes of 8,000 km^2, the EARI's planners argued that the subdivision of the floodplain into hydrologically autonomous compartments was technically achievable, if not necessarily socially acceptable.

Elaborated across more than 40 maps, the EARI's investigation and planning attempted to ground the technical and economic reasoning underpinning the conceptualization of polders with the actual conditions encountered in the floodplain. New detailed maps based on the latest aerial photographs traced the areas of physical and human resources such as water, soils, demography and land uses. Consistent with the 'layer cake' approach taught and practised by the landscape architect Ian McHarg, separately mapping specific qualities or uses of a terrain could potentially reveal new, or confirm, known relationships. Elements such as water could be appreciated as particular natural systems but also in terms of their interrelationship with human activities.[36] McHarg's suggestion of a 'whole' contingent on the condition of its different 'parts' was not immediately apparent in the Mekong's floodplain. Rather than a homogeneous vegetated *atopia*, the EARI's new maps revealed a terrain replete with specific ground conditions. To the extent that the cartographic articulation of acid soils, land uses or population density indicated important characteristics of the floodplain, considered separately these did not necessarily compose a single, distinct geographic area. Without reference to the unifying qualities of the Plain's catchment area, to appreciate these separate layers as parts of specific whole would require this whole to be "constructed" from the accumulation of cartographic information.

The use of maps to notionally unify the parts of the floodplain that would otherwise be considered separate is illustrated in the map of the Plain's physiography (**Figure 8.4**). This representation of the floodplain's terrain used height contours

160 *Liquid Territories*

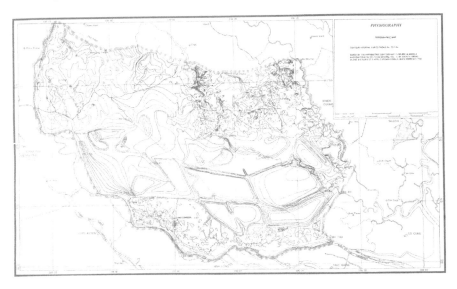

Figure 8.4 **Hydrology of the Plain of Reeds.** One of the 40 maps prepared by the EARI, the articulation of the Plain's topography used contours at 1-metre and at 10-centimetre intervals. Applied to the flattest part of the floodplain, the 10-centimetre contours reveal the otherwise imperceptible landforms of man-made waterways that appear to be 'carved' into the ground's geomorphology. Engineer Agency of Resources Inventories (1968), *Physiography*. [*Source:* Google Books]

that varied in places from intervals of 1 metre to 10 centimetres. As a result of these variations, the same number of contours is concentrated on the floodplain's flattest section as on the higher ground within the Cambodian section of the Plain. Thus, while the map is accurate in its portrayal of information, it also appears to emphasize the straight, shallow landforms produced by existing canals that would otherwise be almost invisible on a contour map. Deliberately or not, the map's suggestion that the floodplain's gradient could be considered an outcome of human activity, also appeared to indicate that there were other ways to imagine what physical characteristics constituted a differentiable geographic space. In this sense, the use of contours to describe the terrain was also an argument *about* that terrain which, if nothing else, posed the possibility of polders as an extension of the floodplain's existing geomorphology. Even without displaying a specific proposal, the cartographic articulation of the Plain's characteristics could suggest a particular course of action.

If the EARI's ambition was to "transform an unstable political base to one of great stability", new soil surveys revealed that only a small part of the Plain could be productively cultivated.[37] This constraint was reflected in the first of six "improvement" plans which limited dikes to an area parallel with the river's mainstream. And while the second and third options limited interventions even further without incorporating water infrastructure, extensive polders were proposed in the three

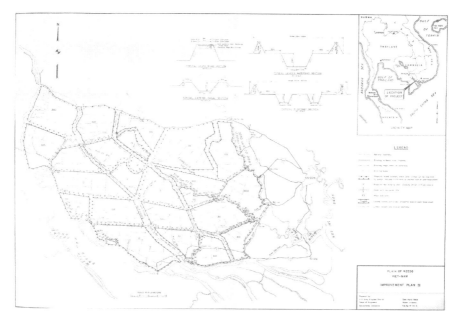

Figure 8.5 **Designing containment.** Illustrating the polder scheme across both South Vietnam and Cambodia, the map shows the entire Plain of Reeds divided into 24 polders by *floodways* reaching a width of up to 1,500 metres. Presumably operated by the state, pumping stations on each polder would distribute water from the *floodways* to the farms. Engineer Agency of Resources Inventories (1968), *Implementation Plan III*. [*Source:* Google Books]

subsequent plans. Dimensioned on the assumption that upstream reservoirs would detain part of the annual volume of inundation for dry season use, the 24 polders presented in "Improvement Plan III" (IP3) were configured to take advantage of the straight edges of existing canals (**Figure 8.5**). Levee walls built at a distance from the edges of waterways, were envisioned to create "floodways" more than 1.5 kilometres wide. These would divert floodwaters separating the hydrology of each interstitial "subarea" from seasonal ground conditions but also from each other. Within each compartment, pumps drawing water from the *floodways* would allow control of the ground's wetness, potentially producing five crops over two years. By confining perennial wetness to the *floodways,* however, the diversion of water for irrigation to a particular farm would require a large-scale mechanical infrastructure that only the state could provide. Stating that control over irrigation and drainage would operate on a "polder-by-polder basis", the EARI's report stipulated that the flows of water in each compartment could be regulated according to "military, political or economic necessity".[38] From this perspective, the almost autonomous management of water that each polder theoretically represented was not conceived purely as a technical operation but also one with the potential to control the activities of people within the polder's confines.

162   *Liquid Territories*

In the maps introducing the plans, the control of water that underpinned the configuration of polders was not confined to South Vietnam. Speculating that the scheme could encompass the entirety of the areas submerged under floodwater, the *floodways* in IP3 continued into Cambodia. Arguments insisting that the development of the Plain should be "contemplated in its entirety" referenced the existing institutional mechanisms for international cooperation in water resource management.[39] Drawing parallels with the basin-wide international planning of the Mekong Committee, the strategic assessment by the Advanced Research Projects Agency recommended that South Vietnam should invite Cambodia for a joint reclamation project of the Plain of Reeds. Similar to the Mekong Committee, the joint project would serve as a framework for international cooperation between the two countries, with the Plain of Reeds substituting the basin as the area of operations. Seen from this perspective, the continuous parallel lines indicating "proposed leveed waterways" on the plan visually construct a very specific geographic entity based on the assemblage of individual polders. Instead of a singular terrain divided into 24 separate compartments, the 24 individual polders could be imagined to collectively construct the Plain of Reeds. Within this Plain, the water infrastructure would act as the barrier to the flows of water as well as weapons, supplies and people.

Conclusion

Examining diachronic plans for polders, Biggs has asserted that *casiers* represented a "containment strategy" attractive to the different political regimes controlling the Vietnamese section of the Mekong's delta.[40] Even within the perimeter of water surrounding each polder, the idea that *floodways* could function as moats to confine people to areas within the polder is less convincing than the 'containment' of water itself. Bounded by the levees and with water distributed to farms by pumps and gates, the area encircled by dikes would remain safe even in the wet season, increasing the agricultural output of an otherwise unproductive terrain. However, the same infrastructure could also withhold water from agricultural use, allowing those with the power to operate the pumps and gates to coerce residents according to political imperatives. The risks related to inundation were therefore replaced by the threat that the water infrastructure serving individual polders could be used to create conditions of artificial dryness, regardless of hydrological conditions in surrounding areas. Alluding to an imbalance in the hydrological equilibrium, this approach to the use of infrastructure was enabled by the diachronic perception that the Plain already had "too much water in the wet season". Quantified with reference to the floodplain's catchment area, the problem of 'excess' water framed the military need to control the border in terms of an environmental anomaly, two different problems which rational scientific planning could mitigate simultaneously. Adopting the floodplain as the extent of these corrective operations did not solely align with the preference of modernist planners to employ 'natural' hydrological scales for water management. Serving as the geographic reference with which to analyse other phenomena, the pictorial articulation of the floodplain also structured hypotheses about how to resolve the uncertainties posed by invasion

Articulating Inundation   163

from water and infiltration from enemies. What could therefore be perceived as the Plain of Reeds entailed more than imagining the sum of its cartographically defined 'contents'. By articulating where ground would be wet or dry, the habitable floodplain identified on maps became contained within the infrastructure controlling inundation.

Notes

1 Gouvernement général de l'Indochine (1931), *Service géographique de l'Indochine. Son organisation – Ses methodes – Ses travaux, Exposition coloniale internationale, Paris 1931*. Hanoi: Impri. d'Extrême-Orient, p. 22.
2 See, for example, Charles Robequain (1926), Gouvernemeni général de l'Indochine. Service géographique. Année 1925. Compte-rendu annuel des travaux exécutés par le Service giographique de l'Indochine. *Bulletin de l'École française d'Extrême-Orient*, v. 26, p. 388.
3 Guy Mercier (2009), Vidal de la Blache, P. In Rob Kitchin & Nigel Thrif (eds.), *International Encyclopaedia of Human Geography*, v. 12. Amsterdam: Elsevier. p. 148.
4 *"car la cartographie, si variés que soient ou que puissent devenir ses moyens d'expression, ne saurait suffire à l'explication des faits. Ces noms assemblés, ces lignes de demarcation tracées sur une feuille de papier recouvrent parfois des différences tells qu'une interprétation attentive des faits qu'ils expriment est seule capable d'introduire la clarté"*. Paul Vidal de la Blache (1898), La Géographie politique, à propos des écrits de M. Frédéric Ratzel. *Annales de Géographie*, v. 7, n. 32, p. 111.
5 John Kleinen (2005), Tropicality and Topicality: Pierre Gourou and the Genealogy of French Colonial Scholarship on Rural Vietnam. *Singapore Journal of Tropical Geography*, v. 26, n. 3, p. 341.
6 Although he fails to mention Delahaye, Singaravelou's research indicates that between 1909 and 1942, three military officers defended theses on colonial geography at French universities. Pierre Singaravelou (2011), The institutionalisation of 'colonial geography' in France, 1880–1940. *Journal of Historical Geography*, n. 37, p. 149.
7 *"Rappelons d'abord la démonstration – faite au chapitre sur l'hydrograpihie – dans laquelle nous avons montré que l'inondation, venant pour la plus grosse partie du Fleuve antérieur – ou plutôt de ses effluents . . . c'est à l'origine même du mal, de Tong Binh à Hong-Ngu, qu'il y a lieu d'intervenir en premier lieu"*. Victor Delahaye (1928), *La Plaine des Joncs (Indochine Française) et sa mise en valeur: Etude géographique*, doctoral thesis, the Faculty of Letters, University of Rennes. Rennes: Impri. de L'Ouest-Éclair, p. 220.
8 *Ibid.*, p. 36.
9 *"La montée se propage presque intégralement, c'est-à-dire, qu'à une montée de cinq centimètres de l'origine, côté Mékong, correspond, quarante-huit heures après une montée identique à l'extrétmité côté Vaïco. Par contre la décrue s'effectue Presque simultanément, sur toute la longueur de la voie considérée. Les differences relevées sont si peu importantes qu'elles ne permettent pas de noter de zones particulières d'écoulement"*. *ibid.*, p. 90.
10 *"Pour que la Plaine des Joncs puisse être mise en valeur, il est évident qu'il faut l'assécher, et, pour cela, éviter les inconvénients de l'inondation périodique, ou mieux, supprimer celle-ci"*. *ibid.*, p. 219.
11 *"Cependant, il faut reconnaître que ce n'est pas tant le travail topographique . . . qui interviendra pour la mise en valeur de la Plaine des Joncs, mais bien plutôt le nivellement dont tout découlera, au vrai sens du mot"*. *ibid.*, p. 17.
12 As Delahaye admitted, between the primary levelling points, the terrain had not been mapped. *"La pente générale ainsi déterminée, reste à considérer les cotes fournies*

164 *Liquid Territories*

par le nivellement général pour toutes les parties qui n', ont pas encore été levées topographiquement, c'est-à-dire tout l'Ouest de la Plaine". ibid., p. 221.

13 It is worth mentioning that the East Vaico was not consistently seen as the limit of the floodplain's catchment area. Writing a few years after Delahaye's thesis was published, the Vietnamese hydrographer Nguyễn Hiến Lê pointed out that from a hydrological perspective the West and East Vaico should be considered separately since the land between them was of a different character from the rest of the floodplain. Nguyễn Hiến Lê (2002), *Bảy Ngày Trong Đồng Tháp Mười.* Nhà xuất bản văn hóa thông.

14 *"Mais celui-ci n'en existe pas moins et son abondance rend, actuellement, nous le répétons, toute culture impossible sur les 4/5 de la région envisage . . . Pourtant le mal n'est pas sans remède. DéJà certains «nhà-qués» [Cultivateurs annamites] sont arrivés à laver leurs terres au moyen de petits canaux recevant les eaux pluviales, chargées de sels après un court séjour à la surface du sol, et les évacuant par la suite dans les «rachs» ou les fleuves voisins".* Delahaye, *op. cit.,* p. 40.

15 *Il figure sur la carte au 1: 500.000-du cadastre de la Cochinchine et porte le nom de "canal projete du song Dinb-Ha à Mylho" bien qu'il u'aboutisse pas à cette ville . . .". Ibid.,* p. 223.

16 David Biggs (2011), Aerial Photography and Colonial Discourse on the Agricultural Crisis in Late-Colonial Indochina, 1930–1945. In C.F. Ax, N. Brimnes, N.T. Jensen & K. Oslund (eds.), *Cultivating the Colonies: Colonial States and Their Environmental Legacies.* Athens: Ohio University Press, p. 184.

17 Due to the separation of hydrological regimes, Segeren comments that this definition would theoretically allow rice paddy or a floodplain to be considered as *polders,* adding that these are rarely (if ever) considered as such. W.A. Segeren (1982), Introduction to Polders of the World. *Water International,* v. 8, n. 2, p. 51.

18 Biggs, *op. cit.,* p. 107.

19 J.Y. Claeys, quoted in Biggs. *Ibid.,* pp. 108–109.

20 *Ibid.,* p. 119.

21 Biggs suggests that settlers unfamiliar with the Mekong's hydrology constructed deep canals that drained water outside the protective dikes. Why the deep canals were required in the first place however is not clear and may have been the result of inadequate planning of the *casier* in the first place. *Ibid.,* p. 20.

22 *Ibid.,* p. 115.

23 Republic of Viet-Nam (1956), *The Dramatic Story of Resettlement and Land Reform in the 'Rice Bowl' of the Republic of Viet-Nam.* Saigon: Secretariat of State for Information, Republic of Viet-Nam, p. 9.

24 *Ibid.,* p. 19.

25 James O'Neal (1967), The Role of the Engineer Agency for Resources Inventories in International Development. *The Professional Geographer,* v. 19, p. 34. Also see James O'Neal & James Bwins (1974), *An Operational Application of ERTS-1 Imagery to the Environmental Inventory Process (Conference Paper),* Goddard Space Flight Center 3d ERTS-1 Symp., v. 1, Sec. A, p. 579.

26 Prepared by Charles Schwartz (geographer), Allen Reimer (soil scientist) and Joseph Brewer (hydraulic engineer), the An Giang report (1969) appears to be an elaboration of the earlier planning study for the Plain of Reeds (1968) and shares the same technical contributors. Engineer Department for Resources Inventories (1969), *A Program to Attain Maximum Agricultural Production in An Gian Province, Viet-Nam.* Washington, DC: Department of the Army.

27 My emphasis. Engineer Agency for Resources Inventories (1968), *Accelerated Development in the Plain of Reeds.* Washington, DC: US Army, Summary of Report, p. vii (Summary).

28 "We are of course aware that the potential benefit/cost ratio of any such reclamation of the Plaine des Joncs would probably be low. But there are abundant social reasons

which might nevertheless mean that the Mekong Committee, and in particular, the governments of Vietnam and Cambodia, might after a detailed feasibility investigation has been carried out, decide to press for such reclamation". Dr. C. Hart Schaff, Chief executive of the Mekong Committee (1964) quoted in Victor Croizat (1969), *The Development of the Plain of Reeds: Some Politico-Military Implications*. Santa Monica, CA: The Rand Corporation, p. 22.

29 EARI (1968), *op. cit.*, p. vii (Summary).
30 *Ibid.*, p. 3.
31 Croizat, *op. cit.*, p. 22.
32 "Therefore, when considering the national security interests of South Vietnam, it becomes apparent that the penetration of the Plain by government forces and its eventual resettlement could help eliminate one major center of communist infection. For this reason the high costs of reclamation could conceivably be accepted, provided the measures taken in the re-settlement process were carefully related to the security situation." *Ibid.*, p. i (Preface).
33 "The establishment of water barriers through the construction of major canals as part of the development program, especially those on an east-west alignment, would provide barriers to infiltration". EARI (1968), *op. cit.,* p. 84.
34 EARI (1969), *op. cit.*, p. 4.
35 The EARI estimated that up to 2,000 km^2 out of about 62,000 km^2 could be used for agriculture simply based on the quantity of available water. EARI (1968), *op. cit.*, p. 22.
36 "A single drop of water in the uplands of a watershed may appear and reappear as cloud, precipitation, surface water . . . in considerations of climate and microclimate, water supply, flood, drought and erosion control, industry, commerce, agriculture, forestry, recreation, scenic beauty, in cloud, snow, stream, river and sea. We conclude that nature is a single interacting system and that changes to any part will affect the operation of the whole". Ian McHarg (1971), *Design with Nature*. New York: Doubleday, Natural History Press, p. 56.
37 EARI (1968), *op. cit.*, p. ix.
38 "The series of canals and levees recommended in this study results in the type of poldering that allows controlled irrigation and drainage on a polder-by-polder basis as dictated by military, political, or economic necessity. The approach also provides for the orderly transition to flood control whenever circumstances warrant". *ibid.*, p. x.
39 Croizat, *op. cit.*, p. 32.
40 Biggs, *op. cit.*, p. 94.

9 The Region's Immergence

The Plain of Reeds could now be renamed the 'Plain of Rice' since the park is surrounded by a 'sea of rice' and human settlements in six surrounding communes and a district town.

Situation Analysis: Plain of Reeds, Viet Nam,
Nguyen Xuan Vinh & Andrew B. Wyatt, 2006

The vast "sea of rice" which today has become almost synonymous with the Mekong's floodplain emerged as water infrastructure gradually reshaped the river's seasonal overflow. Discussions regarding water management have usually been framed as critical to rural development, the sharing of increasingly scarcer resources and more recently the impacts of climate change. Agriculture and its associated irrigation apparatus have been prominent in these conversations. Accounting for nearly 90% of all water abstractions from the Mekong, the magnitude of irrigated land has grown from almost nothing in the 1950s to more than five million hectares by 2015.[1] Of this, almost 80% is situated in the Vietnamese part of the Mekong Delta where individual irrigation units can reach up to 8,000 hectares.[2] Along with the introduction of high-yield varieties of rice (HYV) sparked by the 'green revolution', this has more than doubled the tonnage of rice produced in the south of Vietnam since unification.[3] Especially after the implementation of market-oriented economic policies in the late 1980s, the Delta has been described as Vietnam's 'rice bowl' with the region's rice exports competing for dominance in global markets.

Although credited with bringing widespread socioeconomic benefits across large parts of Southeast Asia, today there is general consensus that the region's irrigation systems have not performed to expectations.[4] Known as *command areas* by agricultural engineers, distinct irrigation units designed to accommodate rice paddy are only partially cultivated and have proven difficult to adapt for growing other crops. Particularly in the Plain of Reeds, the impact of water infrastructure has unfolded beyond individual command areas. Providing water-borne access to homes and protecting nearby fields, the configuration of canals and dikes has underpinned the location of new settlements but also driven the loss of wetlands and consequently reduced the floodplain's capacity to detain inundation.[5] Such rapid changes to the way the hydrological system operates defy the idea of a permanent geographic

DOI: 10.4324/9781032706238-13

The Region's Immergence 167

'background' serving as the setting for human actions and the context of regional planning. As water historians Tvedt and Jacobsson argue, specific water infrastructure projects can have long-term, irreversible downstream impacts as people adapt their lives to the new condition of the ground. Examined from this perspective, the construction of the individual canals and dikes that collectively constitute the floodplain's current hydrology are not just historical episodes taking place within the *longue durée*. How these projects were planned and implemented have redefined the context in which they are considered. Focusing on the changes to surface water flows instigated by the irrigation infrastructure since Vietnam's unification, the chapter asks whether the floodplain's natural catchment area has been replaced by the surface water diversions used to transform the Plain of Reeds into a Plain of Rice.

Isolating Wetness

Beginning in the 1960s, the need to "seal-off" the delta and the floodplain from the river's inundation dominated discussions on the maximization of agricultural production.[6] From the perspective of the Mekong Committee, the control of water in the floodplain was contingent on dams constructed further upstream. Working from their headquarters in Bangkok, the Committee's engineers highlighted the importance of the vast reservoirs planned in Cambodia for agriculture in the Mekong Delta. Designed to store floodwater, maps presented dams at Stung Treng creating a massive artificial inland 'sea' which would exceed Tonle Sap in size.[7] In an attempt to gauge the downstream impact of these projects for dry season cultivation and flood protection, hydrological studies began to employ computerized models. Prepared by a team of Dutch engineers as the regional conflict reached its apex, a 1974 report commissioned by the Committee examined the impact of dikes on the water levels of shallow flooded areas. Using the hydrological model prepared by SOGREAH, the report outlined the results of testing different combinations of the seven proposed dikes throughout the delta. Dividing the delta's flood-affected areas into notional meshes to compartmentalize the computation of water depth, the study concluded that dikes constructed only within the Vietnamese part of delta "would not strongly affect the river stages" at which water might breach manmade barriers.[8] At the same time, the report highlighted that, to a greater or lesser degree, creating flood barriers to direct waterflows anywhere would cause upstream areas in Cambodia to "suffer increases of floodlevels".[9] The impact of new dikes would not just be visible upstream. Even in the scenario where all dikes were simultaneously deployed for their cumulative effect, the depth of inundation in the Plain of Reeds would rise at least 1 metre above baseline levels.[10] The study concluded that without carefully planning their location and dimensions, dikes would almost certainly cause major changes to the flood regime in Cambodia and in disparate sections of the Mekong's floodplain.

The political and military situation that saw the American army leave South Vietnam in 1973 and the dissolution of the Mekong Committee a few years later, brought almost all projects to control the river's mainstream to a standstill. Reconstituted

168 *Liquid Territories*

in 1978 with the participation of Thailand, Laos, a unified Vietnam but not Cambodia, the *Interim Mekong Committee* helped reopen diplomatic discussions on the development of shared water resources. Nonetheless, the political isolation of Vietnam and Laos and civil strife in Cambodia prevented any concerted effort to implement plans for hydroelectric dams and storage reservoirs. Even without the upstream infrastructure, however, irrigation in the delta was considered important. Driven by the need to feed a growing population and reorganize settlement patterns to meet a national programme of 'deurbanization', the Vietnamese state's approach aimed for total water control in the entirety of its domain.[11] Indicative of a strategic approach rather than a technical plan, the map included in the Committee's 1978 report illustrated the imagined relationship between agriculture and water management (**Figure 9.1**). Depicted in relation to the river's surface flows, the map's green shade representing "irrigation areas" appeared to stretch hundreds of kilometres from the coast to the north of the Phnom Penh. Extending beyond the dashed limits of the "flooded area boundary" irrigation was also shown to cover the coastal lowlands where floods were an outcome of tides and monsoonal rains suggesting that agriculture was possible even without the sediment deposits carried by the river. Rather than the floodplain's boundaries the cartographic notation that appeared to be instrumental in determining the extent of irrigation was the basin's watershed. But while on the map this imaginary line appeared to display a hydrological fact, on the ground its descriptive value was non-existent. Not only did the rising floodwaters ignore the hypothetical limits of the river's watershed but even when these eventually receded they did not appear to correspond to any single mapped configuration.

If the watershed crossing the Plain of Reeds did not represent a particular behaviour of water, its value as the critical determinant for the extent of irrigated areas arose from a different angle. A result of the Committee's mandate to focus only on the land within the basin, the alignment of irrigation with this particular mapped limit also indicated where future command areas would *not* to be located. At the same time, the hypothetical watershed differentiated the more densely populated areas located closer to the river from the largely uninhabited swamp further north. The absence of irrigation in the north part of the floodplain however cannot be seen only from the perspective of a convenient alignment between the basin's outline and agriculture. Mapped information regarding the status of ground conditions in the Plain of Reeds was either deficient or contradictory.[12] Important for planning, cartographic records of existing cultivation practices such as floating rice were inconsistent in regard to their extent and location. *Floating rice*, the traditional crop of the floodplain's farmers, was sown directly into sediment deposits, growing long stalks that were visible above the high water level. Adapted to the fluctuations of the annual flood and thus requiring almost no infrastructure, this labour-intensive method yielded far lower quantities of rice than the crop grown on paddy fields.[13] Moreover, given the dependence on annual sediment deposits which could not be precisely predicted, the method also entailed the risk of a poor harvest. In the Plain of Reeds, this cultivation technique encompassed a significant portion of the flooded areas closer to the Mekong's mainstream and along the seasonally submerged border with Cambodia.

Figure 9.1 **The limits of catchments.** A detail from the Interim Mekong Committee's map of basin development published in 1978. The basin's watershed (hatched line) and flooded areas (dashed line) are shown in relation to potential irrigated areas (dark shade) and the national border between Vietnam and Cambodia (thicker opaque line). Similar to the Committee's 1970 indicative basin plan (**Figure 3.6**), north of the river and within Vietnam, irrigation appears to terminate at the watershed. Interim Mekong Committee (1979), *General Map of the Lower Mekong Basin Showing Potential Water Projects*. [*Source:* United Nations]

Estimated by the Mekong Committee to encompass half a million hecatres in the early 1970s, floating rice was identified as a crop that could be replaced with HYVs.[14] Using transplanting techniques where the plants would first be grown in a nursery and then transferred to the field, the HYVs promoted by international organizations required full water control and adequate dry-season irrigation to

170   *Liquid Territories*

harvest two annual crops. On the Committee's maps, the location of transplanted rice appeared to ignore the physiological differences within the floodplain. Shown to cover the majority of the Plain, HYVs appeared further inland where conditions were described as unsuitable for paddy agriculture. Indeed, as a different map published four years later indicated that only the areas adjacent to the mainstream were actually usable for growing rice. Prepared by Japanese agriculture specialists after fieldwork in the region, the map presented the physiographic classification of existing ground conditions and their relationship with cultivation. Diagrammatic rather than technical, the map's depiction of the "backswamp" indicated that agriculture on the Plain of Reeds was possible only in these "marginal parts of the area", where *emplodering* would modify the "original hydrography".[15] Warning that it was of "no use to drain all the water" in the great swamp, the perennially wet grounds of the Plain were considered unsuitable for cultivation and depicted without any information about the soil and only an **R** denoting the Plain's toponymy.[16] Due to the depth of floodwaters and the presence of acid soils, the infrastructure needed to establish agriculture in these areas was too costly in comparison with other parts of the Mekong Delta and therefore a low overall priority. Either as a "backswamp" or as "floating rice", conditions in areas more than 20 kilometres from the mainstream prevented the establishment of paddy agriculture without drainage and irrigation infrastructure. As such the extent of single transplant rice fields on the Committee's map is dubious. Even if only a projection of future conditions rather than a record of existing ones is considered, the 1978 map placing irrigation infrastructure where floating rice was grown appears inherently contradictory. Although it is impossible to deduce if this was an error on the part of the cartographers or a contradiction internal to the plan, the map argued that a productive, irrigated terrain which corresponded to the cartography of water could be extracted from the swamp and differentiated from all other adjacent areas.

The Geography of Irrigation

In the context of the Mekong's lowlands, "irrigation infrastructure" includes control structures such as embankments and water gates as well as water distribution systems such as canals and pump stations.[17] While the limits of distinct command areas are not always spatially defined by waterways, canals provide the surface water needed for cultivation during the dry season and determine how it is accessed by farmers. Following Vietnam's unification, more than 15,000 kilometres of main canals have been constructed in the Mekong Delta.[18] A significant portion of these canals has been built in the Plain of Reeds, extending the network of waterways constructed by the French and the post-colonial administrations of South Vietnam. Arranged to form an irregular 'grid', the main canals visible on maps and aerial images occupy the entirety of the geographic space between the Mekong's mainstream and the border with Cambodia. Constructed incrementally, the arrangement of waterways today is a consequence of multiple plans formulated by the Vietnamese state following the country's unification. The first plan for irrigation in the Delta was articulated in 1976 and intended to counter the impact of unplanned waterways constructed by local farmers that had resulted in the distribution of the

The Region's Immergence   171

toxic water from acid soils.[19] Referencing the water control practices in the Red River Delta, the new plan focused on organizing irrigation and introduced pumping stations along large canals. However, these early attempts faltered. In combination with the lack of petrol and the wide availability of small pumps useable by individual farmers, many pumping stations reached only up to 15% of their design capacity.[20] Along with the lack of dredging equipment which forced canals to be excavated manually, the development of major irrigation infrastructure in the 1970s was severely constrained.

The failure to plan a distribution system suitable to the actual conditions confronted by farmers led to a change in the approach. Adopting the idea that long-term technical plans required both scientific knowledge and political will, the Vietnamese state initiated studies to understand the actual conditions on the ground.[21] Complemented by hydraulic and salinity models to predict water flows, soil surveys and programmes to understand social conditions, the compiled information was used to formulate a new plan for the period 1986–1990.[22] As an important part of the plan, the Delta was subdivided into five irrigation zones, with each zone adopting a different approach to water control. The Plain of Reeds was included in the East Tien River zone that spanned between the hydrological regimes of the Mekong and Vaico rivers. Within the zone, new east-west canals were constructed to drain floodwaters using the Mekong River's flows to wash away the toxic surface water created by immersion of the acid soils. Partially following the route of the Sở Hạ River, the national boundary dividing the Plain of Reeds between Vietnam and Cambodia became the edge of a 'grid', composed of a new drainage infrastructure. According to a Vietnamese map of the Plain available in 1968, acid soils were known to be concentrated inland from the river and had already formed the ground through which important manmade waterways such as the Republic Canal and the Lagrange had been routed. With reference to the planar configuration of these existing waterways, the new primary canals were excavated through areas where acid soils were predominant. The risks entailed in the redistribution of acid water through the canals became a point of contention. Arguing that waterways such as the Hong Ngu canal would pollute the Mekong's mainstream and surrounding paddy fields, Vietnamese researchers and international scientists voiced strong objections to the central government's plans. When concerns were also raised by the party Chairman of Dong Thap Province, the central government halted construction to study the impact more closely, restarting construction only after provincial authorities had been convinced. Completed, the canal began to 'push' acid water into the West Vaico River where it flowed downstream to be diluted in the estuary.[23] Although the adverse impacts eventually dissipated, the state's drainage infrastructure dispersed conditions that were previously concentrated in one part of the floodplain to the distant part of a different river. If before the new canals the Vaico and the Mekong had been discussed as part of the same hydrological system only during the wet season floods, the canals would henceforth unify the flows of the two rivers in the dry season as well.

Joining distant parts of the floodplain into new contiguous geographic areas, the new canals also placed barriers to the movement of water. Raised at a height suitable to direct floodwater in the early part of the *mùa nước nổi*, earth embankments

172 *Liquid Territories*

began to be constructed after 1976. Unlike *casiers* in the Red River's Delta, dikes were not a traditional technique for controlling water by the Mekong Delta's Vietnamese farmers. Describing his experience in An Giang Province in 1976, the former Chairman of the Provincial People's Committee Nhị Minh Nguyễn pointed out that the model for low dikes was inspired by observation of Cambodian farmers during the American War.[24] With the top of the embankments used as roads and the relatively mild flood of 1976 both showing the benefit of these structures, the model of low seasonal dikes was subsequently adopted in the other parts of the Mekong Delta to increase rice harvests. Re-built annually by local farmers, low levee walls called *August dikes* (*bao lung*) protected planted fields when the flood levels rose. Timed with the harvest of a second rice crop, the height of the dikes was designed to overflow with the high water levels in late August. This allowed the nutrient-rich sediment to settle in the fields after the first harvest, with the floodwater detained within the waterworn embankments available until the end of the wet season.

The state-sanctioned proliferation of low dikes throughout the floodplain signified a change in the way floods were managed. Brought into law in 1986, policies to further increase rice production resulted in the government raising the height of existing embankments even further.[25] Encircled by walls and using gates and canals to divert water into and out of the dikes when needed, the dispersion of floodwater was contingent not only on the rhythms of the monsoonal climate but also on the demand for water. With the ability to fill and drain the paddy encircled by dikes more than once each year, the increased control over what and when to plant allowed farmers to cultivate a third rice crop. Following the catastrophic floods of 2000, the construction of high dikes accelerated.[26] Since then, concrete embankments designed at a height to withstand inundation throughout the year have been built throughout the floodplain. In the Plain of Reeds, maps show that these high dikes are concentrated within the administrative boundaries of Dong Thap and Tien Giang provinces where the flood depth is lowest. As a result of the sixfold increase in land dedicated to producing three annual crops, rice yields in the Plain of Reeds have doubled, allowing some to describe the continuous extent of paddy covering the floodplain as a vast "Plain of Rice" stretching to the flat horizon.[27]

Although the control of water within these floodproof 'cells' has become synonymous with industrial-level rice production, in the Plain of Reeds dikes have also become the site of efforts to recreate an almost extinct natural condition. Since perhaps 700,000 hectares of melaleuca swamp forests (*tram*) had been converted into rice farms during the 1980s alone, restoring these forest ecosystems was a key concern of some local officials.[28] The first attempts to preserve the Plain's indigenous biodiversity focused on a dike between four canals which had been designed to detain floodwater rather than to grow crops.[29] As a result of the lack of agriculture activity and preservation of existing melaleuca trees, the rare eastern saurus crane was spotted nesting in the dike and by central government decree, the Tram Chim National Park was established in 1992 to conserve the wildlife and vegetation within the dike. In terms of biodiversity, the forest which has grown within the dike stands in contrast to the rice monocultures in the surrounding fields.

The Region's Immergence   173

Nonetheless, the quality and depth of the water on which the acid-tolerant mela-leuca grow are controlled by the opening and closing of six gates timed to follow the seasonal fluctuations of floodwater.[30] The maintenance of water levels at artifi-cial depths have resulted in biological changes in some species of vegetation, while also dramatically increasing the risk of forest fires during the dry season.[31] From this perspective, Tram Chim's geographically isolated forest ecosystem is not the preserved fragment of a previous pre-dike condition. Encompassed within one of the hydrologically autonomous units created by the subdivision of the terrain, the nature conserved in the park is underpinned by the same technologies which allow farmers to grow rice on a former swamp.

As flood barriers in one place affect flood levels in another, the maintenance of the irrigation system must constantly also account for the changes the system induces in both upstream and downstream. In hydrological models, the catchment area used to quantify the volume of water diverted by these embankments in the Plain of Reeds extends to Tonle Sap (**Figure 9.2**). Studies based on these models have identified the impact of high dikes on the floodplain's hydrology. While the temporary nature of August dikes does not appear to have had measurable effects, high dikes have been connected with higher flood depths further upstream as well as downstream increases in mean water levels.[32] Considering that land subsidence and climate-related changes in tidal levels are also important reasons for these changes, those induced by the construction and use of high dikes have extended the threats posed by destructive floods, dry season drought and salinity intrusion into downstream areas.[33] While these conclusions describe conditions across the entire floodplain, the propagation of rice agriculture which has resulted from the flood control of both high and August dikes has affected the Plain of Reeds more profoundly. Research has pointed out that the disappearance of perennial wetlands in the Plain of Reeds has been driven by the demand for agricultural land, which the drainage of the floodplain has produced.[34] Coupled with the destruction of the melaleuca swamp forests, the capacity of the Plain to detain floodwater has been significantly reduced. If the cartographic delineation of the floodplain is closely associated with defining an area at risk from inundation, then does the redistribu-tion of these risks imply that a more fundamental relationship between water and geographic space has also changed?

An answer to this question is provided in the delineation of catchment areas by the Mekong River Commission (MRC). The organization charged with coordinat-ing exploitation of the river's water across four countries, the MRC is also one of the most important sources of information about the river. Derived digitally by the MRC's cartographers, spatial data of the Mekong's tributary basins and catchment areas are obtained by projecting water flows on a digital elevation model. In the mapping process, this technique of determining boundaries is utilized for catch-ment areas between the river's sources in Tibet and the upper part of Vietnam's Mekong Delta.[35] Throughout the remaining Delta, however, the topographically derived boundaries are combined with "water resource management areas". Thus, while in the Cambodian part of the Plain of Reeds catchment areas appear to follow the irregular features of the terrain, in the Vietnamese part they correspond to the

174 *Liquid Territories*

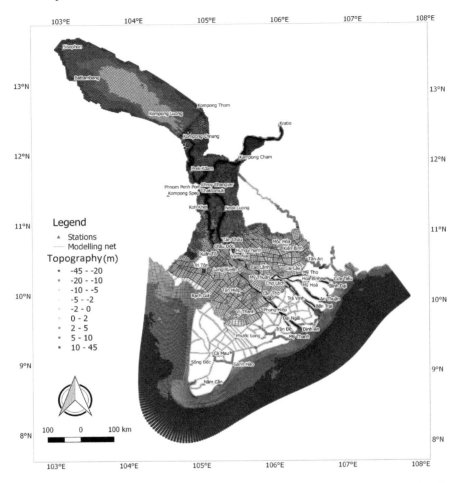

Figure 9.2 **Hydrological parameters.** The map is extracted from the study evaluating the impact of high dikes. It shows the spatial extent used to calibrate the hydraulic model and outlines the floodplain's catchment area (shaded areas showing the flood depth) used for assessment. Vo *et al* (2020), *Mekong Delta Modelling Grid and River Interpolated Topography.* [*Source:* Vo Quoc Thanh]

subunits of the East Tien River irrigation zone. To the extent that the map illustrates a plausible spatial relationship between land and the flows of water, the catchments' outlines suggest that for the MRC's cartographers, the most relevant spatial unit for describing the relationship between water and geographic space equates with the configuration and regulation of water for irrigation. Considering that the hypothetical line dividing the flows of the Mekong and the Vaico now aligns with the straight edges of canals, the configuration of the Plain's irrigation system appears to have substituted the hydrological basin as the reference for water control.

Conclusion

Confronted by such diverse depictions of the catchment's cartographic delineation, it is worth considering what hydrological relationship the catchments are used to describe. Even if the MRC's version can be seen as a purely technocratic response to the question of where the watershed between waterways is located, the conceptualization of catchment areas in terms of an area of water control is consistent with earlier versions published after 1975. Denoting the extent of irrigation in the Mekong Committee's map from 1978, the position of the basin's limit in the Plain of Reeds would have been difficult to reconcile with an observable behaviour of water. Intentionally or not, the watershed's cartographic division of the Plain of Reeds reflected most closely the approximate location of alluvial soils closer to the river that were most favourable for agriculture, leaving a void on the map where most of the acid soils were concentrated. Iterations of the outline still used today have refined the watershed's configuration roughly equidistant between the Vaico and Mekong rivers. But as the catchment of the hydraulic model shows, knowledge of this hypothetical limit has almost no value in the calculation of floodwater volume flowing over the Plain. Even if the Lower Mekong Basin's outline also functions as the MRC's area of operations, the line bisecting the Plain of Reeds is perhaps more symbolic of a hydrological concept rather than instrumental to spatial decisions regarding water control. Similarly, given the proliferation of dikes, the outlines of the irrigation units from which the MRC's catchments are extracted do not necessarily specify a distinct behaviour of water situated only within their limits. From this perspective, the extents of these catchments can also be thought of as imaginary hydrological notations which allude to a particular perception of geographic space. Cartographic references to the irrigation system are therefore equally symbolic of the process of rice cultivation driving the changes observable in the Plain, as much as they are intended to describe the extent of a particular behaviour of water.

Showing the satellite-detected surface water as the flood season peaks in late August, maps constructed from GIS spatial data reveal the degree of control exercised by water infrastructure in the flat lowlands of the Plain of Reeds **(Figure 7.1)**. Prescribing where water flows or stands still, the distribution of the dikes and canals used for irrigating rice produces a visible patchwork of (relatively) dry land, concentrated mostly to the south of the cartographic line indicating the river basin's boundary. If maps showing the location of surface water are intended to present the 'reality' of an existing condition, understanding what environment becomes visible in the cartographic lines of the Plain's catchments is important. Equated with the watersheds of the Mekong's tributary basins, the rectilinear areal forms drawn by the MRC's cartographers suggest that collectively, anthropogenic changes to the flows of water have produced an environment which cannot be described solely through existing hydrological registers like the river's basin, delta or floodplain. What some scholars have called a 'second nature' is closely connected with an understanding that ground conditions have been permanently transformed by human activity.[36] As the socially produced environment of these processes is thought to have "replaced a non-human 'first nature'",[37] the way this

176 *Liquid Territories*

transformation is presented on a map is not limited to the individual alterations to the terrain in subsequent depictions of the same geographic area. Calibrated in relation to the practices of rice agriculture, the MRC's hypothetical catchment areas do not so much replace a pre-existing 'natural' environment but rather present that environment as an outcome of the human labour invested in its control and domestication. To therefore conclude that the irrigation system has become the geographic reference for the physical control of water is also to accept that the terrain visible on the map is not the same floodplain which Delahaye and the EARI's geographers had examined. Yet this is not just because infrastructure, agriculture and settlement have changed the physical conditions the map purports to depict. If references to catchments are also intended to evoke a permanent geographic 'reality' that could conceivably be restored if human maintenance of the system ceased, the 'second floodplain' produced by human activity suggests that the return to a possible 'equilibrium' prescribed purely by natural forces is no longer available.

Notes

1 Mekong River Commission (2019), *State of the Basin Report 2018*. Vientiane: Mekong River Commission, p. 152, Table 6.6.
2 Mekong River Commission (2018), *Irrigation Database Improvement for the Lower Mekong Basin*. Vientiane: Mekong River Commission, p. 11. Data from the MRC indicates that in Vietnam's Mekong Delta two million hectares of irrigated land have been created by 120 schemes averaging more than 16,000 hectares each compared with the whole of Laos (88 hectares/scheme) or Cambodia (390 hectares/scheme).
3 Jean-Francois Le Coq, Marc Dufumier & Guy Trébuil (2001), *History of Rice Production in the Mekong Delta*. Paper presented at Third EUROSEAS Conference, London, September 6–8, p. 5, Figure 4a.
4 Despite the proliferation of irrigation in the Mekong Basin, less than 40% of farmland in the region is irrigated. C.T. Hoanh, T. Facon, T. Thuon, R.C. Bastakoti, F. Molle & F. Phengphaengsy (2009), Irrigation in the Lower Mekong Basin Countries: The Beginning of a New Era? In F. Molle, T. Foran & M. Kakonen (eds.), *Contested Waterscapes in the Mekong Region: Hydropower, Livelihoods and Governance*. London: Earthscan, pp. 149–150.
5 Tanaka describes how migrants to the Plain of Reeds situated their homes and farms along newly built canals, increasing the Plain's population from perhaps one million in 1969 to almost three million today. Koji Tanaka (2001), Agricultural Development in the Broad Depression and the Plain of Reeds in the Mekong Delta: Conserving Forests or Developing Rice Culture? *Southeast Asian Studies*, v. 39, n. 1.
6 Joint Development Group (1969), *The Postwar Development of the Republic of Vietnam: Policies and Programs, v. 1*. Saigon & New York: Postwar Planning Group & Development and Resources Corporation, p. 520.
7 Committee for Coordination of Investigations of the Lower Mekong Basin (1970), *Report on Indicative Basin Plan: A Proposed Framework for the Development of Water and Related Resources of the Lower Mekong Basin (E/CN.ll/WRD/MKG/L.340)*. Bangkok: United Nations, pp. III–20.
8 Netherlands Delta Development Team (1974), *Recommendations Concerning Agricultural Development with Improved Water Control in the Mekong Delta, v. 7*. Working Paper IV, Hydrology. Bangkok: Netherlands Delta Development Team, p. 36.
9 *ibid.*
10 Referencing the table of flood levels, only in scenarios 4 and 7 do flood levels remain the same. In all other diking schemes – including partially diking part of the Plain of Reeds – flood levels rise. *Ibid.*, p. 37.

The Region's Immergence   177

11 H.H. Nguyen, P. Dargusch, P. Moss & D.B. Tran (2016), A Review of the Drivers of 200 Years of Wetland Degradation in the Mekong Delta of Vietnam. *Regional Environmental Change*, v. 16, n. 8, p. 2308.

12 Perhaps due to their strategic nature, the detailed maps of acid sulphate soils in the Plain prepared by the Engineer Agency for Resources Inventories (EARI) in 1968 do not appear to have directly informed maps from other sources.

13 François Molle & D.T. Tuân (2006), Water Control and Agricultural Development: Crafting Deltaic Environments in South-East Asia. In T. Tvedt & E. Jakobsson (eds.), *A History of Water, v. 1: Water Control and River Biographies*. London & New York: Tauris, p. 150.

14 *ibid.*

15 Yoshihiro Kaida (1974), Hydrography of Rice Land in the Vietnamese Part of the Mekong Delta. *Southeast Asian Studies*, v. 12, n. 2, p. 153.

16 *ibid.*

17 MRC (2018), *op. cit.*, p. 11.

18 Nguyen *et al* (2016), *op. cit.*, p. 2308. The length of canals constructed since unification is reported differently in various sources. Marchand *et al* (2014) indicate that 43,000 kilometres of main and secondary canals, and perhaps 50,000 kilometres of tertiary canals were built after 1990.

19 Chu Thai Hoanh, Diana Suhardiman & Le Tuan Anh (2014), Irrigation Development in the Vietnamese Mekong Delta: Towards Polycentric Water Governance? *International Journal of Water Governance*, v. 2, p. 68.

20 MRC (2018), *op. cit.*, p. 11.

21 Hoanh *et al*, *op. cit.*, p. 71.

22 *Ibid.*, p. 70.

23 *ibid.*

24 Initially met with resistance by Vietnamese farmers, for the construction of these dikes each household in the village was mobilized to make mud bricks for the new embankments. https://laodong.vn/phong-su/di-tim-cha-de-mo-hinh-de-bao-dong-bang-song-cuu-long-525727.ldo, accessed 16 June 2020.

25 Van Staveren *et al*, *op. cit.*, p. 286.

26 T.Q. Vo, D. Roelvink, M. van der Wegen, J. Reyns, H. Kernkamp, V.V. Giap & L.P.T. Vo (2020), Flooding in the Mekong Delta: The Impact of Dyke Systems on Downstream Hydrodynamics. *Hydrological Earth System Sciences*, v. 24, p. 191.

27 Nguyen Xuan Vinh & Andrew Wyatt (2006), *Situation Analysis: Plain of Reeds, Viet Nam*. Vientiane: Mekong Wetlands Biodiversity Conservation and Sustainable Use Programme (MWBP), p. 15.

28 Nguyen *et al* (2016), *op. cit.*, p. 2308.

29 Le Cong Kiet (1993), Dong Thap Muoi; Restoring the Mystery Forest of the Plain of Reeds. *Restoration and Management Notes*, v. 11, n. 2, p. 102.

30 Jill Pacovsky (2001), Restoration of wetlands in the Tram Chim Nature Reserve (Dong Thap Province, Mekong River Delta, Vietnam). *Student On-Line Journal*, v. 7, n. 3. Department of Horticultural Science, University of Minnesota.

31 Water levels in the dike have been responsible for reducing the growth rates of the melaleuca trees and for reducing the main source of food for the saurus cranes which have subsequently impacted the bird population nesting in the Park. V.N. Duong, D. Shulman, J. Thompson, T. Tran, T. Thai & M. van der Schans (2006), *Integrated Water and Fire Management Strategy Tram Chim National Park*. UNDP, IUCN, MRC, GEF, p. ii.

32 Vo *et al* (2020), *op. cit.*, p. 189. See also D.D. Tran, G. van Halsema, P. Hellegers, L.P. Hoang, T.Q. Tran, M. Kummu & F. Ludwig (2018), Assessing Impacts of Dike Construction on the Flood Dynamics of the Mekong Delta. *Hydrological Earth System Sciences*, v. 22, p. 1875.

178 *Liquid Territories*

33 V.K.T. Nguyen, V.D. Nguyen, H. Fujii, M. Kummu, B. Merz & A. Heiko (2017), Has Dyke Development in the Vietnamese Mekong Delta Shifted Flood Hazard Downstream? *Hydrology and Earth System Sciences*, v. 21, p. 3992.

34 Nguyen *et al* (2016), *op. cit.*, p. 2308.

35 "Basinwide catchments (4,000 km^2 upstream areas) for the whole Mekong Basin. [The dataset] is derived by burning the classified river dataset into the existing DEM data to update DEM reflecting the patterns of water flow across the landscape and enable upstream area to be calculated to delineate boundary of catchment over the upper part of Vietnam Mekong delta, then combined with projected water resource management area of Vietnam Mekong Delta". https://portal.mrcmekong.org/data-catalogue?q=catchment&size=n_20_n, accessed 22 June 2022.

36 Christian Schmid (2016), The Urbanization of the Territory: On the Research Approach of ETH Studio Basel. In Mathias Gunz & Vesna Jovanovic (eds.), *Territory: On the Development of Landscape and City*. Zurich: Park Books, p. 28.

37 Noel Castree (2000), Marxism and the Production of Nature. *Capital & Class*, v. 24, n. 3, p. 25.

Bibliography

A

Acker, Robert (1998), New Geographical Tests of the Hydraulic Thesis at Angkor. *South East Asia Research*, v. 6, n. 1. pp. 5–47.

Akerman, James (1995), The Structuring of Political Territory in Early Printed Atlases. *Imago Mundi*, v. 47. pp. 138–154.

Andrew, C.M. & Kanya-Forstner, A.S. (1971), The French 'Colonial Party': Its Composition, Aims and Influence, 1885–1914. *The Historical Journal*, v. 14, n. 1. pp. 99–128.

Anh, D.N. (2008), The Mega-Urban Transformations of HCMC in the Era of Doi Moi Renovation. In G.W. Jones & M. Douglas (eds.), *Mega-Urban Regions in Pacific Asia: Urban Dynamics in a Global Era*. Singapore: National University of Singapore Press. pp. 188–217.

B

Banister, Jeffrey (2014), Are You Wittfogel or Against Him? Geophilosophy, Hydro-Sociality, and the State. *Geoforum*, n. 57. pp. 205–214.

Banister, Judith (1993), *Vietnam Population Dynamics and Prospects*. Institute of East Asian Studies. Berkeley, CA: University of California.

Benedikter, Simon (2014), Extending the Hydraulic Paradigm: Reunification, State Consolidation, and Water Control in the Vietnamese Mekong Delta After 1975. *Southeast Asian Studies*, v. 3, n. 3. pp. 547–587.

Biggs, David (2008), Breaking from the Colonial Mold: Water Engineering and the Failure of Nation-Building in the Plain of Reeds, Vietnam. *Technology and Culture*, v. 49, n. 3, Water. pp. 599–623.

Biggs, David (2010), *Quagmire: Nation Building and Nature in the Mekong Delta*. Seattle: University of Washington Press.

Biggs, David (2011), Aerial Photography and Colonial Discourse on the Agricultural Crisis in Late-Colonial Indochina, 1930–1945. In C.F. Ax, N. Brimnes, N.T. Jensen & K. Oslund (eds.), *Cultivating the Colonies: Colonial States and Their Environmental Legacies*. Athens: Ohio University Press. pp. 109–132.

Biswas, Asit (1970), *History of Hydrology*. Amsterdam & London: North-Holland Publishing Company.

Bogle, J.E., Republic of Vietnam, Daniel Mann Johnson & Mendenhall (DMJM) & William C. Rasmussen and Associates (1972), *Dialectics of Urban Proposals for the Saigon Metropolitan Area*. Washington, DC: United States Agency for International Development (USAID).

Bourdeaux, Pascal (2014), Sơn Nam ou la dualité d'une oeuvre: Évocations poétiques et ethnographiques du Viêt Nam meridional. *Moussons*, n. 24. pp. 189–216.

180 *Bibliography*

Bowd, Gavin & Clayton, Daniel (2003), Fieldwork and Tropicality in French Indochina: Reflections on Pierre Gourou's Les Paysans Du Delta Tonkinois, 1936. *Singapore Journal of Tropical Geography*, v. 24, n. 2. pp. 147–168.

Bras, Rafael L. (1999), A Brief History of Hydrology – The Robert E. Horton Lecture. *Bulletin of the American Meteorological Society*, v. 80, n. 6. pp. 1151–1164.

Brenner, Neil & Schmidt, Christian (2014), The 'Urban Age' in Question. *International Journal of Urban and Regional Research*, v. 38, n. 3. pp. 731–755.

Brocheux, Pierre (1995), *The Mekong Delta: Ecology, Economy, and Revolution, 1860–1960.* Madison, WI: Center for Southeast Asian Studies.

Brocklebank, R.A. (1961), The Mekong Survey. *The Canadian Surveyor*, March issue. pp. 402–410.

Buache, Philippe (1752), *Essai de géographie physique.* Mémoires de l'Académie royale des Sciences.

Bulletin Officiel de la Cochinchine française (1870), *Décision du Gouverneur de la Cochinchine du 9 Juillet 1870 portant délimitation des frontières du Cambodge.*

C

Cairns, Stephen (2018), Debilitating City-Centricity. In Rita Padawangi (ed.), *Routledge Handbook of Urbanization in Southeast Asia.* Abingdon, Oxon & New York, NY: Routledge. pp. 115–129.

Carroll, Siobhan (2015), *An Empire of Air and Water: Uncolonizable Space in the British Imagination, 1750–1850.* Philadelphia, PA: University of Pennsylvania Press.

Cassirer, Ernst (1951), *The Philosophy of the Enlightenment.* Princeton, NJ: Princeton University Press.

Castree, Noel (2000), Marxism and the Production of Nature. *Capital & Class*, v. 24, n. 3. pp. 5–36.

Catton, Philip E. (1999), Counter-Insurgency and Nation Building: The Strategic Hamlet Programme in South Vietnam, 1961–1963. *The International History Review*, v. 21, n. 4, pp. 918–940.

Celoria, Francis (1966), Delta as a Geographical Concept in Greek Literature. *Isis*, v. 57, n. 3. pp. 385–388.

Chester, Lucy (2000), The Mapping of Empire: French and British Cartographies of India in the Late Eighteenth Century. *Portugese Studies*, v. 16. pp. 256–275.

Clem, Clayton & Nelson, Jeffrey (2010), *The TVA Transmission System: Facts, Figures and Trends.* Proceedings of the 2010 Institute of Electrical and Electronics Engineers International Conference on High Voltage Engineering and Application, New Orleans, LA, October 11–14. pp. 1–11.

Coedès, Georges (1931), Etudes cambodgiennes. XXV, Deux inscriptions sanskrites du Fou-nan. XXVI, La date de Kôh Ker. XXVII, La date du Bàphûonm. *Bulletin de l'Ecole française d'Extrême-Orient*, v. 31. pp. 1–23.

Committee for Coordination of Investigations of the Lower Mekong Basin (1961), *Brief Description of the Pa Mong Project.* Bangkok: United Nations.

Committee for Coordination of Investigations of the Lower Mekong Basin (1970), *Report on Indicative Basin Plan: A Proposed Framework for the Development of Water and Related Resources of the Lower Mekong Basin (E/CN.ll/WRD/MKG/L.340).* Bangkok: United Nations.

Committee for Coordination of Investigations of the Lower Mekong Basin (1979), *Annual Report 1978 (ST/ESCAP/79).* Bangkok: United Nations.

Cosgrove, Denis (2008), Images and Imagination in 20th-Century Environmentalism: From the Sierras to the Poles. *Environment and Planning A*, v. 40. pp. 1862–1880.

Courrier de Saigon (1865), *Journal officiel de la Cochinchine Francaise*, n. 21, Novembre 5.

Croizat, Victor (1969), *The Development of the Plain of Reeds: Some Politico-Military Implications.* Santa Monica, CA: The Rand Corporation.

Bibliography   181

D

Da Cunha, Dilip (2019), *The Invention of Rivers: Alexander's Eye and Ganga's Descent.* Penn Studies in Landscape Architecture. Philadelphia, PA: University of Pennsylvania Press.

Dang, Trung (2018), *Vietnam's Post-1975 Agrarian Reforms: How Local Politics Derailed Socialist Agriculture in Southern Vietnam.* Canberra: Australia National University Press.

D'Anville, Jean-Baptiste Bourguignon (1753), *Éclaircissemens géographiques sur la carte de l'Inde.* Paris: Impri. Royale.

Dao, Van Tap (1980), On the Transformation and New Distribution of Population Centres in the Socialist Republic of Vietnam. *International Journal of Urban and Regional Research*, v. 4. Translated by Miriam Atlas. pp. 503–515.

Daston, Lorraine & Galison, Peter (1992), The Image of Objectivity. *Representations*, n. 40, Special Issue: Seeing Science. pp. 81–128.

Debarbieux, Bernard (2008), Mountains Between Corporal Experience And Pure Rationality: Buache And Von Humboldt's Contradictory Theories. In Denis Cosgrove & Veronica della Dora (eds.), *High Place Cultural Geographies of Mountains and Ice.* London & New York: IB Tauris. pp. 87–104.

Delahaye, Victor (1928), *La Plaine des Joncs (Indochine Française) et sa mise en valeur: Etude géographique.* Doctoral thesis, the Faculty of Letters, University of Rennes. Rennes: Impri. de L'Ouest-Éclair.

Delta Commission (2008), *Working Together with Water, Findings of the Deltacommissie 2008.* Amsterdam: Government of the Netherlands.

Desbarats, Jacqueline (1987), Population Redistribution in the Socialist Republic of Vietnam. *Population and Development Review*, v. 13, n. 1. pp. 43–76.

Đỗ, Bang (2011), *Hệ Thống Phòng Thủ Miền Trung Dưới Triều Nguyễn (Central Defence System Under the Nguyen Dynasty).* Hanoi: NXB Khoa Học Xã Hội (Social Science Publishing House).

Dooge, James (1974), The Development of Hydrological Concepts in Britain and Ireland Between 1674 and 1874. *Hydrological Sciences Journal*, v. 19, n. 3. pp. 279–302.

Dooge, James (1988), Hydrology in Perspective. *Hydrological Sciences Journal*, v. 33, n. 1. pp. 61–85.

Du, Huynh (2015), The Misuse of Urban Planning in Ho Chi Minh City. *Habitat International*, n. 48. pp. 11–19.

Duffy, Christopher (2017), The Terrestrial Hydrologic Cycle: An Historical Sense of Balance. *WIREs Water*, v. 4, e1216. pp. 1–21.

Duong, V.H.T., Van T.C., Nestmann, F., Oberle, P. & Nam N.T. (2014), *Land Use Based Flood Hazards Analysis for the Mekong Delta.* Proceedings of the 19th IAHR-APD Congress, Hanoi, Vietnam.

Duong, V.N., Shulman, D., Thompson, J., Triet, T., Truyen, T. & van der Schans, M. (2006), *Integrated Water and Fire Management Strategy Tram Chim National Park.* UNDP, IUCN, MRC, GEF.

Duvernoy, Victor (1924), *Monographie de la province de Longauyên (Cochinchine).* Hanoi: Moniteur de l'Indochine.

E

Edmonds, Christopher (2002), *The Role of Infrastructure in Land-Use Dynamics and Rice Production in Viet Nam's Mekong River Delta.* ERD Working Paper n. 16. Vientiane: Asian Development Bank.

Ehlert, Judith (2012), *Beautiful Floods: Environmental Knowledge and Agrarian Change in the Mekong Delta.* Vietnam, ZEF Development Studies, v. 19. Zurich & Berlin: LIT.

Ekbladh, David (2002), 'Mr. TVA'. Grass-Root Development, David Lilienthal, and the Rise and Fall of the Tennessee Valley Authority as a Symbol for U.S. Overseas Development, 1933–1973. *Diplomatic History*, v. 26, n. 3. pp. 335–374.

182   Bibliography

Elden, Stuart (2010), Land, Terrain, Territory. *Progress in Human Geography*, v. 34, n. 6. pp. 799–817.

Elliott, V.L. (1973), *Development Problems in Viet Nam; A Discussion and Definition of the South Viet Nam (Mekong Delta) Economic Region*. Washington, DC: USAID.

Engineer Agency for Resources Inventories (1968), *Accelerated Development in the Plain of Reeds*. Washington, DC: US Army. Summary of Report. p. vii.

Engineer Agency for Resources Inventories (1969), *A Program to Attain Maximum Agricultural Production in An Giang Province, Viet-Nam*. Washington, DC: Dept of the Army.

Evans, D., Pottier, C., Fletcher, R., Hensley, S., Tapley, I., Milne, A. & Barbetti, M. (2007), A Comprehensive Archaeological Map of the World's Largest Preindustrial Settlement Complex at Angkor, Cambodia. *Proceedings of the National Academy of Sciences*, v. 104, n. 36. pp. 14277–14282.

F

Fernández, Pablo & Buchroithner, Manfred (2014), *Paradigms in Cartography: An Epistemological Review of the 20th and 21st Centuries*. Berlin: Springer.

Ferraton, Cyrille (2007), *Associations et coopératives: Une autre histoire économique*. Toulouse: Érès.

Ferretti, Federico (2017), Teaching Anarchist Geographies: Élisée Reclus in Brussels and 'The Art of Not Being Governed'. *Annals of the American Association of Geographers*, v. 108, n. 1. pp. 162–178.

Fletcher, R., Pottier, C., Evans, D. & Kummu, M. (2008), The Development of the Water Management System of Angkor: A Provisional Model. *Bulletin of the Indo-Pacific Prehistory Association*, The Indo-Pacific Prehistory Association. pp. 57–66.

Follansbee, Robert (1994), *A History of the Water Resources Branch, U.S. Geological Survey: Volume I, from Predecessor Surveys to June 30, 1919*. Washington: Government Printing Office.

Francis, G. (1864), *La Cochinchine française en 1864*. Paris: E. Dentu.

Francis, G. (1865), *De la colonisation de la Cochinchine*. Paris: Challamel Aine.

Fry, Albert (1948), *Recent Developments in Hydrology with Respect to Stream Flow Forecasting*. IAHS Congress, Oslo. pp. 143–151.

G

Galison, Peter (2010), *The Objective Image*. Inaugural Address for Treaty of Utrecht Chair at Utrecht University. Universiteit Utrecht, Faculteit Geesteswetenschappen, Utrecht.

Gamond, Thomé (1871), *Mémoire sur le régime général des eaux courantes: Plan d'ensemble pour la transformation de l'appareil hydraulique de la France*. Paris: Dunod.

Garnier, Francis, Doudart de Lagrée, Ernest & Schieble, Erhard (1873), *Exploration de l'Indochine. Dirigée par Mr. le Cape. de frégate Doudart de Lagrée*. Paris: Hachette.

Gottman, Jean (1964), *Megalopolis: The Urbanized Northeastern Seaboard of the United States*. Cambridge, MA: The MIT Press.

Gourou, Pierre (1936), *Les paysans du Delta Tonkinois: Etude de Géographie Humaine*. Paris: EFEO.

Gourou, Pierre (1942), La population rurale de la Cochinchine. *Annales de Géographie*, v. 51, n. 285.

Gourou, Pierre (1950), La succession des paysages humains en Cochinchine occidentale. *Annales de Géographie*, v. 59, n. 313. pp. 79–80.

Gouvernement Général de l'Indochine (1931), *Service géographique de l'Indochine: Son organisation, ses méthodes, ses travaux. Exposition Coloniale Internationale*. Hanoi: Impri. d'extrême-Orient.

Government of the Netherlands & Government of Vietnam (2013), *Mekong Delta Plan*. Consortium Royal Haskoning DHV, WUR, Deltares, Rebel.

Bibliography 183

Groslier, Bernard-Philippe (1974), Agriculture et religion dans l'Empire angkorien. *Études rurales*, n. 53–56. pp. 95–117.

Gupta, Avijit (2009), Geology and Landforms of the Mekong Basin. In Ian Campbell (ed.), *The Mekong: Biophysical Environment of an International River Basin*. New York, NY: Academic Press. pp. 29–51.

H

Hahn, H. Hazel (2013), Abstract Spaces of Asia, Indochina, and Empire in the French Imaginaire. In Vimalin Rujivarcharkul, H. Hazel Hah, Ken Oshima & Peter Christensen (eds.), *Architecturalized Asia*. Hong Kong: Hong Kong University Press. pp. 85–100.

Harley, John (1989), Deconstructing the Map. *Cartographica*, v. 26, n. 2. pp. 1–20.

Harmand, Jules (1874), *Aperçu pathologique sur la Cochinchine*. Versailles: Impri. de E. Aurbert.

Harms, Erik (2019), Megalopolitan Megalomania: Ho Chi Minh City, Vietnam's Southeastern Region and the Speculative Growth Machine. *International Planning Studies*, v. 24, n. 1. pp. 53–67.

Hartshorne, Richard (1936), *The Nature of Geography: A Critical Survey of Current Thought in the Light of the Past*. Lancaster, PA: The Association of American Geographers.

Harvey, H.R. & Williams, B.J. (1980), Aztec Arithmetic: Positional Notation and Area Calculation. *Science*, v. 210. pp. 499–510.

Hasan, S., Evers, J., Zegwaard, A. & Zwarteveen, M. (2019), Making Waves in the Mekong Delta: Recognizing the Work and the Actors Behind the Transfer of Dutch Delta Planning Expertise. *Journal of Environmental Planning and Management*, v. 62, n. 9. pp. 1583–1602.

Heffernan, Michael (2014), Geography and the Paris Academy of Sciences: Politics and Patronage in Early 18th-Century France. *Transactions of the Institute of British Geographers*, v. 39, n. 1. pp. 1–14.

Hien, Luong Quang (2020), French Educational Reforms in Indochina Peninsula and the Appearance of the Western Intellectual Hierarchy in Vietnam in the Early Twentieth Century. *American Journal of Educational Research*, v. 8, n. 4. pp. 208–213.

Hoang, H.N., Dargusch, P., Moss, P. & Tran, D.B. (2016), A Review of the Drivers of 200 Years of Wetland Degradation in the Mekong Delta of Vietnam. *Regional Environmental Change*, v. 16, n. 8. pp. 2303–2315.

Hoanh, C.T., Facon, T., Thuon, T., Bastakoti, R.C., Molle, F. & Phengphaengsy, F. (2009), Irrigation in the Lower Mekong Basin Countries: The Beginning of a New Era? In F. Molle, T. Foran & M. Kakonen (eds.), *Contested Waterscapes in the Mekong Region: Hydropower, Livelihoods and Governance*. London: Earthscan. pp. 143–171.

Hoanh, C.T., Suhardiman, D. & Anh, L.T. (2014), Irrigation Development in the Vietnamese Mekong Delta: Towards Polycentric Water Governance? *International Journal of Water Governance*, v. 2. pp. 61–82.

Hori, Hiroshi (2000), *The Mekong: Environment and Development*. Hong Kong: United Nations University Press.

Horton, Robert E. (1933), *The Role of Infiltration in the Hydrologic Cycle*. Transactions of the American Geophysical Union Fourteenth Annual Meeting. Washington, DC: National Research Council. pp. 445–460.

Huddle, Franklin (1972), *The Mekong Project: Opportunities and Problems of Regionalism*. Science, Technology, and American Diplomacy. Washington, DC: U.S. Government Printing Office.

Husson, Olivier (1998), *Spatio-Temporal Variability of Acid Sulphate Soils in the Plain of Reeds, Vietnam: Impact of Soil Properties, Water Management and Crop Husbandry on the Growth and Yield of Rice in Relation to Microtopography*. Unpublished PhD thesis. Delft University of Technology.

184   *Bibliography*

I

Inspection générale des travaux publics (1930), *Dragages de Cochinchine: Canal Rachgia-Hatien.* Saigon: Gouvernement général de l'Indochine.

J

Jacobs, Jane (1969), *The Economy of Cities.* New York: Random House.

Jammer, Max (1954), *Concepts of Space, the History of Theories of Space in Physics.* Cambridge, MA: Harvard University Press.

Jenkins, David (1968), The Lower Mekong Scheme. *Asian Survey,* v. 8, n. 6. pp. 456–464.

Joint Development Group (1969), *The Postwar Development of the Republic of Vietnam: Policies and Programs,* v. 1. Saigon & New York: Postwar Planning Group & Development And Resources Corporation.

K

Kagawa, Ayako & Le Sourd, Guillaume (2017), Mapping the World: Cartographic and Geographic Visualization by the United Nations Geospatial Information Section (Formerly Cartographic Section). *Proceedings of the International Cartographic Association,* n. 1. pp. 1–7.

Kaida, Yoshihiro (1974), Hydrography of Rice Land in the Vietnamese Part of the Mekong Delta. *Southeast Asian Studies,* v. 12, n. 2. pp. 143–156.

Kasprzyk-Istin, Marie-Cécile (2018), *De la navigation maritime à la navigation aérienne: Transferts de méthodes mathématiques et de connaissances en France dans la première moitié du XXe siècle.* Unpublished PhD thesis. Université de Nantes.

Kelley, Liam (2016), From a Reliant Land to a Kingdom in Asia: Premodern Geographic Knowledge and the Emergence of the Geo-Body in Late Imperial Vietnam. *Cross-Currents: East Asian History and Culture Review (E-Journal),* n. 20. pp. 7–39.

Kish, George (1976), Early Thematic Mapping: The Work of Philippe Buache. *Imago Mundi,* v. 28. pp. 129–136.

Kleinen, John (2005), Tropicality and Topicality: Pierre Gourou and the Genealogy of French Colonial Scholarship on Rural Vietnam. *Singapore Journal of Tropical Geography,* v. 26, n. 3. pp. 339–358.

Kuenzer, C., Guo, H., Huth, J., Leinenkugel, P., Li, X. & Dech, S. (2013), Flood Mapping and Flood Dynamics of the Mekong Delta: ENVISAT-ASAR-WSM Based Time Series Analyses. *Remote Sensing,* n. 5. pp. 687–715.

Kuhn, Thomas (1970), *The Structure of Scientific Revolutions,* 2nd edition. Chicago: Chicago University Press.

Ký, Trương Vĩnh (Petrus) (1875), *Petit cours de géographie de la Basse-Cochinchine.* Saigon: Impri. du Gouvernment.

Ký, Trương Vĩnh (Petrus) (1885), *Dictionnaire Français Annamite.* Saigon: Impri. de la Mission, à Tân-Định.

Ký, Trương Vĩnh (Petrus) (1887), *Dư đồ thuyết lược. Précis de géographie.* Impri. de la Mission à Tân-Định.

L

Laeni, N., van den Brink, M.A., Trel, E.M. & Arts, E.J.M.M. (2021), Going Dutch in the Mekong Delta: A Framing Perspective on Water Policy Translation. *Journal of Environmental Policy & Planning,* v. 23, n. 1. pp. 16–33.

Bibliography 185

Lagendijk, Vincent (2019), Streams of Knowledge: River Development Knowledge and the TVA on the River Mekong. *History and Technology*, v. 35, n. 3. pp. 316–337.

La Loubère, Simon (1693), *A New Historical Relation of the Kingdom of Siam.* London: Printed by F.L. for Tho. Horne, Francis Saunders, & Tho. Bennet.

Le, Cong Kiet (1993), Dong Thap Muoi: Restoring the Mystery Forest of the Plain of Reeds. *Restoration & Management Notes*, v. 11, n. 2. pp. 102–105.

Le, T.V.H., Shigeko, H., Nguyen, H.H. & Cong, T.C. (2008), Infrastructure Effects on Floods in the Mekong River Delta in Vietnam. *Hydrological Processes*, v. 22. pp. 1359–1372.

Le Coq, J.F., Dufumier, M. & Trébuil, G. (2001), *History of Rice Production in the Mekong Delta.* Paper presented at Third EUROSEAS Conference, London, September 6–8. pp. 1–27.

Lepage, Jean-Denis G.G. (2010), *Vauban and the French Military Under Louis XIV: An Illustrated History of Fortifications and Strategies.* Jefferson, NC & London: McFarland & Co.

Les Armées Françaises D'outre-Mer (1931), *La Carte de l'Empire Colonial Français, Exposition Coloniale Internationale.* Paris: Impri. Georges Lang.

Li, Tana (2004), The Water Frontier: An Introduction. In Nola Cooke & Li Tana (eds.), *Water Frontier: Commerce and the Chinese in the Lower Mekong Region, 1750–1880.* Singapore: Rowman & Littlefield. pp. 1–20.

Lilienthal, David (1940), The TVA and Decentralization. *Survey Graphic*, v. 24, n. 6.

Lilienthal, David (1944), *TVA Democracy on the March.* New York & London: Harper Brothers.

Lilienthal, David (1951), Another Korea in the Making? *Collier's Weekly*, August 4.

Logan, William (2009), Hanoi, Vietnam. *City*, v. 13, n. 1. pp. 87–94.

M

Maki, Fumihiko & Ohtaka, Masato (1964), *Investigations in Collective Form.* Special Publication n. 2. St Louis: Washington University School of Architecture.

Malleret, Louis (1951), Les fouilles d'Oc-èo: Rapport préliminaire. *Bulletin de l'Ecole française d'Extrême-Orient*, v. 45, n. 1. pp. 75–88.

Malte-Brun, Conrad (1827), *Universal Geography or a Description of All Parts of the World on a New Plan, According to the Natural Division of the Globe*, v. 2. Philadelphia, PA: Anthony Finley.

Malte-Brun, Conrad (1829), *Universal Geography.* Philadelphia, PA: Anthony Finley.

Mantienne, Frédéric (2003), The Transfer of Western Military Technology to Vietnam in the Late Eighteenth and Early Nineteenth Centuries: The Case of the Nguyễn. *Journal of Southeast Asian Studies*, v. 34, n. 3. pp. 519–534.

Marchand, M., Pham, D. & Le, T. (2014), Mekong Delta: Living with Water, But for How Long? *Built Environment*, v. 40, n. 2. pp. 230–243.

Mathevet, R., Peluso, N. L., Couespel, A. & Robbins, P. (2015), Using Historical Political Ecology to Understand the Present: Water, Reeds, and Biodiversity in the Camargue Biosphere Reserve, Southern France. *Ecology and Society*, v. 20, n. 4.

McCarthy, James (1900), *Surveying and Exploring in Siam.* London: William Clowes & Sons.

McDole, Catherine (1969), *A Report on Socio-Cultural Conditions in the Pa Mong Study Area of Northeast Thailand. A.I.D. Contract No. AID-493–461.* Bangkok: USAID.

McGee, Terry (2009), Interrogating the Production of Urban Space in China and Vietnam Under Market Socialism. *Asia Pacific Viewpoint*, v. 50, n. 2. pp. 37–50.

McGee, Terry & Shaharudin, I. (2016), Reimagining the 'Peri-Urban' in the Mega-Urban Regions of Southeast Asia. In B. Maheshwari, B. Thoradeniya & V.P. Singh (eds.), *Balanced Urban Development: Options and Strategies for Liveable Cities.* Water Science and Technology Library, v. 72. Cham: Springer. pp. 499–516.

186 Bibliography

McGee, William J. (1909), Water as a Resource. *The Annals of the American Academy of Political and Social Science*, v. 33, n. 3, Conservation of Natural Resources. pp. 228–246.

McHarg, Ian (1971), *Design with Nature*. New York: Doubleday, Natural History Press.

Mekong River Commission (2015), *Annual Mekong Flood Report 2013*. Vientiane: Mekong River Commission.

Mekong River Commission (2018), *Irrigation Database Improvement for the Lower Mekong Basin*. Vientiane: Mekong River Commission.

Mekong River Commission (2019), *State of the Basin Report 2018*. Vientiane: Mekong River Commission.

Mercier, Guy (2009), Vidal de la Blache, P. In Rob Kitchin & Nigel Thrif (eds.), *International Encyclopaedia of Human Geography*, v. 12. Amsterdam: Elsevier. pp. 389–412.

Miller, Edward (2013), *Misalliance: Ngo Dinh Diem, the United States, and the Fate of South Vietnam*. Cambridge, MA: Harvard University Press.

Minkman, E. & van Buuren, A. (2019), Branding in Policy Translation: How the Dutch Delta Approach Became an International Brand. *Environmental Science and Policy*, n. 96. pp. 114–122.

Molle, François (2006), River-Basin Planning and Management: The Social Life of a Concept. *Geoforum*, n. 40. pp. 484–494.

Molle, François, Floch, P., Promphakping, B. & Blake, D. (2009), The 'Greening of Isaan': Politics, Ideology and Irrigation Development in the Northeast of Thailand. In François Molle, Tira Foran & Mira Kakonen (eds.), *Contested Waterscapes in the Mekong Region: Hydropower, Livelihoods and Governance*. London & Sterling, VA: Earthscan. pp. 253–282.

Molle, François, Mollinga, P. & Wester, P. (2009), Hydraulic Bureaucracies and the Hydraulic Mission: Flows of Water, Flows of Power. *Water Alternatives*, v. 2, n. 3. pp. 328–349.

Molle, François & Tuân, D.T. (2006), Water Control and Agricultural Development: Crafting Deltaic Environments in South-East Asia. In T. Tvedt & E. Jakobsson (eds.), *A History of Water, v. 1: Water Control and River Biographies*. London & New York: Tauris. pp. 144–171.

N

Netherlands Delta Development Team (1974), *Recommendations Concerning Agricultural Development with Improved Water Control in the Mekong Delta*, v. 7. Working Paper IV, Hydrology. Bangkok: Netherlands Delta Development Team.

Nguyễn, Đình Đầu (1991), Remarques préliminaires sur les registres cadastraux (địa bạ) des six provinces de la Cochinchine (Nam Kỳ Lục Tỉnh). *Bulletin de l'École française d'Extrême-Orient*, v. 78. pp. 275–285.

Nguyễn, Hiến Lê (1954), *Bảy Ngày Trong Đồng Tháp Mười (Seven Days in Dong Thap Muoi)*. Saigon: NXB văn hóa thông.

Nguyễn, Hữu Hiếu (2018), *Văn hóa dân gian vùng Đồng Tháp Mười (Folklore in the Dong Thap Muoi region)*. Ho Chi Minh City: NXB Văn hóa – Văn nghệ.

Nguyen, Thu Dieu (1999), *The Mekong River and the Struggle for Indochina*. Westport, CT: Greenwood Publishing Group.

Nguyen, V.K.T., Nguyen, V.D., Fujii, H., Kummu, M., Merz, B. & Apel, H. (2017), Has Dyke Development in the Vietnamese Mekong Delta Shifted Flood Hazard Downstream? *Hydrology and Earth System Sciences*, v. 21. pp. 3991–4010.

Nguyễn, Văn Nở (2014), Tìm hiểu cách vận dụng thành ngữ, tục ngữ trong tác phẩm Sơn Nam (Study on the Use of Locutions and Proverbs in the Work of Son Nam). In Dao Huu Vinh & Pham Duc Binh (eds.), *Ngôn ngữ Miền sông nước (Language of the River Region)*. Hanoi: NXB Chính trị quốc gia.

Nguyen, Xuan Vinh & Wyatt, Andrew (2006), *Situation Analysis: Plain of Reeds, Viet Nam*. Vientiane: Mekong Wetlands Biodiversity Conservation and Sustainable Use Programme (MWBP).

Bibliography   187

O

O'Neal, James (1967), The Role of the Engineer Agency for Resources Inventories in International Development. *The Professional Geographer*, v. 19. pp. 34–35.

O'Neal, James & Bwins, James (1974), *An Operational Application of ERTS-1 Imagery to the Environmental Inventory Process (Conference Paper)*. Goddard Space Flight Center, 3d ERTS-1 Symposium, v. 1, Sec. A. pp. 579–584.

Osborne, Milton (1965), *Strategic Hamlets in South Viet-Nam*. Ithaca, NY: Cornell Southeast Asia Program Publications.

Ozouf-Marignier, Marie-Vic (2002), Bassins hydrographiques et divisions administratives en France (XIXe–XXe siècle). *Trames*, n. 10. pp. 63–76.

P

Pacovsky, Jill (2001), Restoration of Wetlands in the Tram Chim Nature Reserve (Dong Thap Province, Mekong River Delta, Vietnam). *Student On-Line Journal*, v. 7, n. 3. Department of Horticultural Science, University of Minnesota. pp. 1–7.

Paris, Pierre (1941), Autres canaux reconnus à l'Est du Mékong par examen d'autres photographies aériennes (provinces de Châudôc et de Long-xuyên). *Bulletin de l'Ecole française d'Extrême-Orient*, v. 41. pp. 371–372.

Pelletier, Monique (2003), L'ingénieur militaire et la description du territoire: Du XVIe au XVIIIe siècle. In *Cartographie de la France et du monde de la Renaissance au Siècle des lumières [en ligne]*. Paris: Éditions de la Bibliothèque nationale de France. pp. 45–68.

Pelletier, Monique (2007), Representations of Territory by Painters, Engineers, and Land Surveyors in France During the Renaissance. In David Woodward (ed.), *The History of Cartography, v. 3, Part 2, Cartography in the European Renaissance*. Chicago, IL: University of Chicago Press. pp. 1522–1537.

Perrault, Pierre (1674), *De l'origine des fontaines*. Paris: Pierre le Petit.

Petto, Christine Marie (2007), *When France Was King of Cartography: The Patronage and Production of Maps in Early Modern France*. Lanham, MD: Lexington Books.

Pham, T.H.L. (2010), The Legislative Framework for Urban Design and Planning in Vietnam. In K. Shannon, B. De Meulder, D. Derden, T.H.L. Pham & D.T. Pho (eds.), *Urban Planning & Design in an Era of Dynamic Development Innovative and Relevant Practices for Vietnam*. Hanoi: Ministry of Construction.

Pichard, Georges (2005), La découverte géologique de la Camargue, du XVIe siècle au début du XIXe siècle. *Travaux du Comité français d'Histoire de la Géologie, Comité français d'Histoire de la Géologie*, 3ème série, v. 19. pp. 113–136.

Pichard, Georges, Provansal, M. & Sabatier, F. (2014), Les embouchures du Rhône. *Méditerranée*, n. 122.

Pottier, Nathalie (2000), Risque d'inondation, réglementation et territoires. *Hommes et Terres du Nord, 2000/2. Hydrosystèmes, paysages et territoires*. pp. 93–101.

Pouyanne, Albert Armand (1926), *Inspection générale des travaux publics*. Hanoi: Impri. d'Extrême-Orient.

Powell, John Wesley (1891), *Eleventh Annual Report of the Director of the United States Geological Survey. Part II – Irrigation: 1889–1890*. Washington: Government Printing Office.

Prescott, J., Collier, H. & Prescott, D. (1977), *Frontiers of Asia and Southeast Asia*. Melbourne: Melbourne University Press.

R

Raffestin, Claude (2012), Space, Territory and Territoriality. *Environment and Planning D: Society and Space*, v. 30. pp. 121–141.

Reclus, Elisée (1882), *Histoire d'un Ruisseau*. Paris: J. Hetzel & Co.

188   *Bibliography*

Rénaud, Jacques (1880), Étude d'un projet de canal entre le Vaico et le Cua-Tieu. *Excursions et Reconnaissances*, n. 3.

Republic of Viet-Nam (1956), *The Dramatic Story of Resettlement and Land Reform in the 'Rice Bowl' of the Republic of Viet-Nam.* Saigon: Secretariat of State for Information, Republic of Viet-Nam.

Republic of Viet-Nam (1963), *Viet Nam's Strategic Hamlets.* Saigon: Directorate General of Information.

Ritter, Carl (1865), *Comparative Geography*, translated for the Use of Schools and Colleges by William L. Gage. Philadelphia, PA: J.B. Lippincott & Co.

Robequain, Charles (1926), Gouvernement général de l'Indochine. Service géographique. Année 1925. Compte-rendu annuel des travaux exécutés par le Service giographique de l'Indochine. *Bulletin de l'École française d'Extrême-Orient*, v. 26. pp. 385–389.

Royal Haskoning & Deutsche Gesellschaft fur Inter-nationale Zusammenarbeit (GIZ) (2020), *Mekong Delta Integrated Regional Plan MDIRP-RHD-D4-XX-RP-Z-0007.*

S

Sahlins, Peter (1990), Natural Frontiers Revisited: France's Boundaries Since the Seventeenth Century. *The American Historical Review*, v. 95, n. 5. pp. 1423–1451.

Schmid, Christian (2016), The Urbanization of the Territory: On the Research Approach of ETH Studio Basel. In Mathias Gunz & Vesna Jovanovic (eds.), *Territory: On the Development of Landscape and City.* Zurich: Park Books. pp. 22–48.

Schmidt, Jeremy (2014), Historicising the Hydrosocial Cycle. *Water Alternatives*, v. 7, n. 1. pp. 220–234.

Schwartzberg, Joseph E. (1995a), Introduction to Southeast Asian Cartography. In *The History of Cartography, v. 2, b. 2, Cartography in the Traditional East and Southeast Asian Societies.* Chicago, IL: University of Chicago Press. pp. 689–700.

Schwartzberg, Joseph E. (1995b), Southeast Asian Geographical Maps. In J.B. Harley & David Woodward (eds.), *The History of Cartography, v. 2, b. 2: Cartography in the Traditional East and Southeast Asian Societies.* Chicago, IL: University of Chicago Press. pp. 741–827.

Scott, James C. (1998), *Seeing Like a State: How Certain Schemes to Improve the Human Condition Have Failed.* New Haven, CT: Yale University Press.

Segeren, W.A. (1982), Introduction to Polders of the World. *Water International*, v. 8, n. 2. pp. 51–54.

Sewell, W.R. Derrick (1968), The Mekong Scheme: Guideline for a Solution to Strife in Southeast Asia. *Asian Survey*, v. 8, n. 6. pp. 448–455.

Sherman, LeRoy (1932), The Relation of Hydrographs of Runoff to Size and Character of Drainage-Basins. *Eos Transactions, American Geophysical Union*, v. 13, n. 1. pp. 332–339.

Simon, M., Budke, A. & Schäbitz, F. (2020), The Objectives and Uses of Comparisons in Geography Textbooks: Results of an International Comparative Analysis. *Heliyon*, n. 6. pp. 1–13.

Singaravelou, Pierre (2011), The Institutionalisation of 'Colonial Geography' in France, 1880–1940. *Journal of Historical Geography*, n. 37. pp. 149–157.

Smith, C.T. (1971), The Drainage Basin as an Historical Basis for Human Activity. In Richard J. Chorley (ed.), *Introduction to Geographical Hydrology: Spatial Aspects of the Interactions Between Water Occurrence and Human Activity.* London: Taylor & Francis. pp. 220–230.

Smith, Neil (1990), *Uneven Development: Nature, Capital and the Production of Space.* Oxford: Blackwell. pp. 34–65.

Sneddon, Chris (2012), The 'Sinew of Development': Cold War Geopolitics Technical Expertise, and Water Resource Development in Southeast Asia, 1954–1975. *Social Studies of Science*, v. 42, n. 4, Water Worlds. pp. 564–590.

Sneddon, Chris & Fox, Coleen (2006), Rethinking Transboundary Waters: A Critical Hydropolitics of the Mekong Basin. *Political Geography*, n. 25. pp. 181–202.

Socialist Republic of Vietnam (2008), *Decision No. 589/QD-TTg Dated May 20, 2008 of the Prime Minister Approving the Master Plan on Construction of the Ho Chi Minh City Region Up to 2020, with a Vision Toward 2050.* Hanoi: Government of Vietnam.

Socialist Republic of Vietnam (2017a), *Decision 2076/QĐ-TTg: Decision on the Approval of the Adjustment of the Ho Chi Minh City Construction Planning to 2030 and Vision to 2050.* Hanoi: Government of Vietnam. pp. 1–20.

Socialist Republic of Vietnam (2017b), *Resolution 120/NQ-CP: On Sustainable and Climate-Resilient Development of the Mekong River Delta.* Hanoi: Government of Vietnam.

Socialist Republic of Vietnam (2018), *Decision No. 68/QD-TTg: On Approving the Revision of the Construction Plan of the Mekong Delta Region by 2030 with Vision Towards 2050.* Hanoi: Government of Vietnam.

Socialist Republic of Vietnam (2019), *Proceedings of the Conference on Evaluation of Two-Year Implementation of Governments Resolution on Climate Resilient and Sustainable Development of the Mekong Delta of Viet Nam.* Hanoi: Government of Vietnam.

Sơn, Nam (1973), *Lịch Sử Khẩn Hoang Miền Nam (A History of Settlement in the South).* Saigon: NXB Chưa Cập Nhật.

Stencel, R., Gifford, F. & Morón, E. (1976), Astronomy and Cosmology at Angkor Wat, *Science*. New Series, v. 193, n. 4250. pp. 281–287.

Sternstein, Larry (1993), The London Company's Envoys Plot Siam. *The Journal of the Siam Society*, v. 81, n. 2. pp. 11–95.

Stuart-Fox, Martin (1995), The French in Laos, 1887–1945. *Modern Asian Studies*, v. 29, n. 1. pp. 111–139.

T

Taillefer, Oswald (1865), *La Cochinchine: Ce qu'elle est, ce qu'elle sera: deux ans de séjour dans ce pays de 1863 à 1865.* Perigeaux: Impri. Dupont.

Tanaka, Koji (2001), Agricultural Development in the Broad Depression and the Plain of Reeds in the Mekong Delta: Conserving Forests or Developing Rice Culture? *Southeast Asian Studies*, v. 39, n. 1. pp. 81–96.

Taylor, Philip (2014), Water in the Shaping and Unmaking of Khmer Identity on the Vietnam-Cambodia Frontier. *TRaNS: Trans – Regional and – National Studies of Southeast Asia*, v. 2, n. 1. pp. 103–130.

Tennessee Valley Authority (1936), *Report to the Congress on the Unified Development of the Tennessee River System.* Knoxville, TN: Tennessee Valley Authority.

Tertrais, Hugues (2002), L'électrification de l'Indochine. *Outre-mers*, v. 89, n. 334–335, L'électrification Outremer de la fin du XIXe siècle aux premières décolonisations. pp. 589–600.

Teulières, Roger (1962), Les paysans vietnamiens et la réforme rurale au Sud Viêt-Nam. *Cahiers d'outre-mer*, n. 57–15e année. pp. 47–84.

Thai, D.V.H., Cong, V.T., Nestmann, F., Oberle, P. & Trung, N.N. (2014), *Land Use Based Flood Hazards Analysis for the Mekong Delta.* Proceedings of the 19th IAHR-APD Congress, Hanoi, Vietnam.

Thornbury, W.D. (1968), *Principles of Geomorphology*, 2nd edition. New York: Wiley.

Tran, Anh Hoai (2019), From Socialist Modernism to Market Modernism? Master-Planned Developments in Post-Reform Vietnam. In Rita Padawangi (ed.), *Routledge Handbook of Urbanization in Southeast Asia*. Abingdon, Oxon & New York, NY: Routledge. pp. 249–264.

Tran, D.D., van Halsema, G., Hellegers, P., Hoang, L.P., Tran, T.Q., Kummu, M. & Ludwig, F. (2018), Assessing Impacts of Dike Construction on the Flood Dynamics of the Mekong Delta. *Hydrological Earth System Sciences*, v. 22. pp. 1875–1896.

190   *Bibliography*

Trần, Hữu Quang & Nguyễn, Nghị (2016), Reframing the 'Traditional' Vietnamese Village: From Peasant to Farmer Society in the Mekong Delta. *Moussons [Online]*, v. 28. pp. 61–88.

Turnbull, David (1996), Cartography and Science in Early Modern Europe: Mapping the Construction of Knowledge Spaces. *Imago Mundi*, v. 48. pp. 5–24.

Tvedt, Terje & Jacobsson, Eva (2006), Introduction: Water History Is World History. In T. Tvedt & E. Jakobsson (eds.), *A History of Water, v. 1: Water Control and River Biographies*. London & New York: Tauris. pp. ix–xxiii.

Tvedt, Terje, McIntyre, O. & Woldetsadik, T.K. (2011), Sovereignty, the Web of Water and the Myth of Westphalia. In Terje Tvedt, O. McIntyre & T.K. Woldestsadik (eds.), *A History of Water, Series 3, v. 2, Sovereignty and International Water Law*. London & New York: IB Tauris. pp. 3–26.

U

United Nations (1958), Completion of the Mekong Field Survey. *Ekistics*, v. 5, n. 30. p. 149.

United Nations (1968), *Economic Survey of Asia and the Far East 1967: Economic Bulletin for Asia and the Far East (E/CN.11/825)*. Bangkok: United Nations.

United Nations Department of Economic and Social Affairs (1958), *Integrated River Basin Development: Report by a Panel of Experts*. New York: United Nations.

United Nations Economic Commission for Asia and the Far East (1957), *Development of Water Resources in the Lower Mekong Basin*. Bangkok: United Nations.

United Nations Economic Commission for Latin America (1959), *Preliminary Review of Questions Relating to the Development of International River Basins in Latin America (E/CN.12/511)*. Panama City: United Nations.

United Nations Educational, Scientific and Cultural Organization (UNESCO) (1956), *The Definition of Community Development*. Working Paper n. 3. New York: United Nations.

United Nations Office of Public Information (1959), *Yearbook of the United Nations 1958*. New York: United Nations.

U.S. Bureau of the Census (1950), *Population of Standard Metropolitan Areas: April 1, 1950. Census of Population, Preliminary Counts*. Series PC-3, n. 3. Washington, DC: US Department of Commerce.

U.S. Bureau of Reclamation (1956), *Reconnaissance Report: Lower Mekong River Basin*. Denver, CO: United States Department of the Interior, Bureau of Reclamation.

U.S. Bureau of Reclamation (1969), *Pa Mong Project Lower Mekong River Basin, Stage One Interim Report*. Denver, CO: United States Bureau of Reclamation.

U.S. Bureau of Reclamation (1970), *Pa Mong Stage One Feasibility Report, Appendix V – Plans and Estimates*, v. 1. Denver, CO: United States Bureau of Reclamation.

U.S. Congress (1920), *United States Code: Federal Power Act* [June 10, 1920, ch. 285, pt. III, § 321, Formerly § 320, as Added Aug. 26, 1935, ch. 687, title II, § 213, 49 Stat. 863]. Part II – Regulation of Electric Utility Companies Engaged in Interstate Commerce, Sec. 202 (a).

U.S. Congress (1925). *United States Code: Muscle Shores Act*, 16 U.S.C. §§ 831–831 cc Suppl. 7.

V

Van Staveren, M.F., van Tatenhove, J.P.M. & Warner, J.F. (2018), The Tenth Dragon: Controlled Seasonal Flooding in Long-Term Policy Plans for the Vietnamese Mekong Delta. *Journal of Environmental Policy & Planning*, v. 20, n. 3. pp. 267–281.

Vial, Paulin (1874), *Les Premières années de la Cochinchine. colonie française*. Paris: Challamel Aine.

Vickery, Michael (1994), *What and Where Was Chenla?* Paris: Recherches nouvelles sur le Cambodge, École française d'Extrême-Orient. pp. 197–212.

Bibliography 191

Vidal de la Blache, Paul (1898), La Géographie politique, à propos des écrits de M. Frédéric Ratzel. *Annales de Géographie*, v. 7, n. 32. pp. 97–111.

Vidal de la Blache, Paul (2015), *Principes de géographie humaine: Publiés d'après les manuscrits de l'auteur par Emmanuel de Martonne*. Paris: ENS Éditions.

Vietnam General Statistics Office (2020), *Completed Results of the 2019 Viet Nam Population and Housing Census (Tổng điều tra dân số và nhà ở năm 2019)*. Hanoi: Statistical Publishing House.

Vitruvius (1934), *On Architecture, v. II, b. 6–10*, translated by Frank Granger. Loeb Classical Library 280. Cambridge, MA: Harvard University Press.

Vo, Q.T., Roelvink, D., van der Wegen, M., Reyns, J., Kernkamp, H., Giap, V.V. & Vo, T.P.L. (2020), Flooding in the Mekong Delta: The Impact of Dyke Systems on Downstream Hydrodynamics. *Hydrological Earth System Sciences*, v. 24. pp. 189–212.

Von Humboldt, Alexander (1827), *Personal Narratives of Travel to the Equinoctial Regions of the New Continent During the Years 1799–1804 by A. de Humboldt and Aimé Bonpland with Maps and Plans*. London, Longman, translated by H.M. Williams, 2nd edition, 7 vols., v. 5. London: Longman, Hurst, Rees, Orme and Brown.

Vu, Duc Liem (2017), Boundary on the Move: Border Making in Vietnamese-Cambodian Frontier, 1802–1847. *Mekong Review*, v. 2, n. 2. pp. 2–7.

Vu, T.H.H. & Duong, V. (2018), *Morphology of Water-Based Housing in Mekong Delta, Vietnam*. MATEC Web of Conferences, n. 193. pp. 1–12, 04005.

W

Warner, J., Wester, P. & Bolding, A. (2008), Going with the Flow: River Basins as the Natural Units for Water Management? *Water Policy*, n. 10, Supplement 2. pp. 121–138.

White, Gilbert (1957), A Perspective of River Basin Development. *Law and Contemporary Problems*, v. 22, n. 2, River Basin Development. pp. 157–187.

White, Gilbert (1963), The Mekong River Plan. *Ekistics*, v. 16, n. 96. pp. 310–316.

White, Gilbert, de Vries, E., Dunkerley, H. & Krutilla, J. (1962), *Economic and Social Aspects of Lower Mekong Development (Report for the Committee for Co-Ordination of Investigations of the Lower Mekong Basin)*. Bangkok: United Nations.

Whitmore, John (1994), Cartography in Vietnam. In J.B. Harley & David Woodward (eds.), *The History of Cartography, v. 2, b. 2: Cartography in the Traditional East and Southeast Asian Societies*. Chicago, IL: University of Chicago Press. pp. 478–508.

Whitmore, John (2013), Transformations of Thăng Long: Space and Time, Power and Belief. *International Journal of Asian Studies*, v. 10, n. 1. pp. 1–24.

Winichakul, Thongchai (1994), *Siam Mapped: A History of the Geo-Body of a Nation*. Honolulu: University of Hawaii Press.

Wittfogel, Karl (1981), *Oriental Despotism*. New York: Random House.

Wolters, O.W. (1974), North-Western Cambodia in the Seventh Century. *Bulletin of the School of Oriental and African Studies, University of London*, v. 37, n. 2. pp. 355–384.

Wolters, O.W. (1999), *History, Culture and Religion in Southeast Asian Perspectives*. Revised edition. Ithaca, NY: Southeast Asia Program Publications (SEAP).

Wood, Denis & Fels, John (2008), The Natures of Maps: Cartographic Constructions of the Natural World. *Cartographica*, v. 43, n. 3. pp. 189–202.

World Bank (2011), *Vietnam Urbanization Review: Technical Assistance Report*. Hanoi: World Bank.

World Bank (2016), *International Development Association Project Appraisal Document on a Proposed Credit in the Amount of SDR 218.8 Million (us$310 Million Equivalent) to the Socialist Republic of Vietnam for a Mekong Delta Integrated Climate Resilience and Sustainable Livelihoods Project (English)*. Washington, DC: World Bank Group.

192 *Bibliography*

Z

Zasloff, Joseph J. (1962a), Rural Resettlement in South Viet Nam: The Agroville Program. *Pacific Affairs*, v. 35, n. 4. pp. 327–340.

Zasloff, Joseph J. (1962b), *Rural Resettlement in Vietnam: An Agroville in Development.* Washington, DC: Agency for International Development.

Cartography

Part A: Basin

Figure A.1 Christoforos Romanos (2022), *The Mekong River's flows.* [source: Author]

Chapter 1

Figure 1.1 Jacques Cassini (1723), *Carte de France ou sont marquez les triangles qui ont servi determiner la Meridiene de Paris.* [source: Bibliothèque nationale de France]
Figure 1.2 Philippe Buache (1752), *Carte Physique et Profil de la Manche.* [source: Bibliothèque nationale de France]

Chapter 2

Figure 2.1 John Walker (1830), *Map of the Kingdoms of Siam and Cochin China.* [source: Bibliothèque nationale de France]
Figure 2.2 Thomé de Gamond (1871), *Carte de France indiquant la division des principaux bassins hydrographiques pour la transformation et l'exploitation du Regime des Eaux courantes* [source: T. de Gamond]
Figure 2.3 Francis Garnier (1873), *Carte itinéraire No. 6. Vallée de K. Kay á Xieng Khong.* [source: Bibliothèque nationale de France]
Figure 2.4 James McCarthy (1888), *Map of the Kingdom of Siam and Its Dependencies.* [source: National Library of Australia]

Chapter 3

Figure 3.1 Tennessee Valley Authority (1936), *Location of Dams and Reservoirs.* [source: TVA]
Figure 3.2 UN Economic Commission for Asia and the Far East (1957), *Stage Hydrographs of the Lower Mekong 1950.* [source: United Nations]
Figure 3.3 Gilbert White (1957), *Major International Drainage Areas 1956 & Major Integrated River Development Programs 1956.* [source: Law and Contemporary Problems]
Figure 3.4 Gilbert White, Egbert de Vries, Harold Dunkerley & John Krutilla (1962), *Lower Mekong Basin – Population Density.* [source: United Nations]
Figure 3.4 UN Economic Commission for Asia and the Far East (1957), *Map Showing Development Projects in the Lower Mekong Basin Recommended for Detailed Investigation.* [source: United Nations]
Figure 3.5 Mekong Committee (1970), *General Map of the Lower Mekong Basin Showing Potential Water Projects.* [source: United Nations]

194   *Cartography*

Part B: Delta

Figure 4.1 Christoforos Romanos (2022), *Mekong delta soil differentiations.* [source: Author]

Chapter 4

Figure 4.2 L. Manen, F. Vidalin & G. Héraud (1867), *Carte generale de la Basse Cochinchine et du Cambodge.* [source: Université Bordeaux Montaigne-1886. Res 09110803]
Figure 4.3 Unknown painter (1890s), *Manusyaloka, map of the world of man, according to Jain cosmological traditions.* [source: Library of Congress]
Figure 4.4 Service géographique de l'Indochine (1939), *Carte archéologique de la région d'Angkor* [source: Bibliothèque nationale de France]
Figure 4.5 J.E. Duhamel (1773), *Carte militaire, ou sont representees les principales parties d'une place fortifiee.* [source: Bibliothèque nationale de France]
Figure 4.5 Unknown cartographer (1861), *Carte de la basse Cochinchine.* [source: Bibliothèque nationale de France]

Chapter 5

Figure 5.1 Albert Pouyanne (1911), *Voies d'eau d'Intérêt general.* [source: ODSAS]
Figure 5.2 Service Géographique de l'Indochine (1940), *Villages du Delta Cochinchinois.* [source: Université Bordeaux Montaigne-1886. Res 09110703]
Figure 5.3 Ministère de la réforme agraire (1956), *Plan du remise en culture de la región de Cai-San.* [source: Republic of Viet-Nam]
Figure 5.4 Defense Mapping Agency (1966), *Hong Ngu Vietnam; Cambodia, (Sheet 6030 I), Series L7014.* [source: University of Texas Libraries, The University of Texas at Austin]

Chapter 6

Figure 6.1 Mekong Committee (1970), *Limit of Flooding in Lowland Floodplain.* [source: United Nations]
Figure 6.2 Gov. Vietnam (1982), *NC 48–7.* [source: Virtual Saigon]
Figure 6.3 Christoforos Romanos (2022), *HCMC Metropolitan region.* [source: Author]
Figure 6.4 MDP (2013) [source: Mekong Delta Plan, 2013]
Figure 6.5 MDP (2013) [source: Mekong Delta Plan, 2013]

Part C: Floodplain

Figure 7.1 Christoforos Romanos (2022), *Mekong delta soil differentiations.* [source: Author]

Chapter 7

Figure 7.2 M. Bertaux (1882), *Carte de la Cochinchine francaise divisee en quatre zones.* [source: Bibliothèque nationale de France]
Figure 7.3 Albert Pouyanne (1911), *Inondation.* [source: ODSAS]
Figure 7.4 Camouilly & Boisson (1885), *Plan topographique de l' arrondissement de Sa Dec.* [source: Bibliothèque nationale de France]

Cartography 195

Chapter 8

Figure 8.1 Henri Brenier (1914), *Schema Hypsometrique* [Source: Cirad]
Figure 8.2 Victor Delahaye (1928), *Topographie* [source: V. Delahaye]
Figure 8.3 Engineer Agency of Resources Inventories (1968), *Surface water resources.* [source: Google Books]
Figure 8.4 Engineer Agency of Resources Inventories (1968), *Physiography.* [source: Google Books]
Figure 8.5 Engineer Agency of Resources Inventories (1968), *Implementation Plan III.* [source: Google Books]

Chapter 9

Figure 9.1 Committee for Coordination of Investigations of the Lower Mekong Basin (1979), *General Map of the Lower Mekong Basin showing potential Water Projects.* [source: United Nations]
Figure 9.2 Vo Quoc Thanh et al (2020), *Mekong Delta modelling grid and river interpolated topography.* [source: Vo Quoc Thanh]

Index

Note: Page numbers in *italic* indicate a figure on the corresponding page.

Ackerman 75, 89
agglomeration 94, 97, 104–109, 114–116
Agricultural Development Centers 101; *see also* dinh điền
agriculture: basin 15, 45–47; delta 74–78, 94–98, 101–104, 114–123, *121*, *124*, 125–129, *127*; floodplain 141–145, 153–157, *161*, 162, 166–177
agrovilles 102–105
Angkor (settlement) 74, 79, 81–82, *81*, 86–88, 139
Angkor Wat 79–82, 90
Annales de Géographie 110, 146, 163
Annam: colony 37, 39; country of 40
Annamite mountains 38–41, 43, 44, 79
Anville (cartographer) 74, 140
archaeology 80–82, 145–146
area (concept of) 15
area of operations 49, 117, 143, 146, 162, 175
arid region 45, 47, 69
atlas 40, 74–75, 78, 88, 89, 151
atopia 5, 141, *144*, 146–147, 151, 153, 159

Bangkok (settlement) *62*, 167
baray 80–81, 82
basin 2–6, 9, *10*, 11–12, 24–25, 27–28, 41–42, 45–46, 66; and delta 119–122; drainage area and development unit 51–56, *55*; and floodplain 157–158, 168, 173–175; 'lower basin' as a construct 56–58; nature's frontiers 16–18, *18*; planning 46–51, *48*, *50*, 54, 58–65, *59*, 61, *62*, *64*; theorizing 19–24
Bassac River 85, 102–103, *102*, *118*, 133
Bastide 76

Bénabenq 153, 155
Bertaux (cartographer) *142*
Biggs 110, 112, 148, 155, 162, 164
Bogle 115–116, 130, 131
Brenier (cartographer) *151*
Buache (cartographer) 19–24, *20*, 28, 41
Burma 28, 29, 34, 37, 41, 90, 91

Cairns x, 129, 134
Cái Sắn (settlement) 102–104, *102*, 107–108, 156
Camargue 75, 76, 87, 89
Cambodia 33–34, 82–84, 86, 106–109, 117–119, 139–141, 155–162, 170–173
Camouilly (cartographer) *144*
canals *see* waterways
canalization 85, 94–96, 101, 144
Cần Thơ (settlement) 104, 123, 125–127, *127*
Cartes des Deltas de l'Annam 97
cartography 2–6; aerial photography 60, 97, 111, 129, 145, 155, 159; Burmese 28, 82, 91; catchment areas 17–22; conventions 28, 78, 112; hydrography 22, 34; levelling 97, 153, *154*, 163; practice 17, 19, 29; surveying 19, 22, 27, 37–39, 44, 60–61, 153–155; technique 39, 112; *see also* maps/mapping
casier 98, 110, 112, 148, 155–156, 159, 162, 164
Cassini, Jean-Dominique (cartographer) 16–17, 28–29
Cassini, Jacques (cartographer) 17, *18*
Cassirer 21, 24, 26
catchment area 2–4, 11–16, 19–24, *20*, 42; arid region 46; Lower Mekong Basin

52–54, 57, 61–66, *64*, 69; Mekong delta 12, 108–118, 124, 129, 159; Plain of Reeds *136*, 151–159, 162, 173–176, *174*; Tennessee Valley 47–49
Celoria 74, 88
Chao Phraya River 28, 29, 35, 38, 39, 41, 43
Châu Đốc (settlement) 86
Chenla 140
China 11, 56–58, 68; ambassadors 33, 139–140; border 41, 44; cartography 40, 78, 82; Ming dynasty 40, 78; Qing dynasty 28, 34, 57; state planning 120, 123; Tang dynasty 81, 139; trade route 34, 37
citadels 83–84, *85*, 86
Cochinchina 28, *30*, 76, 86, 93–94, 99–100, *101*, 108, 141–146, *143*, 150–155
Coedès 145, 148
Cold War 45–46, 52, 54, 57, 63, 66
Columbia River 69
command areas 61, 166, 168, 170
Committee for Coordination of Investigations of the Lower Mekong Basin see Mekong Committee
community development 101
Compagnie Nationale du Rhône 56
continuity (principle of) 12–16
contours 3, 153–154, *154*, 159–160, *160*
cosmography/ cosmology: Chinese 82; Hindu 79, *80*, 82; Khmer 73–74, 78–82, 88, 90; Vietnamese 39–40, 78–79
Courrier de Saigon 148
créments 76, 87

Da Cunha 6, 7
Dalton 42
dams: Hoover 69; Mekong Basin 57–58, 61–66, *62*, 69, 167–168; Pa Mong 60, 63, 65, 68–69, 119; Sambor 63, 65; Stung Treng 65, 69, 119, 167; Tennessee Valley 48, *48*
Dao 120, 131
Daston 21, 23, 75
defence: military 83–86, *85*, 104, 112, 114; flood 98, *106*, 119, *126*, 148, 156
Delahaye (cartographer) 151–155, 157, 163–164, 176
delta 1–6, 71; Indus 74–75, 90; Mekong *72*, 73–74, 76–77, *77*, 93–94, 108–109, 114–115, 129–130; mapping 75, *77*, 84, *85*, 99–101, *100*; Orinoco 22, 75; planning 123–129, *124*,

126–127; Nile 73–74, 77, 87, 89; Tonkin/ Red River 97–99, 110, 111, 112, 143, 148, 150, 152, 155, 171; *see also* Camargue
deurbanization 114, 120, 128, 168
development unit 51–56, *55*
dikes: August/ low 172–173, 175; Cái Sắn 112, 156; Camargue 76; catchment areas 159–160, 175; high dikes 173–174; Tonkin 98, 155; Tram Chim National Park 172–173; Plain of Reeds 135, 157–164, 166–167; *see also* casier
dinh điền 101, *106*, 107
đồn điền (garrisoned plantations) 83, 84, 105, *106*, 112
Dong Thap (province) 135, 171–172
Đồng Tháp Mười 135; *see also* Plain of Reeds
Dooge 14–15, 42
Đức Huệ (settlement) 104
Duhamel (cartographer) *83*

East Tien River 171, 174
ECAFE *see* UN Economic Commission for Asia and the Far East (ECAFE)
Elliott 117, 130, 131
Engineer Agency of Resources Inventories (EARI) 150, 157, *158*, 159–161, *160*, *161*, 165, 176, 177
English Channel 20, *31*
equilibrium 5, 12–16, 45, 48, 51, 151, 162, 176; *see also* water balance

First Indochina War 56, 130, 156
floating rice 112, 168–170
Flood Control Bureau 56, 58
floodplain 1–6, 135, *136*, 146–147, 150–151, *151*, 162–163, 166–167, 175–176; planning 154–155, 160–162, 168, 170–172; *see also* Plain of Reeds
floodways 161–162, *161*
Fontana da Meli 14
fortifications 83–84, *83*, 104–105
Francis *see* Garnier
French Academy of Sciences *(Académie des sciences)* 17
French Indochina 5, 41, 56, 97, 145, *151*, 152
flood 135–136; agriculture 112, 168–170, 172–173, 175; control 47–48, 56–58, 65, 67, 76, 128, 131, 146, 151; modelling 49, *50*, 119, 155, 167, *174*; infrastructure 48, 98, 107, 117, 119, 128, 153–156, 166–167, 171–173; mapping

19, *136*, 140, 143, *143*, *151*, 153; season 147, 150, 172, 175; Southeast Asia 56–57, 60, 68; submersion 87, 135, 144, *151*, 158–159, 162, 168
frontières naturelles (natural frontiers) 5, 11, 16–18, 21, 28–29
frontiers (political) 37–42, *38*, 44, 54, 79, 84, 91, 105–108, 142, 148, 159
Frontinus 14
Fry 48, 51, 67
Funan 33, 145

Galison 21, 23, 24, 75
Gamond 31–32, *31*, 42
garden lands (*miệt vườn*) 73, 78, 141
Garnier (cartographer) 34–39, *36*, 43, 86, 91
geography (science) 4, 23–24, 35, 97, 152
geomancy 78, 82, 84, 91
geomorphology 27, *160*
Gia Dinh (settlement) 34, 83–84, 88
Gottman 116
Gourou 97–101, *100*, 108–111, 146, 149, 152, 155, 163
Groslier 80, 90
Gulf of Thailand (Siam) *30*, *85*, 90, 96, 102, 135

Hamilton 28
hamlet 96–98, 104–108, 112, 131
Hanoi 78, 120–123
Hapsburg dynasty 16
Harmand 141
Hartshorne 4, 26
Hà Tiên (settlement) 86
Héraud (cartographer) *77*
hinge cities 100–104, *102*, 108
Ho Chi Minh City (settlement) 114–115, 120–127, *121*, *124*, *126–127*, 129–130
Huế (settlement) 3, 40, 44, 79, 83, 88, 91
Humboldt (cartographer) 11, 12, 22, 26–27, 32, 42, 75
hydraulic/hydrological models 60–63, 81, 92, 119, 167, 171, 172, 173, *174*, 175
hydrograph 48–49, *50*
hydrology 2–5; hydrological cycle 12, 14, 56; Lower Mekong Basin 57–58, 66; Mekong Valley 27, 38, 42; delta 94, 101, 125–127, *126*, 133, 143–145, 148; Plain of Reeds 144, 153, 157, 158–161, *158*, *160*, 162, 164, 166–168, 171; science 9, 11–16, 22, 42, 152–158; Tennessee Valley 48–49, 51; Tonkin 98, 155; Vinh Tế canal 86, 92
hydropower 51, 56–57, 63, *64*, 67

imperial geography 39, 44, 78, 79, 83–84, 88, 91, 112
India 11, 28, 52, 74, 79, 145
Indochina 5, 34, 41, 45, 46, 97, 102–103, 143, 145, 146, *151*, 152
infrastructure: autonomy 46, 159, 161, 173; control 51–53, 61, 76, 82–84, 98, 104, 161–162, 167, 175–176; drainage 82, 117, 122, 154–155, 157, 170–171; groups 32, 45–48, *48*, 63, 65–66; impact 96, 100–101, 122, 146, 166–167, 171–173; multi-purpose *31*, 54, 61; planning 63–66, 97, 116–117, 122–125, 128, 153, 162, 168; settlement 81, 99–101, 104, 107, 117, 146; spatial subdivision 61, 65, 76, 82, 87, 119–120, 155, 160–162; transport 81, 104, 115, 122, 125; *see also casiers*; dams; dikes; hydropower; irrigation; military; polders; waterways
Integrated River Basin Development 54–56, 66
integration (concept of) 49, 61, 63, 68
Interim Mekong Committee 168, *169*
inundation *see* floods
Irrawaddy River 29
irrigation: districts 46, 117; floodplain 166–176, *169*; infrastructure 56, 61, 63–65, 76, 82, 117–119, 122, 161, 166

Jammer 15
Joint Development Group (JDG) 115–119, 156–157

Kelley 78, 89
Khmer: cartography 82; cosmology 79; empire 34, 43, 73–74, 79, 86–87, 96, 140, 150; people 73, 92, 97, 152; Rouge 120
Khone (rapids) 60, 65
khu trù mật *see* agrovilles
Korean Peninsula 57
Ký 73, 77–78, 89, 140

La Loubère 28–29, 42
Lancang River 57–58
Laos 41, 57–60, 65, 168
Lê dynasty 78
Les Armées Françaises D'outre-Mer 109–111
levees *see* dikes
Lilienthal 49, 51, 52, 65–67, 115, 131
Loire River 20, *20*

Index 199

Long An (province) 116, 122, 132, 133
Lower Mekong Basin 56–58, *59*, 60–61, *62*, *64*, 65–66, 119, 175
Luang Prabang 35, *36*, 37, 41

Maingnyaung 82, 90–91
Malaya 34, 37, 105
Malleret 145, 146
mandala polities 5, 27, 33–34, 43, 44, 145
Manen (cartographer). *77*
maps/mapping 2–6; agriculture 117, *118*, 143, 157, 168, *169*, 175–176; basin 37, *38*, 45–46, 53–56, *55*, 57, 60–61, 65, 66, 68; catchment areas 11–12, 19–25, 45, 173–174; delta 73–76, *77*, 87, 96–97; floodplain 140–141, *142–143*, 153, *154*, 157–160, 172; hydrology 140, 157, *160*; hydrography 34, 43; Indochina 97, 102–103, 111, 152; itinerary 78–79, 87; layer cake 159; military 58, 84, *106*, 107, 112, 113; natural frontiers 16–17, *18*; settlements 94, 97–99, *100*, 108–109, 120, *124*, 129–130, 156; valley 27, 34–39, *36*, *38*; voids 140–141, 144–145, 175; *see also* atlas; cartography
Mariotte 12, 16, 24
McCarthy (cartographer) 37–39, 44, *38*
McHarg 159, 165
Mega Urban Regions 123
Mekong Committee 60–61, *64*, *118*, 119, 157, 162, 167–169, *169*, 175
Mekong Delta *see* delta
Mekong Delta Plan (MDP) 123–128, *126–127*
Mekong Delta Development Authority (MDDA) 117
Mekong River Commission (MRC) 173, 176
Mekong Scheme 61
melaleuca (*tram*) 96, 139, 141, 148, 149, 152, 172–173, 177
Menam River *see* Chao Phraya River
metropolitan area 81, 114–116, 123, *124*, 130
Middle Delta 125, *126*, 129
military: districts 84, 108, 116; infrastructure 74, 83–88, *85*; maps 96, 106, 108, 113
Mount Meru *80*, 90
muangs 37, 39–41, 43

Nam Bộ 77, 79, 83, 86, 91, 109, 112
natural frontiers *see frontières naturelles*
Netherlands 31, 123–125, 155

new urban areas (NUAs) 114, 121–122
Ngo 93, 108, 112
Nguyễn, Đình Đâu 96, 109
Nguyen dynasty 78, 83, 140
Nile Delta 73–74, 77, 87, 89
North Vietnam 37, 40, 68, 98, 101, 105, 119, 132, 155

Pa Mong 60, 63, 65, 68–69, 119
Paris (cartographer) 145
Paris (settlement) 12, 16, *18*, 19–20
Perfume River 74, 79, 88
Perrault 12, 14, 16, 24, 25
Phan (cartographer) 40, 41
Phnom Penh (settlement) 34, 43, *77*, 86, 168
Plain of Reeds/Plaine des Joncs 135–136, *136*, 139–148, *142*, *144*, 150–151, *151*, 156–158, *158*, 161–163, 164, 166–175, 176; mapping 140–141, *142–144*, 153, *154*, 157–160, 172
plans/planning 2–5; Lower Mekong Basin 46–51, *48*, *50*, 54, 58–65, *59*, 61, *62*, *64*; Mekong Delta 102–104, 107–108, 114–116, 120–129, *124*, *126–127*; Plain of Reeds 156–162, 167–168; urban 119–123
polders 155–162, *161*, 164, 165; *see also* casiers
population density 58, *59*, 81, 90, 93, 101, 111, 133, 134, 159; and overpopulation 99, 155
Pouyanne (cartographer) 95, *95*, 142–143, *143*, 148
Powell (cartographer) 46–49, 60, 117
precipitation/rainfall 12–14, 42, 46, *50*, 60, 117, 135
Program for Mekong Delta Development 116, 156–157

Rach Gia-Bassac (canal) *102*
Raffestin 66
Reclus 27, 32–33
Red River Delta *see* Tonkin Delta
Rénaud 87, 92
reservoirs 48, *48*, 61, 65, 82, 119, 158, 161, 167–168; *see also* baray
resettlement 99–104, *102*, 108–109, 115, 120, 129, 130, 155–156, 165
Rhine River 16–17, *18*
Rhône River 56, 75
rice cultivation 114–117, *118*, 119–122, 128–129, 166–176; *see also* agriculture; floating rice
Ritter 23, 24

200 *Index*

Robequain 152, 163
Rousseau 17–18
rural: agricultural hinterland 115–116, 119,
    123–124; differentiation with urban
    119–120, 134; land uses 123, 129;
    population 103–105, 107; revolution
    105; rurality 129
Royal Haskoning 123

Saigon River 84, 116
Saigon (settlement) 34, 56, *62*, 83–84, *84*,
    91, 102, 119, 141, 159; metropolitan
    area 114–116, 123, *124*, 129–130
Sa Rài (settlement) *106*
Scott 66, 105, 107
Seine River 12, 19–20, *20*
Service géographique de l'Indochine *81*,
    96–97, 99, *100*, 110
settlement: compact 116, 128, 129; density
    58, *59*, 81, 99, 103, 111, 132; dispersed
    95–96, 103, 106, 108, 120; patterns
    71, 81, 94, 107, 116, 121; planning
    104, 107–108, 112; system 81, 95–96;
    typology 96, 98–101, 110, 111, 112;
    unit 82, 107; *see also* agglomeration;
    agrovilles; Cái Sắn; hinge cities;
    resettlement; strategic hamlets;
    urbanization; village
Shen-Yi 56
Sherman 48
Siam 9, 28–29, *30*, 34–42, *38*, 43, 57, 86,
    91; *see also* Thailand
soil 3; acid sulphate 145–146, 151,
    154–157, 159, 170–171, 175, 177;
    alluvial 77–78, 175; cultivation 78, 87,
    94, 97; settlement 93, 94, 97, 103, 104,
    107, 115; surveys 160, 171; types *72*,
    117, 119
Sơn Nam 95–96, 101, 103, 109, 147
South Vietnam (Republic of Viet-nam)
    58, 93, 94, 101–108, 112, 119, 131,
    157–158, 162, 165, 167, 170
strategic hamlets 102, 105–109, *106*, 112

Taberd (cartographer) 40–41
Taillefer 76, 89, 141, 148
Tan 56, 57
Tân Lược (settlement) 104
territory 4–6, 47, 65, 73–74, 82, 84, 87,
    103, 119, 139
Tennessee Valley Authority (TVA) 45,
    47–53, *48*, 56, 65, 69, 101, 117, 124
Thailand 1, 119, 168
Tháp Mười 141, 145

Thất Sơn 86–87
Tien Giang (province) 172
Tonkin Delta 37, 39, 97, 99, 110, 111, 145
Tonle Sap 64–65, *72*, 82–84, 150, 157,
    167, 173
Tram Chim National Park 172–173
Trần 84, 90
Tvedt 17, 25, 167, 177

U.N. Economic Commission for Asia and
    the Far East (ECAFE) *50*, 52, 56–57,
    60, *62*
United Nations 46, 52–57, 101, 122
unity 45–51, *48*, *50*, 65, 97–98
urbanization *10*, 114–116, 120–125, *121*,
    126–127, 128–130
U.S. Agency for International Development
    (USAID) 52, 115, 117, 130, 157
U.S. Bureau of Reclamation 63, 69
U.S. Corps of Engineers 48, 69, 157
U.S. Defense Mapping Agency *106*, *121*
U.S. Geological Survey 46, 60

Vaico River (East and West) 116, 119, 135,
    143, 153–155, *158*, 171, 174–175
valley 22, 26, 27–28, 41–42, 71, 97;
    common 32–33; Damodar 52; Kashmir
    52; Indus 52; Mekong 27, 34–39, 42,
    43, 44; Nile 27; Tennessee *31*, 45, 47,
    48, 49, 51, *62*, 65, 67
Vauban 83
Vial 76, 139, 148
Vidal 93–94, 97–98, 108, 152–153,
    155
Vidalin (cartographer) *77*
Vietnam: Empire 34, 37, 39–40, 43, 44,
    78–79, 83–84, 88; North 37, 40, 68,
    98, 101, 105, 119, 132, 155; Socialist
    Republic of 114, 120, *121*, 124–125;
    South 58, 93, 94, 101–108, 112,
    119, 131, 157–158, 162, 165, 167,
    170; unification 114, 120, 128, 131,
    166–167, 171
village: Khmer 74, 86, 6; mapping 99–101,
    100; model 105–106, 108, 113; limits
    37, 95–96, 99, 106, 109, 111; Tonkin
    96–98, 101; typologies 88, 97, *100*,
    98–101, 110–111; villagization 107
Vinh Long (settlement) 73, 77, *77*, 89, 140
Vinh Tế (canal) 86–87, 92, 142
Vị Thanh (settlement) 104, 107–108, 112
Vitruvius 15
Võ Duy Dương 141
Vũ Quốc Thúc 115

Walker (cartographer) 28–30, *30*, 35, 37–38
water *see* hydrology
water balance 5, 42, 69
water management: arid region 45; Europe 61; floodplain 136, 167–168; Mekong Delta 123–126
watersheds 38–39, 41–42, 47, *48*, *62*, 65, *158*, 158–159, *169*, 175
waterways: boundary/ border 37, 82, 86–87, 91, 107, 158, 173, 175; canals 76, 86, *95*, 140, 144–145, 153–155, 160–161, 165, 170–171, 176, 177; Duperré 143; Lagrange 143, 155, 171; network 32, 76, 81–82, 88, *95*, 96, 128, 143, 170; planning 31–32, 65, 108, 154–156, 159; prehistoric 145–146; Republic 171; settlement 86, 94–96, 103–104, 106; strategic 34, 84, 103; *see also* floodways; infrastructure; Vinh Té (canal)
Westphalian peace treaty 16
White (cartographer) 53–54, 58, *59*
Winichakul 38–39
Wolters 33, 43, 140
working object 4, 12, 23–25, 47

Yangtze River 56